Somewhere Special

WHERE TO STAY
ENGLAND 1999

ENGLISH
TOURIST BOARD

Where to Stay in England 1999 *'Somewhere Special'*

Published by: **Jarrold Publishing,** Whitefriars, Norwich NR3 1TR, *in association with the* **English Tourist Board,** Thames Tower, Black's Road, Hammersmith, London W6 9EL *and* **Celsius,** St Thomas House, St Thomas Street, Winchester SO23 9HE.

Managing Editor, ETB: Lucy Duke
Design, Compilation and Production: Celsius
Editorial Contributors: Tessa Lecomber, Hugh Chevallier
Illustrations: Jeffy Salt
Cartography: Colin Earl
Typesetting: Celsius
Colour Origination: Spectrum LithoScan
Printed and bound in Great Britain

Display Advertisement Sales: Madison Bell Ltd, 3 St. Peter's Street, Islington Green, London N1 8JD. Telephone: (0171) 359 7737.

© English Tourist Board (except where stated), 1998

ISBN 0-7117-1059-7

Important:

The information contained in this guide has been published in good faith on the basis of information submitted to the English Tourist Board by the proprietors of the premises listed, who have paid for their entries to appear. Jarrold Publishing, the English Tourist Board and Celsius cannot guarantee the accuracy of the information in this guide and accept no responsibility for any error or misrepresentation. All liability for loss, disappointment, negligence or other damage caused by reliance on this guide, or in the event of bankruptcy, or liquidation, or cessation of trade of any company, individual or firm mentioned, is hereby excluded. Please check carefully all prices and other details before confirming a reservation.

The English Tourist Board

The Board is a statutory body created by the Development of Tourism Act 1969 to develop and market England's tourism. Its main objectives are to provide a welcome for people visiting England to take their holidays there; to encourage the provision of tourist amenities and facilities in England. The Board has a statutory duty to advise the Government on tourism matters relating to England and, with Government approval and support, administers the national classification and grading schemes for tourist accommodation in England.

Front cover: Lavenham Priory (page 101)
Back cover: The Stonor Arms Hotel (page 164), Coulsdon Manor Hotel (page 189)

TO BEGIN

All you need to know about
the guide and how to use it

Contents

PLUS... USEFUL INFORMATION

Welcome
to the guide

Somewhere Special is the guide for the discerning traveller, featuring over four hundred hotels, guesthouses, B&Bs and inns all offering their guests that little bit extra. The format is easy to use, with attractive, detailed entries cross-referenced to full-colour maps, plus articles and features as well as helpful hints. Whatever your budget, and whether you want a short get-away or a longer break, *Somewhere Special* offers a choice of accommodation that promises a warm welcome and a stay that's special.

YOUR SURE SIGN OF WHERE TO STAY

As in other English Tourist Board *Where to Stay* accommodation guides, all accommodation included in this invaluable title has been classified under the Board's quality grading and classification scheme (see page 6). In *Somewhere Special*, however, you are promised something extra, for every single entry has achieved a top quality grading of *Highly Commended* or *De Luxe* (see page 8). This means that whatever range of facilities are on offer, they are presented with exceptional care, individuality and quality of service.

QUALITY FIRST

Whether you're looking for no-holds-barred luxury on a grand scale, a short break in a small hotel with character or an intimate bed and breakfast that gives personal attention to perhaps only three or four guests, you're looking in the right guide. The criterion for inclusion in *Somewhere Special* is excellence rather than the range of facilities available – though of course you'll be able to see at a glance exactly what's on offer.

HOW TO CHOOSE

To help you choose somewhere to stay, each entry is illustrated by both a colour photograph and a detailed description. Also displayed are its quality grading, Crown classification and estimated 1999 prices. Facilities are indicated by clear, at-a-glance symbols – see the back flap for a key. You'll also find important details such as meal times, number of bedrooms, parking spaces and which credit/debit cards are accepted, together with address, telephone and fax numbers.

REGIONAL DIVISIONS

To make finding somewhere special even easier, the guide is divided into four sections, each with its own map: England's North Country, England's Heartland, England's West Country and South and South East England. At the start of each section is a regional introduction followed by a detailed map, cross-referenced to the geographical list of accommodation. Features on topics as varied as the Angel of the North and one of the most flawless pieces of Norman architecture in Europe – Romsey Abbey – are interspersed throughout the entries to make perusal even more absorbing.

HIGHLY COMMENDED AND DE LUXE

Those establishments awarded a *Highly Commended* or *De Luxe* grading represent only a small percentage of all Tourist Board quality-graded accommodation. So whether you're looking for somewhere large or small, you can expect to find accommodation of the very highest standard, accompanied by those personal touches which can transform a guesthouse, B&B, inn or hotel into *somewhere really special*.

Crown classifications
and quality gradings

The English Tourist Board's accommodation rating scheme has become recognised as the authoritative indicator of the level of service you can expect to find at your selected guesthouse, B&B, inn or hotel. Our team of assessors has visited over 11,000 establishments throughout England to carry out objective assessments of the facilities and services offered and their overall quality standard.

THE CROWN SYSTEM EXPLAINED

A system of Crown classifications may be applied to any type of establishment offering 'serviced' accommodation – hotels, guesthouses, inns, B&Bs and farmhouses. The number of Crowns is an indication of the range of facilities and services on offer – quite simply, the more Crowns, the wider the range of facilities available. There are six classification bands starting at **Listed**, and then increasing in line with the facilities from **One** to **Five Crown**. The Tourist Board lays down strict rules about how these Crown classifications are applied, stipulating, for example, that every classified establishment meets standards for the size of bed, type of bed linen and even the extent of illumination in each room. Assessment for higher bands of classification includes the provision of tourist information, the number – and location – of colour televisions, the use of 13-amp power outlets, the availability of room service and much, much more.

CROWN CLASSIFICATIONS – A QUICK GUIDE

Listed You can be sure that the accommodation will be clean and comfortable, but the range of facilities and services may be limited.

⌲ You will find additional facilities, including washbasin and chair in your bedroom and you will have use of a telephone.

≋ ≋ There will be a colour TV in your bedroom (or in a lounge) and you can enjoy morning tea/coffee in your bedroom. At least some of the bedrooms will have a private bath (or shower) and WC.

≋ ≋ ≋ At least half of the bedrooms will have private bath (or shower) en-suite. You will also be able to order a hot evening meal.

≋ ≋ ≋ ≋ Your bedroom will have a colour TV, radio and telephone, there will be lounge service until midnight and evening meals can be ordered up to 2030 hours. At least 90% of the bedrooms will have private bath and/or shower and WC en-suite.

≋ ≋ ≋ ≋ ≋ Every bedroom will have a private bath, fixed shower and WC en-suite. The restaurant will be open for breakfast, lunch and dinner (or you can take meals in your room from breakfast until midnight) and you will benefit from an all-night lounge service. A night porter will also be on duty.

QUALITY GRADINGS

A separate quality grading indicates the overall standard of services and facilities. In order to determine which of the four quality grades (APPROVED, COMMENDED, HIGHLY COMMENDED and DE LUXE) should be awarded, a highly-trained Tourist Board assessor inspects every aspect of the accommodation. Those establishments awarded a *Highly Commended* or *De Luxe* grading represent only a small, select percentage of all Tourist Board quality-graded accommodation.

From August 1999 a new rating system for hotel and guest accommodation will be introduced in England.

Following extensive consumer research, the English Tourist Board, the AA and the RAC have developed a new system for rating serviced accommodation based on quality and facilities. There will be two categories – one for 'hotels' and one for 'guest accommodation' which includes guesthouses, B&Bs, inns and farmhouses.

Based on the internationally recognised 1–5 symbols rating, the new system will put greater emphasis on quality and will be very easy to use. All three organisations will assess accommodation to the same agreed rating system, replacing those currently operated in parallel by the English Tourist Board, the RAC and the AA. Hotels will be rated from One to Five Stars and guest accommodation will be rated from One to Five Diamonds.

This is the last edition of *Somewhere Special* to feature the current ratings – future editions will use the new system.

The rigorous and objective annual English Tourist Board assessment takes into account such factors as warmth of welcome, atmosphere, efficiency, as well as the quality of furnishings and equipment, and the standard of meals and their presentation. Consideration is also given to the style and nature of the accommodation. This means that all types of establishment, whatever their Crown classification, can achieve a high quality grade if the facilities and services they provide, even if limited in scope, are to a very high standard. You will therefore find that *Somewhere Special* features accommodation, from **Listed** to **Five Crown**, that has all been awarded a top quality grading of **Highly Commended** or **De Luxe**. Since only a small percentage of establishments are awarded these top two gradings, you know that if your chosen accommodation is in this guide, it is clearly somewhere very special indeed.

AN ASSESSOR CALLS

Before a quality grading is awarded, one of over 55 Tourist Board assessors visits the guesthouse, B&B, farmhouse, inn or hotel for an assessment. The assessor books in advance, but does not reveal his or her identity on arrival. Sadly for those contemplating a career move, the assessor does not have a lazy time; he or she is busy noting the standard of decor, the state of the grounds, the quality of the food and the courtesy of the staff. Once the bill has been paid the next morning, the assessor announces his or her identity to the management and tours the building. At the end of the tour, they discuss the conclusions, with the assessor making suggestions where helpful. Only after the visit does the assessor arrive at a conclusion for the quality grade – so the assessment is 100 per cent independent and reliable.

ACCESSIBILITY

It's all very well deciding exactly where you'd like to stay, but if you find difficulty in walking or are a wheelchair user, then you also need to know how accessible a particular establishment is. If you book your accommodation at an establishment displaying the Accessible symbol, there's no longer any guesswork involved. The National Accessibility Scheme forms part of the *Tourism for All* campaign that is being promoted by all three National Tourist Boards. The Tourist Boards recognise three categories of accessibility, based upon what are considered to be the practical needs of wheelchair users:

 Category 1: accessible to all wheelchair users including those travelling independently

 Category 2: accessible to a wheelchair user with assistance

 Category 3: accessible to a wheelchair user able to walk short distances and up at least three steps.

Additional help and guidance for those with special needs can be obtained from: Holiday Care Service, 2nd Floor, Imperial Buildings, Victoria Road, Horley, Surrey RH6 7PZ. Telephone (01293) 774535, Fax (01293) 784647, Minicom (01293) 776943.

How to use this
guide

Somewhere Special will enable you to find that special place to stay in – whichever part of the country you are planning to visit. Even if you only have a rough idea of where you wish to go, you can easily use this guide to locate a quality place to stay.

The guide is divided into four distinct sections: England's North Country, England's Heartland, England's West Country, and South and South East England. On page 12 you will find a comprehensive break-down of which county is in which region, together with an accompanying 'England-at-a-Glance' map. At the start of each section is a full-colour regional map which clearly plots by number the location of all the *Somewhere Special* entries, as well as the positions of major roads, towns, stations and airports. If you know the area you want to visit, first locate the possible establishments on the regional map and then turn to the appropriate pages in the regional section. The entries are listed by their geographical position, so you'll find that the places you're interested in are usually close to each other in the listing.

Each entry provides detailed information on the nature of the establishment together with the facilities provided and a colour photograph so that you can easily determine whether the place meets the criteria you have in mind. It also lists 1999 estimated prices, so you immediately know whether the entry falls within your price range.

THE ENTRIES IN MORE DETAIL

The entries are designed to convey as much information as possible in a clear, attractive and easy-to-read format. The first line contains the name of the inn, hotel, guesthouse or B&B, together with its Crown classification and quality grading. In *Somewhere Special*, of course, every entry will have a quality grading of either **Highly Commended** or **De Luxe**. Below these come the full address and telephone number of the establishment and, where applicable, its fax number and e-mail address.

Each entry features a full-colour photograph of the establishment and a short description of its main attractions. These details have been supplied by the proprietors themselves and although this information has been checked for accuracy, you are advised to confirm all relevant details at the time of booking. At the foot of each entry comes the all-important practical information:

- A guide to 1999 prices for bed & breakfast and for half board, for both single and double rooms. Prices can sometimes change after the guide has gone to press, so please check when making a booking.

- Mealtimes for both lunch and evening meal, when available.

- The numbers of bedrooms and bathrooms, and whether the latter are en-suite, private or shared.

- The number of parking spaces.

- The range of any credit and charge cards accepted.

In the bottom right-hand corner of the entry is a list of symbols representing in greater detail the range of facilities and services offered. The key explaining exactly what these mean is conveniently located on the back of the cover flap, which can be kept open while you're browsing through the entries. The symbols cover everything from the provision of private shooting rights to whether or not there's a sauna for guests' use. Most importantly, they allow you to see at a glance whether any special requirements you may have can be met.

OTHER FEATURES OF THE GUIDE

As well as the entries – 390 in all – you'll find many features on a wide variety of subjects scattered throughout the book. The four informative introductions to the regions appear on pages 13, 57, 105 and 153. At the back of the book (pages 193–197) you will find more detailed information about booking accommodation. You are strongly recommended to read this before committing yourself to any firm arrangements, bearing in mind the fact that all details have been supplied by proprietors themselves.

In this guide, England is divided into four main sections. A map of the area, showing each entry and its nearest town or city, as well as nearby major roads or motorways, can be found after the regional introduction.

England
at a glance

ENGLAND'S NORTH COUNTRY

Cheshire, Cumbria, Durham, East Riding of Yorkshire, Greater Manchester, Lancashire, Merseyside, North & North East Lincolnshire, North, South & West Yorkshire, Northumberland, Tees Valley and Tyne & Wear.

ENGLAND'S HEARTLAND

Bedfordshire, Cambridgeshire, Derbyshire, Essex, Gloucestershire, Herefordshire, Hertfordshire, Leicestershire, Lincolnshire, Norfolk, Northamptonshire, Nottinghamshire, Rutland, Shropshire, Staffordshire, Suffolk, Warwickshire, West Midlands, and Worcestershire.

ENGLAND'S WEST COUNTRY

Bath & North East Somerset, Bristol, Cornwall, Devon, Isles of Scilly, North Somerset, Somerset, South Gloucestershire, Western Dorset and Wiltshire.

SOUTH AND SOUTH EAST ENGLAND

Berkshire, Buckinghamshire, East & West Sussex, Eastern Dorset, Hampshire, Isle of Wight, Kent, London, Oxfordshire and Surrey.

England's North Country

England's Heartland

South and South East England

England's West Country

England

England's North Country

Alnwick

▶ Humber Bridge

Parliament approved construction of a Humber bridge in 1959, but it took 22 years to open, and cost £98 million, almost four times the original estimate. The result, however, is impressive. With a central span of almost a mile (4,626ft - 1,410m), the Humber Bridge was until very recently the longest unsupported section of bridge in the world. Visitor facilities include viewing areas at both ends; the northern side also has a tourist information centre and country park; views of and from the bridge are magnificent.

▶ Bowes Museum

In the entrance hall, on the stroke of every hour, a large silver swan whirrs into action, slowly bending its articulated silver neck to swallow a silver fish. This bizarre mechanical toy is one of many valuable treasures amassed by John Bowes, Earl of Strathmore, who in 1869 began building this outrageously inappropriate French château-style mansion to house his possessions. The imposing rooms contain paintings by El Greco, Goya, Boucher and Courbet, together with superb displays of furniture, ceramics and tapestries (tel: 01833 690606).

Peak after peak

The soul of England's North Country lies in the Pennines, England's mountainous backbone stretching from the borders of Scotland to the borders of the Midlands. The North boasts the Lake District, two glorious coastlines, countless imposing castles and, in York, one of the most perfect cities one could ever wish for, but somehow the sheer scale of the Pennine ridge dominates. The mountains run for around 200 miles (322km), the peaks rising above 2,000ft (610m), too many to count.

Exploring on foot

The most famous way to savour the Pennine experience, fitness and time permitting, is to walk Britain's oldest long-distance path. About 10,000 people each year complete the 268 miles (431km) of the Pennine Way, though many more – perhaps 300,000 – join it for a mile or two from one of 535 separate access points. Two of these are intersections with other waymarked paths. The Coast-to-Coast Walk, as its name suggests, links the Irish Sea with the North Sea, traversing the Lake District, Yorkshire Dales and North York Moors national parks on its 190-mile (306km) route, while the Dales Way (81 miles - 130km) is a low-level path along the banks of the Wharfe, Dee, Lune and Kent rivers. The Cumbria Way (Ulverston to Carlisle) guides you through Lakeland grandeur. The Cleveland Way falls almost entirely within the North York Moors national park, but still extends over 100 miles (161km). Roughly following the river from its source high in the Dales to the sea, from near Preston, the wise walker tackles the Ribble Way in a downhill direction. Altogether quieter and less dramatic is the Wolds Way, wending from near Hull to Filey, where it joins the Cleveland Way. Needless to say, all these – as well as Hadrian's Wall, which can be walked for its entire length – explore scenery of the utmost beauty. All make an ideal starting point for shorter strolls, too.

Mills to museums

Towards the southern end of the Pennines the valleys become more populated. The fast-flowing rivers that long ago powered the mills are lined with the characterful small houses built for the workers. Once reviled, but now revered, towns such as Holmforth and Hebden Bridge have justly become visitor attractions in their own right. And the factories have in many instances been turned into imaginative museums and galleries. The Armley Mills Industrial Museum, Leeds, occupies what was once the largest woollen mill in the world; Saddleworth Museum and Art Gallery houses working woollen textile machinery; much of Salts Mill, near Bradford is devoted to the works of the artist, David Hockney; and, at Macclesfield, Paradise Mill produced silk until the 1980s. At Sheffield, those with an interest in industrial archaeology can indulge themselves at either the Abbeydale Industrial Hamlet or Kelham Island Industrial Museum. If you prefer more modern scientific endeavour, then try the Jodrell Bank Science Centre & Arboretum, south of Manchester, home of a massive steerable radio telescope.

On a grand scale

A few miles from Jodrell Bank lies Tatton Park, one of the finest country houses of the North and on a decidedly grand scale. Other lesser-known properties to explore include: medieval Raby Castle with its nine towers (near Staindrop, County Durham); the very Victorian Lady Waterford Hall, decorated with murals depicting familiar Bible stories (Ford, Northumberland); Dalemain, a stately home intriguingly adapted from the original pele tower, now home of the Westmorland and Cumberland

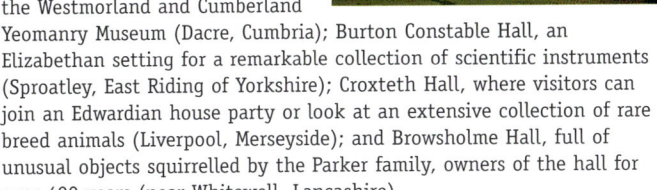

Yeomanry Museum (Dacre, Cumbria); Burton Constable Hall, an Elizabethan setting for a remarkable collection of scientific instruments (Sproatley, East Riding of Yorkshire); Croxteth Hall, where visitors can join an Edwardian house party or look at an extensive collection of rare breed animals (Liverpool, Merseyside); and Browsholme Hall, full of unusual objects squirrelled by the Parker family, owners of the hall for over 400 years (near Whitewell, Lancashire).

For art's sake

The North Country has a range of arts and music festivals to rival the rest of England. As always, the breadth of entertainment is prodigious. For concerts devoted to early music – and played in some of England's most glorious medieval churches – visit either the York Early Music Festival (July) or, 25 or so miles (40km) further east, the Beverley and East Riding Early Music Festival (May). At the other end of the spectrum, go south to Huddersfield in November for the Contemporary Music Festival. The Lake District hosts jazz, orchestral and chamber concerts at a number of venues as part of its Summer Music festivities (August), while Chester does broadly the same – as well as adding a fringe element, too – in July. Bradford (late June and early July) and Harrogate (late July and early August) both add comedy and street theatre to a range of musical concerts. Manchester, meanwhile, devotes three weeks in May to its Streets Ahead festival. Circus events and fireworks provide alternatives to the music, dance and theatre – and everything is free. And, if you thought the Aldborough Festival was exclusive to Suffolk, look closely at the spelling. A village near Boroughbridge, North Yorkshire, holds the Northern Aldborough (not Aldeburgh) Festival each July; classical music is once again the subject.

Fishing villages and golden sands

The coastline of Northumberland, England's north-eastern extremity, bears intriguing resemblance to Cornwall, in the extreme south-west. Fine sandy beaches, a history peopled by saints and martyrs, and a rural interior characterise both. In Northumberland, it is never difficult to escape the throng, but take a trip to the Farne Islands, and you will be outnumbered by both birds and seals. The golden shores south of Bamburgh and north of

▶ Grace Darling

Few women have attracted such uninvited public adulation as Grace Darling. Daughter of a lighthouse keeper, Grace lived a lonely life on the Farne Islands, off the Northumberland coast. On 7 September 1838 she and her father risked their lives to rescue nine survivors from the wrecked steamer *Forfarshire*, putting out in heavy seas in a tiny rowing-boat. The newspapers made her a national heroine overnight. At Bamburgh are the Grace Darling Museum and the cottage where she was born. Weather permitting, a boat trip around the Farne Islands is an unforgettable experience (tel: 01665 720884).

▶ Lawnmowers on display

The British Lawnmower Museum (tel: 01704 501336) is based in the seaside resort of Southport, Merseyside. Prized exhibits include some of the first machines dating from the early 19th century, mowers once belonging to Nicholas Parsons and to Prince Charles, another capable of cutting a 2-inch (5cm) wide strip, and what is believed to be the only hand-powered rotary lawnmower in existence. Also on view is the world's largest collection of toy mowers and one of the oldest surviving racing lawnmowers (built by the curator).

Dunstanburgh, two glorious beaches that never seem busy, have the added attraction of offering views of their respective castles. Further south, into the North York Moors national park, the coastline is more for the fossil hunter and the walker – the Cleveland Way here follows the sea – than the sun-seeker. Many of the picturesque villages, such as Ravenscar, Runswick Bay, Staithes and Robin Hood's Bay, tumble down cliffs that yield an array of fossils. Then come the famous resorts of Scarborough, Filey and Bridlington, each with magnificent sandy beaches ideal for family outings. Southport, on the southern Lancashire shores, has endless sand, as does its illustrious neighbour, Blackpool, over the Ribble Estuary. North again is Morecambe Bay, at low tide around 150 square miles (38,850 hectares) of gleaming but potentially treacherous sand. Away from the bustle of Blackpool and the teaming birdlife of Morecambe Bay, try Annaside or Gutterby Spa, two of the region's remoter beaches.

Former glories

Hidden away on Cumbria's westernmost point is an elegant port that, 250 years ago, was busier than Liverpool. Retaining many 17th- and 18th-century buildings, and with pleasure craft bobbing up and down in the old harbour, Whitehaven makes an unusual excursion from the Lake District. The North has countless towns that invite unhurried exploration. One is Hexham, whose focal point is the magnificent abbey, dating largely from the 12th-century, but it also has Georgian streets surrounding the Shambles, the shelter for the lively Tuesday market. Others to consider are: Rothbury, also in Northumberland, an attractive small market town with a medieval bridge; Barnard Castle (County Durham), where visitors can marvel at the exhibits in the Bowes Museum then clamber over the ruins of the lofty castle to admire the views of the River Tees; Beverley (East Riding of Yorkshire), a superb mixture of medieval and Georgian architecture; Pickering (North Yorkshire), whose ancient coaching inns reflect its heyday as an important stop on the way to Scarborough and Whitby; Clitheroe (Lancashire), where a diminutive Norman castle watches over the stone-built houses; and Macclesfield (Cheshire), a former weaving centre in the shadow of the southern Pennines with fine 18th-century townhouses.

North country fare

The region produces a number of edible specialities, confectionery and cheeses in particular. Cumbria, renowned for its coiled, smoky sausage, also produces Cumberland rum butter – originally eaten to celebrate the arrival of a newborn child and still made in Whitehaven – as well as Kendal mint cake, famously taken on expeditions to Mount Everest. Pontefract was once the centre of liquorice cultivation and, although the plant is no longer grown, Pontefract cakes are manufactured in the town. Nantwich Museum devotes a room to Cheshire cheese, while three Yorkshire Dales – Swaledale, Wensleydale and Coverdale – give their names to crumbly cheeses made within the national park. The finest kippers are traditionally sold on the quayside at Whitby.

A Northern miscellany

The North Country can also offer many other curiosities. Around Ingleton are a number of cave systems, of which the vast Gaping Ghyll cavern is one of the most impressive. Also in North Yorkshire, but west of Masham, is the Druid's Temple, a 19th-century folly built in imitation of a miniature Stonehenge. Hale, just over the Mersey from Runcorn, boasts the grave of John Middleton, a local giant reputedly 9 ft 3 inches (2.8m) tall, while at Lower Heysham, near Morecambe, on a promontory above the sandy beach, are some strange rock 'coffins', perhaps carved by 9th-century missionaries from Ireland. And in one of England's furthest-flung spots, high up in the Pennines where Cumbria and Durham meet, is Cauldron Snout, a magnificent waterfall and series of cataracts.

Contact numbers

Lake District National Park (tel: 01539 446601)
Yorkshire Dales National Park (tel: 01756 752774)
North York Moors National Park (tel: 01439 770657)
Hadrian's Wall (tel: 01434 344363)
The Armley Mills Industrial Museum, Leeds (tel: 0113 263 7861))
Saddleworth Museum and Art Gallery, Uppermill (tel: 01457 874093)
Salts Mill, Bradford (tel: 01274 531163)
Paradise Mill, Macclesfield (tel: 01625 618228))
Abbeydale Industrial Hamlet, Sheffield (tel: 0114 236 7731)
Kelham Island Industrial Museum, Sheffield (tel: 0114 272 2106)
Jodrell Bank Science Centre & Arboretum (tel: 01477 571339)
Tatton Park, Knutsford (tel: 01565 654822)
Raby Castle, Staindrop (tel: 01833 660202)
Lady Waterford Hall, Ford (tel: 01890 820224)
Dalemain, Dacre (tel: 01768 486450)
Burton Constable Hall, Sproatley (tel: 01964 562400)
Croxteth Hall, Liverpool (tel: 0151 228 5311)
Browsholme Hall, Whitewell (tel: 01254 826719)
York Early Music Festival (tel: 01904 645738)
Beverley and East Riding Early Music Festival (tel: 01904 645738)
Huddersfield Contemporary Music Festival (tel: 01484 472103)
Lake District Summer Music (tel: 01539 733411)
Chester Summer Festival (tel: 01204 320722)
Bradford Festival (tel: 01274 309199)
Harrogate International Festival (tel: 01423 562303)
Manchester Streets Ahead (tel: 0161 953 4238)
Northern Aldborough Festival (tel: 01423 324899)
Nantwich Museum (tel: 01270 627104)

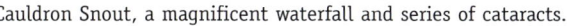

▶ Grizedale Sculpture Trail

A walk through Grizedale Forest offers an intriguing trail of discovery in the hunt for 80 or so large-scale sculptures dotted along its pathways. The Sculpture Trail began as an opportunity for sculptors to develop diverse works on the theme of the Forest, and the sculptures are inspired by the materials and forms which naturally occur there: wildlife, rock formations, drystone walls, and, of course, trees. Most are sited on the Silurian Way, a 9½-mile (15km) circular walk starting at the Visitor Centre (tel: 01229 860010) where maps (that include short-cuts) may be purchased.

▶ Berwick-upon-Tweed

Berwick-upon-Tweed, though still in England, is further north than much of the Hebridean island of Islay. Oddly, it is cut off from the county which bears its name, for Berwickshire lies in Scotland. Not surprisingly, Berwick's history is intractably bound up with the struggle between the English and the Scots; between 1147 and 1482, the town changed hands 13 times. The 16th century saw the town walls comprehensively fortified against a Scots-French attack which never materialised, hence their amazing state of preservation. A two-mile (3km) walk around these ramparts gives spectacular views of the historic town.

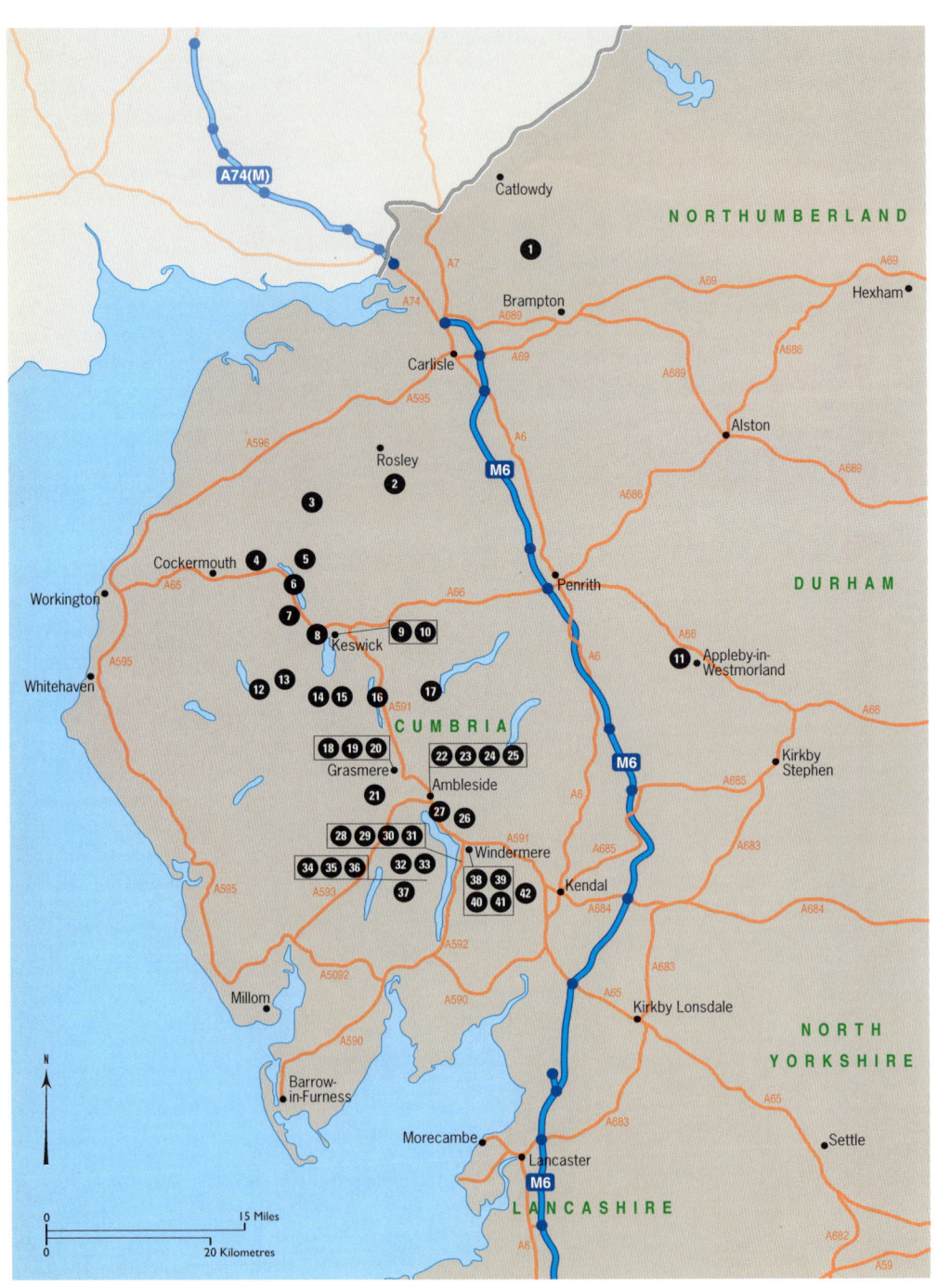

Colin Earl Cartography

1 NEW PALLYARDS

≋ ≋ ≋ HIGHLY COMMENDED

Hethersgill, Carlisle, Cumbria CA6 6HZ Tel (01228) 577308 Fax (01228) 577308

Relax and see beautiful North Cumbria and the Borders. A warm welcome awaits you in our country farmhouse where you have the benefit of en-suite rooms with colour television (some ground floor rooms). Also enjoy our own nature trail and nearby woodland walks. Long or short stays. Ideal Scotland stop-off. Out of season special breaks. Peak of Perfection Salon Culinaire Gold Award winner for the Best Breakfast in Britain.

Bed & Breakfast per night: single occupancy from £22.00–£27.00; double room from £42.00–£44.00
Dinner, Bed & Breakfast per person, per night: £32.15–£36.50 (special week breaks)
Evening meal 1900 (last orders 1930)

Bedrooms: 1 double, 1 twin, 1 triple
Bathrooms: 3 en-suite, 1 public
Parking for 7
Cards accepted: Mastercard, Visa

2 SWALEDALE WATCH

≋ ≋ HIGHLY COMMENDED

Whelpo, Caldbeck, Wigton, Cumbria CA7 8HQ Tel (016974) 78409 Fax (016974) 78409

Swaledale Watch is a busy sheep farm just outside picturesque Caldbeck and within the Lake District National Park. Enjoy great comfort, excellent food, a warm welcome and peaceful, unspoilt surroundings. A central location for touring, walking or exploring the rolling northern fells. All rooms are beautifully decorated, homely, and have private facilities. Chilly evenings mean open fires in the lounges with books for every interest. A magical, memorable walk lies within 150 yards of the house. Your happiness is our priority.

Bed & Breakfast per night: single occupancy from £18.00–£21.00; double room from £34.00–£40.00
Dinner, Bed & Breakfast per person, per night: £28.00–£32.00
Evening meal 1900 (last bookings 1400)

Bedrooms: 2 double, 2 triple
Bathrooms: 4 en-suite
Parking for 10

3 WOODLANDS COUNTRY HOUSE

≋ ≋ ≋ HIGHLY COMMENDED

Ireby, Cumbria CA5 1EX Tel (016973) 71791 Fax (016973) 71482 E-mail hj@woodlnd.u-net.com

Woodlands is a most elegant Victorian house, tastefully refurbished throughout to reflect the period. It enjoys fine views and is set within carefully maintained and spacious grounds. Ireby, a truly unspoilt Cumbrian village, is an ideal base for exploring the Northern Lakes. John and Helen Payne have established a reputation for fine food, affordable wines, the warmest of welcomes and a highly personal service. Residential licence. Non smoking. Vegetarian alternatives. Pets welcome. Suitable for wheelchair users. CATEGORY 2

Bed & Breakfast per night: single occupancy from £30.00–£33.00; double room from £55.00–£60.00
Dinner, Bed & Breakfast per person, per night: £46.00–£49.00
Evening meal 1900 (last bookings 1600)

Bedrooms: 3 double, 2 twin, 2 triple
Bathrooms: 7 en-suite
Parking for 12
Open: February–November and Christmas
Cards accepted: Mastercard, Switch/Delta

Entries are cross referenced by number to the maps on pages 18–19

4 HIGH SIDE FARM

 HIGHLY COMMENDED

Embleton, Cockermouth, Cumbria CA13 9TN Tel (017687) 76893

A 17th-century farmhouse, perched over 600ft up Ling Fell, looking west over the Embleton Valley to the Solway, Scottish mountains and the setting sun, and backing onto the Lake District fells. The farmhouse is in a forgotten part of the National Park, three quarters of a mile up a private road. The area is hardly touched by tourism, yet within twenty minutes you can be by Derwentwater, Buttermere, Crummock Water, Loweswater or Bassenthwaite.

Bed & Breakfast per night: double room from
£40.00–£45.00

Bedrooms: 1 double, 1 twin
Bathrooms: 2 en-suite
Parking for 2

5 RAVENSTONE LODGE

 HIGHLY COMMENDED

Bassenthwaite, Keswick, Cumbria CA12 4QG Tel (017687) 76629 or (017687) 76638 Fax (017687) 76629

A warm and friendly welcome awaits you at Ravenstone Lodge, our 19th-century stone-built property nestling at the foot of Ullock Pike, just four miles north of Keswick on the A591. The lodge is set in five acres of spectacular countryside with a private terrace, a large walled garden and ample off-the-road parking space. Enjoy the relaxed atmosphere of our stable dining room, bar and large Victorian-style conservatory.

Bed & Breakfast per night: single occupancy from
£30.50–£32.50; double room from £57.00–£61.00
Dinner, Bed & Breakfast per person, per night:
£43.50–£47.50
Evening meal 1900 (last bookings 1800)

Bedrooms: 7 double, 2 twin, 1 family room
Bathrooms: 9 en-suite
Parking for 12
Cards accepted: Mastercard, Visa, Switch/Delta

6 THE PHEASANT

 HIGHLY COMMENDED

Bassenthwaite Lake, Cockermouth, Cumbria CA13 9YE Tel (017687) 76234 Fax (017687) 76002

A tranquil, traditional, north Lake District inn, adjacent to Bassenthwaite Lake, and surrounded by gardens and woodland providing a wealth of wildlife. Three lounges feature antiques, beams, open fires and fresh flowers. Commended by major guides for high quality English food and service, The Pheasant also has twenty individually-decorated bedrooms with private facilities. Dogs welcome – kennels available. CATEGORY 3

Bed & Breakfast per night: single room from
£59.00–£66.00; double room from £90.00–£104.00
Dinner, Bed & Breakfast per person, per night:
£67.00–£74.00 (2 sharing)
Lunch available: 1230–1400

Evening meal 1900 (last orders 2030)
Bedrooms: 5 single, 8 double, 7 twin
Bathrooms: 20 en-suite
Parking for 80
Cards accepted: Mastercard, Visa

At-a-glance symbols are explained on the flap inside the back cover

7 THWAITE HOWE HOTEL

 HIGHLY COMMENDED

Thornthwaite, Keswick, Cumbria CA12 5SA Tel (017687) 78281 Fax (017687) 78529

Situated in its own grounds, with superb views across the Derwent Valley to the Skiddaw range, our hotel is in a very peaceful position, but in easy reach of all the Lake District's attractions. Mary's delicious, award-winning home cooking is complemented by fine wines, or followed by one of Harry's cask-strength malt whiskies. Red squirrels feed in the garden daily and, together with guests, enjoy the friendly informal atmosphere. AA Rosette for cuisine. RAC restaurant award.

Dinner, Bed & Breakfast per person, per night:
£44.00–£49.50 (2 sharing)
Evening meal 1900

Bedrooms: 5 double, 3 twin
Bathrooms: 8 en-suite
Parking for 12
Open: March–October
Cards accepted: Mastercard, Visa, Switch/Delta

8 DERWENT COTTAGE

HIGHLY COMMENDED

Portinscale, Keswick, Cumbria CA12 5RF Tel (017687) 74838

Gleaming silver, cut glass, spacious en-suite bedrooms and elegant furnishings are all to be found at Derwent Cottage. This Lakeland house, dating from the 18th century, stands in an acre of secluded gardens in the quiet village of Portinscale, one mile from Keswick. A four-course, candle light table d'hôte is served at 1900 each evening with classical music in the background. A residential licence is held, and drinks and wine are available throughout the evening. We are a totally non-smoking establishment.

Bed & Breakfast per night: double room from
£66.00–£78.00
Dinner, Bed & Breakfast per person, per night:
£47.00–£53.00 (less for longer stays)
Evening meal 1900

Bedrooms: 4 double, 2 twin
Bathrooms: 6 en-suite
Parking for 10
Open: March–October
Cards accepted: Mastercard, Visa

9 SKIDDAW HOTEL

HIGHLY COMMENDED

Main Street, Keswick, Cumbria CA12 5BN Tel (017687) 72071 Fax (017687) 74850

Overlooking Keswick's historic market square, the Skiddaw Hotel provides the perfect location in the heart of the English Lake District for that special break. Try one of our 'Summit' rooms for that extra touch of luxury and dine in our new restaurant '31 The Square'. Complimentary facilities exclusive to our residents include in-house saunas, mid-week golf, and access to a nearby (eight miles outside Keswick) leisure club with fully equipped gym and swimming pool.

Bed & Breakfast per night: single room from
£38.00–£45.00; double room from £70.00–£84.00
Lunch available: 1200–1430
Evening meal 1800 (last orders 2200)

Bedrooms: 7 single, 14 double, 11 twin, 8 triple
Bathrooms: 40 en-suite
Parking for 8
Cards accepted: Mastercard, Visa, Amex, Switch/Delta

Entries are cross referenced by number to the maps on pages 18–19

10 THE GRANGE COUNTRY HOUSE

〰〰〰〰 HIGHLY COMMENDED

Manor Brow, Ambleside Road, Keswick, Cumbria CA12 4BA Tel (017687) 72500

Grange Country House is situated in its own grounds, with excellent parking, overlooking Keswick-on-Derwentwater and the surrounding mountains. Lovely bedrooms with those extra touches, together with comfort, care, quality furnishings and relaxed hospitality, makes our award-winning home a perfect holiday base. The exceptional breakfast menu will give you an ideal start to your day in Lakeland. Walkers, birdwatchers, golfers (free golf) and lovers of the countryside will find the area 'somewhere special'.

Bed & Breakfast per night: single occupancy from £28.00–£38.00; double room from £56.00–£76.00
Evening meal 1930

Bedrooms: 7 double, 3 twin
Bathrooms: 10 en-suite, 1 public
Parking for 13
Open: February–November
Cards accepted: Mastercard, Visa

11 APPLEBY MANOR COUNTRY HOUSE HOTEL

〰〰〰〰 HIGHLY COMMENDED

Roman Road, Appleby-in-Westmorland, Cumbria CA16 6JB Tel (017683) 51571 Fax (017683) 52888 E-mail appleby.manor@btinternet.com

Probably the most relaxing and friendly hotel you'll ever stay at! Set amidst breathtaking beauty, you'll find spotlessly clean accommodation; satellite television and video films; a splendid indoor leisure club that has a small swimming pool, jacuzzi, steam-room, sauna and sunbed; magnificent lounges, and great food in the AA Rosette award-winning restaurant – all in a genuine country house. Golf, squash, horse-riding and all the delights of the Lake District and Yorkshire Dales are close by.
www.btinternet.com/~appleby.manor

Bed & Breakfast per night: single occupancy from £69.00–£78.00; double room from £98.00–£116.00
Dinner, Bed & Breakfast per person, per night: £59.00–£89.00 (min 2 nights)
Lunch available: 1200–1400

Evening meal 1900 (last orders 2100)
Bedrooms: 13 double, 8 twin, 1 triple, 8 family rooms
Bathrooms: 30 en-suite Parking for 51
Cards accepted: Mastercard, Visa, Diners, Amex, Switch/Delta

12 BRIDGE HOTEL

〰〰〰〰 HIGHLY COMMENDED

Buttermere, Cockermouth, Cumbria CA13 9UZ Tel (017687) 70252 Fax (017687) 70215

An 18th-century coaching inn, beautifully situated between two lakes in Lakeland's loveliest valley. Superb unrestricted walking country and breathtaking scenery. Complimentary afternoon tea is served near the log fire in our very comfortable residents' lounge. Two well-stocked bars serve expertly-kept real ales. Four-poster beds. Dogs welcome. Special breaks offered throughout the year.

Bed & Breakfast per night: single room from £39.00–£45.00; double room from £78.00–£90.00
Dinner, Bed & Breakfast per person, per night: £49.00–£67.00 (min 2 nights)
Lunch available: 1200–1430

Evening meal 1900 (last orders 2030)
Bedrooms: 2 single, 8 double, 12 twin
Bathrooms: 21 en-suite, 2 private, 1 public
Parking for 60
Cards accepted: Mastercard, Visa, Switch/Delta

At-a-glance symbols are explained on the flap inside the back cover

13 ## SWINSIDE LODGE
 DE LUXE

Newlands, Keswick, Cumbria CA12 5UE Tel (017687) 72948 Fax (017687) 72948

Swinside Lodge is a delightful Victorian house in a beautiful and tranquil corner of the Lake District, just beneath Cat Bells and a five-minute stroll from the shores of Derwent Water. Relax in this most comfortable and elegantly furnished house where you can enjoy superb award-winning food served by friendly staff in the candle-lit dining room. The hotel, which is personally run, is totally no smoking and is unlicensed but please bring your own favourite wines. A warm welcome awaits you.

Bed & Breakfast per night: single occupancy from £52.00–£59.00; double room from £78.00–£115.00
Dinner, Bed & Breakfast per person, per night: £62.50–£81.00 (min 2 nights)
Evening meal 1930 (last orders 2000)

Bedrooms: 5 double, 2 twin
Bathrooms: 7 en-suite
Parking for 12
Open: February–November and Christmas

Lady Anne Clifford and her monuments

'THEY THAT SHALL be of thee shall build the old waste places' reads the quotation (from Isaiah 58:12) above the door of Outhgill church near Kirkby Stephen. The message, carved at the instigation of Lady Anne Clifford who restored the church in the 17th century, was one which she took to heart. When at the age of 60 she inherited lands in Cumberland, Westmorland and Yorkshire, she embarked upon a frenzy of building, repairs and restoration with a near-religious zeal.

Her enthusiasm was engendered by long years of frustration. She was just 15 in 1605 when her father died and, as his only surviving child, she confidently expected to inherit his extensive northern estates. Instead she found they had been left to his brother and nephew, and she immediately began a long and fruitless campaign to regain her inheritance. In 1643, however, her cousin Henry died without heir and the estates, at long last, passed to her, his only legitimate successor.

Neglect and the Civil War had taken their toll on her many castles. Those of Appleby, Skipton, Brough, Brougham (shown here), Pendragon and Barden Tower had all fallen into decay, but during the next two decades Lady Anne restored them to their original splendour. She also repaired churches at Skipton, Brough, Brougham and Appleby and built almshouses and monuments, a display of wealth not altogether wise in the puritan atmosphere of Commonwealth England.

To celebrate the restoration of her inheritance Lady Anne commissioned a remarkable painting – depicting herself and all the major characters from her eventful life. Known as the Great Picture, this now hangs in the keep of Appleby Castle (tel: 017683 51402). Also in the town, she built the St Anne's almshouses and the white pillars at either end of the main street, while her tomb and that of her beloved mother, Margaret, Countess of Cumberland, lie in St Lawrence's church. On the road to Brougham is the Countess Pillar marking the spot where Lady Anne last saw her mother alive.

Skipton Castle, lovingly restored by Lady Anne, remains one of the most complete and best preserved medieval castles in England (tel: 01756 792442). But, despite all her efforts Barden Tower and the castles of Pendragon, Brough and Brougham are all ruins once more. (Details from Kirkby Stephen Tourist Information Office, tel: 017683 71199).

A 100-mile (161km) walk, Lady Anne's Way, takes in all the buildings and monuments associated with this redoubtable lady.

14 GREENBANK

HIGHLY COMMENDED

Borrowdale, Keswick, Cumbria CA12 5UY Tel (017687) 77215 Fax (017687) 77215

Greenbank is a lovely Victorian house in a peaceful setting. Here you can enjoy magnificent views of Derwentwater and the Borrowdale Valley. There are ten comfortable well-appointed bedrooms, each with an en-suite bathroom. Log fires, honesty bar, newspapers to browse through. We particularly enjoy providing imaginatively presented meals, with interesting menus using lots of local fresh produce.

Bed & Breakfast per night: single room from £22.00; double room from £44.00–£66.00
Dinner, Bed & Breakfast per person, per night: £34.00–£45.00
Evening meal 1900 (last bookings 1700)

Bedrooms: 1 single, 6 double, 2 twin, 1 triple
Bathrooms: 10 en-suite
Parking for 15
Open: all year except Christmas
Cards accepted: Mastercard, Visa

15 HAZEL BANK

HIGHLY COMMENDED

Rosthwaite, Borrowdale, Keswick, Cumbria CA12 5XB Tel (017687) 77248 Fax (017678) 77373 E-mail enquiries@hazelbankhotel.demon.co.uk

Standing on an elevated site overlooking the village of Rosthwaite, there are unsurpassed views of the Borrowdale Valley and central Lakeland peaks. The peaceful location makes Hazel Bank an ideal base for walkers, birdwatchers and lovers of the countryside, with direct access to many mountain and valley walks. The Victorian residence has been carefully and sympathetically converted to provide quality country house accommodation. Non-smokers only. Vegetarians welcome.

Dinner, Bed & Breakfast per person, per night: from £45.00
Evening meal 1900

Bedrooms: 1 single, 3 double, 3 twin
Bathrooms: 7 en-suite
Parking for 12
Cards accepted: Mastercard, Visa, Switch/Delta

16 DALE HEAD HALL LAKESIDE HOTEL

HIGHLY COMMENDED

Thirlmere, Keswick, Cumbria CA12 4TN Tel (017687) 72478 Fax (017687) 71070 E-mail holiday@dale-head-hall.co.uk

With Helvellyn rising majestically behind, the hotel stands alone on the shores of Lake Thirlmere. At Dale Head Hall we offer a friendly home, a place of relaxation and beauty, set apart from the increasing pace of the modern world. Little can compare to a delicious dinner, prepared with love and care, particularly when wholesome ingredients come from the hotel's walled garden. AA 2 Rosettes, RAC Restaurant Award.
www.dale-head-hall.co.uk

Bed & Breakfast per night: single occupancy from £37.50–£45.00; double room from £75.00–£90.00
Dinner, Bed & Breakfast per person, per night: £65.00–£72.50
Evening meal 1930 (last orders 2030)

Bedrooms: 6 double, 2 twin, 1 triple
Bathrooms: 9 en-suite
Parking for 20
Open: February–December
Cards accepted: Mastercard, Visa, Amex, Switch/Delta

At-a-glance symbols are explained on the flap inside the back cover

17 GLENRIDDING HOTEL

HIGHLY COMMENDED

Glenridding, Penrith, Cumbria CA11 0PB Tel (017684) 82228 Fax (017684) 82555

Perfectly placed to explore the Lake District! We are surrounded by mountains and Ullswater, with fabulous walks and beautiful views literally on our doorstep. We offer two restaurants, traditional pub, coffee house, library and lounges with log fires in winter. Our new indoor swimming pool and sauna will provide the ideal place to relax after a day on the fells. Take advantage of one of our special breaks. We look forward to welcoming you!

Bed & Breakfast per night: single room from £68.00–£74.00; double room from £94.00–£102.00
Dinner, Bed & Breakfast per person, per night: £65.00–£67.00 (min 2 nights)
Lunch available: 1200–2130

Evening meal 1900 (last orders 2030)
Bedrooms: 3 single, 21 double, 11 twin, 5 family rooms
Bathrooms: 40 en-suite
Parking for 30
Cards accepted: Mastercard, Visa, Diners, Amex, Switch/Delta

18 OAK BANK HOTEL

HIGHLY COMMENDED

Broadgate, Grasmere, Ambleside, Cumbria LA22 9TA Tel (015394) 35217 Fax (015395) 35685

This elegant and comfortable country house hotel has been run by the Savasi family for nineteen years. Every care has been taken to ensure our guests long to return, from the award-winning Cordon Bleu cuisine, to the well-fitted bedrooms. Our two ground floor lounges each boast a log-burning fire, whilst the dining room has a fashionable conservatory which overlooks the garden and the River Rothay. A 70% customer return each year speaks for itself. Try us!

Bed & Breakfast per night: single room from £30.00–£46.00; double room from £60.00–£92.00
Dinner, Bed & Breakfast per person, per night: £38.00–£56.00
Evening meal 1900 (last orders 2300)

Bedrooms: 1 single, 9 double, 4 twin, 1 family rooms
Bathrooms: 15 en-suite
Parking for 15
Open: February–December
Cards accepted: Mastercard, Visa, Switch/Delta

19 THE GRASMERE HOTEL

HIGHLY COMMENDED

Grasmere, Ambleside, Cumbria LA22 9TA Tel (015394) 35277 Fax (015394) 35277

An elegant Victorian Lakeland stone-built country house set in the quiet location of Grasmere village, in an acre of secluded natural gardens bordered by the River Rothay. Renowned for our cuisine, our beautiful AA Rosette award-winning restaurant offers a four-course dinner with a varied choice of culinary delights that are imaginatively presented with only fresh produce used. A place for all seasons, The Grasmere Hotel extends a warm welcome and all the comfort you could wish for.

Bed & Breakfast per night: single room from £30.00–£55.00; double room from £60.00–£110.00
Dinner, Bed & Breakfast per person, per night: £40.00–£57.00
Evening meal 1930 (last orders 2030)

Bedrooms: 1 single, 9 double, 2 twin
Bathrooms: 12 en-suite
Parking for 16
Open: February–December
Cards accepted: Mastercard, Visa, Amex, Switch/Delta

Entries are cross referenced by number to the maps on pages 18–19

20 WOODLAND CRAG GUEST HOUSE

HIGHLY COMMENDED

Howe Head Lane, Grasmere, Ambleside, Cumbria LA22 9SG Tel (015394) 35351

A warm welcome and an informal atmosphere are found in this delightful house, situated on the edge of Grasmere near Dove Cottage. Secluded but with easy access to all facilities, the accommodation has fine tastefully-decorated bedrooms, all with individual character and wonderful views of the lake, fells or gardens. Ideal for walking and centrally placed for the motorist (enclosed parking). All major outdoor activities are catered for nearby, including sailing, fishing, wind surfing and pony trekking. Totally non-smoking.

Bed & Breakfast per night: single room from £25.00–£27.00; double room from £54.00–£58.00

Bedrooms: 2 single, 2 double, 1 twin
Bathrooms: 3 en-suite, 1 public
Parking for 5

21 LANGDALE HOTEL & COUNTRY CLUB

HIGHLY COMMENDED

Great Langdale, Ambleside, Cumbria LA22 9JD Tel (015394) 37302 Fax (015394) 37694 E-mail info@langdale.co.uk

The Langdale Estate is a haven of peace and tranquillity, an ideal touring base to discover and enjoy all that the Lake District has to offer. Founded on the site of an abandoned 19th-century gunpowder works, it is dotted with massive millstones and other carefully preserved reminders of its history. The hotel has two restaurants, a traditional Lakeland pub and leisure facilities. So much to do and so much to remember... the scenery, the comfort, the good food and the warm and friendly service. www.langdale.co.uk

Bed & Breakfast per night: single occupancy from £90.00–£120.00; double room from £140.00–£200.00
Dinner, Bed & Breakfast per person, per night: £85.00–£115.00 (2 sharing)
Evening meal 1900 (last orders 2200)

Bedrooms: 29 double, 36 twin
Bathrooms: 65 en-suite
Parking for 120
Cards accepted: Mastercard, Visa, Diners, Amex, Switch/Delta

22 LAUREL VILLA

HIGHLY COMMENDED

Lake Road, Ambleside, Cumbria LA22 0DB Tel (015394) 33240

Centrally situated in the heart of the Lake District, this elegant Victorian house, once visited by Beatrix Potter, is now personally run by resident proprietors, and is within easy walking distance of the village of Ambleside and Lake Windermere. Spacious, luxurious rooms decorated in William Morris style, and all the bedrooms overlook the fells. Private car park.

Bed & Breakfast per night: single occupancy £50.00; double room from £60.00–£80.00
Evening meal 1900 (last bookings 1700)

Bedrooms: 7 double, 1 twin
Bathrooms: 8 en-suite
Parking for 10
Cards accepted: Mastercard, Visa, Amex

23 THE SALUTATION HOTEL

HIGHLY COMMENDED

Lake Road, Ambleside, Cumbria LA22 9BX Tel (015394) 32244 Fax (015394) 34157

Being situated in the centre of Ambleside makes us the ideal base for exploring the Lake District. We offer tastefully decorated en-suite rooms, a superb new lounge, and a restaurant serving à la carte and table d'hôte meals. We're proud of our friendly, efficient service and good food. Whilst staying, take advantage of free membership of a nearby luxury leisure club to make your holiday complete.

Bed & Breakfast per night: single room from
£35.50–£48.50; double room from £71.00–£97.00
Dinner, Bed & Breakfast per person, per night:
£48.50–£62.00 (min 2 nights, 2 sharing)
Evening meal 1900 (last orders 2100)

Bedrooms: 3 single, 25 double, 8 twin, 4 triple
Bathrooms: 40 en-suite
Parking for 53
Cards accepted: Mastercard, Visa, Amex, Switch/Delta

24 ROTHAY MANOR HOTEL

HIGHLY COMMENDED

Rothay Bridge, Ambleside, Cumbria LA22 0EH Tel (015394) 33605 Fax (015394) 33607 E-mail hotel@rothaym.demon.co.uk

Rothay Manor, an elegant Regency house run by the Nixon family for over 25 years, stands in its own grounds a quarter mile from the head of Lake Windermere. The drawing rooms and candle-lit dining room still retain the relaxed atmosphere of a private house. Care, consideration and comfort are evident throughout. The menu is varied and meals are prepared and served with flair and imagination to the highest of standards, complemented by a comprehensive wine list. Residents have free use of a nearby Leisure Centre, with swimming pool, sauna, steam room and jacuzzi, and free fishing permits are also available.

Bed & Breakfast per night: single room from
£65.00–£70.00; double room from £105.00–£130.00
Dinner, Bed & Breakfast per person, per night:
£55.00–£85.00
Lunch available: 1230–1400 (1245–1330 on Sundays)

Evening meal 1945 (last orders 2100)
Bedrooms: 2 single, 5 double, 3 twin, 5 triple, 3 family rooms
Bathrooms: 18 en-suite   Parking for 50
Open: February–December
Cards accepted: Mastercard, Visa, Diners, Amex, Switch/Delta

25 AMBLESIDE LODGE

HIGHLY COMMENDED

Rothay Road, Ambleside, Cumbria LA22 0EJ Tel (015394) 31681 Fax (015394) 34547 E-mail cherryho@globalnet.co.uk

Ambleside Lodge is an elegant Lakeland home situated just a minute's walk from the village centre and 3–4 minutes' stroll from Lake Windermere. Set in two and a half acres of peaceful grounds, we provide a fine blend of high quality accommodation and excellent value for money. The Lodge offers a choice of beautifully furnished double rooms, king size four-posters with jacuzzi spa baths and complimentary private leisure club facilities.
www.ambleside-lodge.com

Bed & Breakfast per night: single room from
£30.00–£40.00; double room from £50.00–£130.00
Dinner, Bed & Breakfast per person, per night: from
£50.00
Evening meal 1900 (last orders 2100)

Bedrooms: 2 single, 16 double, 1 twin
Bathrooms: 19 en-suite
Parking for 25
Cards accepted: Mastercard, Visa, Switch/Delta

26 BROADOAKS COUNTRY HOUSE

Listed HIGHLY COMMENDED

Bridge Lane, Troutbeck, Windermere, Cumbria LA23 1LA Tel (015394) 45566 Fax (015394) 88766

A Victorian mansion house set in acres of its own grounds, surrounded by open countryside and with magnificent views of the lake and fells. Decorated in true Victorian fashion with many antiques as well as modern luxury features. Victorian bedrooms with four-poster beds, en-suite jacuzzis and whirlpool spas. Delicious food and wine with a choice of à la carte or table d'hôte menus. Licensed for civil wedding ceremonies. Our award-winning country house is simply somewhere special!

Bed & Breakfast per night: single occupancy from £67.50–£112.50; double room from £90.00–£150.00
Dinner, Bed & Breakfast per person, per night: £75.00–£105.00
Lunch available: 1130–1400 (by reservation only)

Evening meal 1900 (last orders 2000)
Bedrooms: 10 double
Bathrooms: 10 en-suite
Parking for 40

27 WATEREDGE HOTEL

HIGHLY COMMENDED

Waterhead Bay, Ambleside, Cumbria LA22 0EP Tel (015394) 32332 Fax (015394) 31878

Wateredge is a delightfully situated family-run hotel on the shores of Windermere, with gardens leading to the lake edge. It was developed from two 17th-century fishermen's cottages which are still part of the charm of the whole building. Relax in comfortable lounges overlooking the lake, or on our lakeside patio where teas and light lunches are served. In the evening, dine under oak beams and enjoy exquisitely cooked food. Cosy bar, pretty bedrooms and relaxed friendly service.

Bed & Breakfast per night: single room from £48.00–£68.00; double room from £74.00–£156.00
Dinner, Bed & Breakfast per person, per night: £57.00–£98.00
Lunch available: 1215–1400 (light lunches in lounges or lakeside patio)

Evening meal 1900 (last orders 2030)
Bedrooms: 3 single, 11 double, 8 twin
Bathrooms: 22 en-suite
Parking for 25
Cards accepted: Mastercard, Visa, Amex, Switch/Delta

28 CRAG BROW COTTAGE HOTEL

HIGHLY COMMENDED

Helm Road, Bowness-on-Windermere, Cumbria LA23 3BU Tel (015394) 44080 Fax (015394) 46003

Perfectly situated overlooking the old village of Bowness, the lake and Claife Heights. Within two minutes' walk of the lake shore and with ample car parking. All bedrooms are tastefully furnished and en-suite, with colour television, radio, tea/coffee facilities, hairdryer and telephone. Our restaurant has a reputation locally for excellence and we have an extensive wine list and well-stocked bar where you can relax in warmth by a log fire.

Bed & Breakfast per night: single occupancy from £35.00–£50.00; double room from £60.00–£90.00
Dinner, Bed & Breakfast per person, per night: £40.00–£60.00 (2 sharing)
Lunch available: 1200–1345

Evening meal 1800 (last orders 2030)
Bedrooms: 10 double, 1 family room
Bathrooms: 11 en-suite
Parking for 30
Cards accepted: Mastercard, Visa, Switch/Delta

At-a-glance symbols are explained on the flap inside the back cover

29 BURNSIDE HOTEL

HIGHLY COMMENDED

Kendal Road, Bowness-on-Windermere, Windermere, Cumbria LA23 3EP Tel (015394) 42211 or (015394) 44530 Fax (015394) 43824

Set in mature gardens with views over Lake Windermere, three hundred yards from the steamer pier and bustling village centre, the Burnside offers you the perfect location. Parklands Country Club, our all-weather leisure facility, has something for everyone – swimming pool, gymnasium, snooker and squash. All bedrooms have en-suite facilities. Licensed for civil ceremonies. Excellent conference facilities. Pets welcome. Restaurants, two bars and function rooms. Christmas and New Year programme available. &CATEGORY 1

Bed & Breakfast per night: single occupancy from £75.00–£80.00; double room from £106.00–£120.00
Dinner, Bed & Breakfast per person, per night: £93.50–£110.00
Evening meal 1830 (last orders 2145)

Bedrooms: 31 double, 11 twin, 11 triple, 4 family rooms
Bathrooms: 57 en-suite
Parking for 80
Cards accepted: Mastercard, Visa, Diners, Amex, Switch/Delta

30 LINDETH HOWE COUNTRY HOUSE HOTEL

HIGHLY COMMENDED

Longtail Hill, Bowness-on-Windermere, Windermere, Cumbria LA23 3JF Tel (015394) 45759 Fax (015394) 46368 E-mail lindeth.howe@kencomp.net

'A little gem hidden away' – set in six beautiful acres overlooking Lake Windermere, we are 'Somewhere Special' for people looking for peace and tranquillity within comfortable surroundings with excellent AA Rosette food and fine wines. Every bedroom is en-suite, some have four-poster beds and jacuzzi baths and many have beautiful lake views. Leisure facilities are provided free to all residents at the exclusive Spinnaker Club in Windermere Marina just opposite the hotel grounds.

Bed & Breakfast per night: single occupancy from £48.50–£55.00; double room from £68.00–£130.00
Dinner, Bed & Breakfast per person, per night: £51.50–£85.00
Evening meal 1900 (last orders 2030)

Bedrooms: 10 double, 2 twin, 3 triple
Bathrooms: 15 en-suite
Parking for 30
Cards accepted: Mastercard, Visa, Switch/Delta

31 LINTHWAITE HOUSE HOTEL

DE LUXE

Crook Road, Windermere, Cumbria LA23 3JA Tel (015394) 88600 Fax (015394) 88601 E-mail admin@linthwaite.com

Country house hotel, twenty minutes from the M6, situated in fourteen acres of peaceful hilltop grounds, overlooking Lake Windermere and with breathtaking sunsets. The eighteen rooms have en-suite bathrooms, satellite television, radio, telephone and tea/coffee-making facilities. The AA 2 Rosette restaurant serves modern British food using local produce complemented by fine wines. There is a tarn for fly-fishing, croquet, golf practice hole and free use of nearby leisure spa. Romantic breaks feature a king-size double bed with canopy, champagne, chocolates and flowers. English Tourist Board 'Hotel of the Year' 1994. www.linthwaite.com ♠CATEGORY 3

Bed & Breakfast per night: single room from £75.00–£95.00; double room from £75.00–£230.00
Dinner, Bed & Breakfast per person, per night: £49.00–£137.00 (min 2 nights)
Lunch available: 1230–1330

Evening meal 1915 (last orders 2045)
Bedrooms: 1 single, 13 double, 4 twin
Bathrooms: 18 en-suite
Parking for 30
Cards accepted: Mastercard, Visa, Amex, Switch/Delta

32 YEWFIELD VEGETARIAN GUEST HOUSE

HIGHLY COMMENDED

Yewfield, Hawkshead Hill, Ambleside, Cumbria LA22 0PR Tel (015394) 36765 Fax (015394) 36096 E-mail yewfield@compuserve.com

A peaceful and quiet retreat, ideally situated for walking and enjoying this exquisite region of rare natural beauty. The house is set in 25 acres of private grounds where a ten minute stroll leads you to a magnificent viewpoint overlooking Tarn Hows. All rooms are individually appointed to a very high standard with en-suite bath and shower, colour television, radio and tea-making facilities.

Bed & Breakfast per night: single occupancy from £27.00–£33.00; double room from £44.00–£56.00

Bedrooms: 2 double, 1 twin
Bathrooms: 3 en-suite
Parking for 10
Open: February–October

33 BORWICK LODGE

HIGHLY COMMENDED

Outgate, Hawkshead, Ambleside, Cumbria LA22 0PU Tel (015394) 36332 Fax (015394) 36332

1998 winner of the AWARD for 'Accommodation of the Highest Standards'. A leafy driveway entices you to a rather special 17th-century country house with magnificent panoramic lake and mountain views, quietly secluded in the heart of the Lakes. The beautiful en-suite bedrooms include 'Special Occasions' and 'Romantic Breaks' with king-size four-poster beds. Rosemary and Colin Haskell welcome you to this most beautiful corner of England. TOTALLY NON-SMOKING.

Bed & Breakfast per night: single occupancy from £45.00–£55.00; double room from £48.00–£72.00

Bedrooms: 5 double, 1 family room
Bathrooms: 6 en-suite
Parking for 8

34 WEST VALE COUNTRY GUEST HOUSE

HIGHLY COMMENDED

Far Sawrey, Hawkshead, Ambleside, Cumbria LA22 0LQ Tel (015394) 42817

West Vale is superbly situated on the edge of the picturesque village of Far Sawrey, between Windermere Ferry and Hawkshead, in the heart of Beatrix Potter country. Excellent accommodation and a very warm welcome await you at this peaceful, family-run guest house. The meals are all home cooked, using local produce and complemented by a list of selected wines. Full central heating and a log fire in the lounge. All rooms are en-suite.

Bed & Breakfast per night: single occupancy £24.00; double room £48.00
Dinner, Bed & Breakfast per person, per night: £36.00
Evening meal 1900 (last bookings 1600)

Bedrooms: 3 double, 2 triple, 1 family room
Bathrooms: 6 en-suite
Parking for 8
Open: March–October

At-a-glance symbols are explained on the flap inside the back cover

35 EES WYKE COUNTRY HOUSE

 HIGHLY COMMENDED

Sawrey, Ambleside, Cumbria LA22 0JZ Tel (015394) 36393 Fax (015394) 36393

This Georgian house, with its idyllic setting, is a perfect choice for that special break away. Most of our spacious bedrooms have a wonderful view of Esthwaite Water – all have the comfort you would expect from a hotel with a well-established reputation. Beatrix Potter made Ees Wyke her holiday home, the surrounding scenery providing the inspiration for the illustrations in her books. Our delicious dinners and hearty breakfasts are served in our delightful restaurant overlooking the lake.

Bed & Breakfast per night: single occupancy from £44.00–£56.00; double room from £88.00
Dinner, Bed & Breakfast per person, per night: £56.00–£58.00
Evening meal 1900 (last orders 1930)

Bedrooms: 5 double, 3 twin
Bathrooms: 6 en-suite, 2 private, 1 public
Parking for 12
Open: March–December
Cards accepted: Amex

Piel Island

Ray Chatfield

Just offshore from Barrow in Furness is Piel Island, a small rocky outcrop in the sea surmounted by the brooding ruins of a castle. Tiny and unimportant it may be, but it still has its ferry service, pub – even its own king.

The island has a colourful history. It is separated from the mainland yet remains fairly accessible, so making it a useful haven in troubled times. From the 14th century it was the centre of a lively smuggling trade largely orchestrated by the monks of Furness Abbey. They built the impressive castle as a fortified warehouse to keep their cargoes safe from raiders, and to keep the king's customs men at bay. The island's most historic moment arrived in June 1487, when Lambert Simnel, pretender to the English throne, landed at Piel with 8,000 men. Simnel was an impostor, a baker's son claiming to be the Earl of Warwick (then imprisoned in the Tower of London) who, backed by Margaret of Burgundy, gathered a force of German mercenaries and Irish recruits, intending to take the throne by force. Leaving Piel, he set off across Furness towards London, but was defeated at the Battle of Stoke on June 16th. In contrast, the 18th century brought more prosperous and settled times to the island, with Piel's busy harbour servicing Furness's thriving shipping and iron industries. The island's pub and its few houses were built at this time.

The Ship Inn continues to flourish, a useful watering-hole for sailors and day trippers from the mainland. The landlord is traditionally known as the 'King of Piel', a reference, it is supposed, to Lambert Simnel's claim to the throne. Anyone who sits in a particular old wooden chair in the pub, becomes a 'Knight of Piel', and must carry out certain gallant duties – such as buying everyone a drink, being a moderate smoker, a lover of the opposite sex, and generally of good character. If shipwrecked, a Knight of Piel has the right to free board and lodging in the pub.

The ferry from Roa runs from April to October, 11am–5pm weather permitting (telephone in advance: 01229 835809), making the island an easy day trip. Facilities are minimal (the island has neither electricity nor telephone) but for those wishing to stay longer, camping is permitted anywhere on the island by arrangement, on arrival, with the Ship Inn.

36 SAWREY HOUSE COUNTRY HOTEL

HIGHLY COMMENDED

Near Sawrey, Ambleside, Cumbria LA22 0LF Tel (015394) 36387 Fax (015394) 36010 E-mail sawreyhous@aol.com

Situated in three acres of grounds in the centre of the Lake District National Park, this family-run hotel offers a very special combination of elegance and comfort. It directly overlooks both Grizedale Forest and Esthwaite Water, nestling in the peaceful conservation hamlet which won the heart of Beatrix Potter, whose house 'Hilltop' lies nearby. We place special emphasis on our delicious five-course dinners, complemented with a well-stocked cellar offering reasonably priced wines.

Bed & Breakfast per night: single room £42.00; double room from £84.00–£106.00
Dinner, Bed & Breakfast per person, per night: £50.00–£68.00
Evening meal 1900 (last orders 2000)

Bedrooms: 1 single, 5 double, 4 twin, 1 triple
Bathrooms: 11 en-suite
Parking for 20
Open: February–December
Cards accepted: Mastercard, Visa

37 GRIZEDALE LODGE HOTEL AND RESTAURANT IN THE FOREST

HIGHLY COMMENDED

Grizedale, Hawkshead, Ambleside, Cumbria LA22 0QL Tel (015394) 36532 Fax (015394) 36572

Idyllically situated, this former shooting lodge provides a perfect escape and a timeless sense of ease, whilst being at the heart of all Lakeland has to offer. Attractive rooms, including four-posters with a special atmosphere, are complemented by an intimate lounge and restaurant with beautiful forest views, where lovingly-prepared and varied menus are served. Close by are the famous sculpture trails and the Theatre in the Forest. Unobtrusive personal attention completes a pleasing package.

Bed & Breakfast per night: single occupancy from £42.50–£47.50; double room from £60.00–£75.00
Dinner, Bed & Breakfast per person, per night: £49.50–£65.00 (2 sharing)
Lunch available: 1230–1330

Evening meal 1900 (last orders 1930)
Bedrooms: 7 double, 2 twin
Bathrooms: 9 en-suite
Parking for 25   Open: February–December
Cards accepted: Mastercard, Visa, Amex, Switch/Delta

38 HOLBECK GHYLL COUNTRY HOUSE HOTEL

DE LUXE

Holbeck Lane, Windermere, Cumbria LA23 1LU Tel (015394) 32375 Fax (015394) 34743

Peacefully located in eight acres of grounds with breathtaking views across Lake Windermere. 19th-century hunting lodge, former home of Lord Lonsdale, with log fires and intimate candle-lit oak-panelled restaurant serving AA 3 Rosette food. Luxurious bedrooms with vases of fresh flowers, decanters of sherry and fluffy bathrobes. Young, caring staff offering genuine hospitality. Holbeck Ghyll is 'Something Special' for that eagerly-awaited important anniversary or birthday celebration. Rated by all guide books in their highest category. Central Lakes location. Luxury health spa and tennis court. Cumbria Tourist Board 'Hotel of the Year' 1998.

Dinner, Bed & Breakfast per person, per night: £79.00–£145.00
Lunch available: 1200–1400
Evening meal 1900 (last orders 2045)

Bedrooms: 11 double, 8 twin, 1 triple
Bathrooms: 20 en-suite
Parking for 26
Cards accepted: Mastercard, Diners, Amex, Switch/Delta

39 GILPIN LODGE COUNTRY HOUSE HOTEL AND RESTAURANT

 DE LUXE

Crook Road, Windermere, Cumbria LA23 3NE Tel (015394) 88818 Fax (015394) 88058 E-mail hotel@gilpin-lodge.co.uk

A friendly, elegant, relaxing hotel in twenty acres of woodlands, moors and delightful country gardens. Twelve miles from the M6, two miles from Lake Windermere and almost opposite the golf course. Sumptuous bedrooms – many with jacuzzi baths, split-level sitting areas and four-poster beds. Exquisite cuisine (AA 3 Rosettes, RAC Blue Ribbon). Attentive service. Guests have free use of nearby leisure club. Year-round breaks.
www.gilpin-lodge.co.uk

Dinner, Bed & Breakfast per person, per night:
£50.00–£110.00
Lunch available: 1200–1430
Evening meal 1900 (last orders 2045)

Bedrooms: 14 double
Bathrooms: 14 en-suite
Parking for 40
Cards accepted: Mastercard, Visa, Diners, Amex, Switch/Delta

40 LINDETH FELL COUNTRY HOUSE HOTEL

 HIGHLY COMMENDED

Windermere, Cumbria LA23 3JP Tel (015394) 43286 or 44287 Fax (015394) 47455

'One of the most beautifully situated hotels in Lakeland'. In a magnificent garden setting above Lake Windermere, Lindeth Fell offers brilliant lake views, peaceful surroundings and superb modern English cooking – at highly competitive prices. Lawns are laid for croquet and putting, and Windermere Golf Club is one mile away. Good fishing is available free and interesting walks start from the door. Call for a brochure from the resident owners.

Bed & Breakfast per night: single room from
£50.00–£70.00; double room from £100.00–£140.00
Dinner, Bed & Breakfast per person, per night:
£62.50–£82.50
Lunch available: Sunday lunch 1300

Evening meal 1930 (last orders 2030)
Bedrooms: 2 single, 3 double, 6 twin, 4 triple
Bathrooms: 15 en-suite
Parking for 20
Cards accepted: Mastercard, Visa

41 CEDAR MANOR HOTEL

HIGHLY COMMENDED

Ambleside Road, Windermere, Cumbria LA23 1AX Tel (015394) 43192 Fax (015394) 45970

Situated close to Windermere village and the lake, Cedar Manor Hotel is a haven for food lovers and those who enjoy the good things in life. Personally run by Lynn and Martin Hadley, the hotel has won many awards for food and service over the past twelve years. For those who like to work off the calories gained in the restaurant we have facilities at the nearby Spinnaker Club for their enjoyment.

Bed & Breakfast per night: single occupancy from
£28.50–£45.00; double room from £57.00–£90.00
Dinner, Bed & Breakfast per person, per night:
£34.00–£58.00
Lunch available: 1230–1500, Wednesday–Sunday

Evening meal 1930 (last orders 2030)
Bedrooms: 9 double, 3 twin
Bathrooms: 12 en-suite
Parking for 16

42 TULLYTHWAITE HOUSE

 HIGHLY COMMENDED

Underbarrow, Kendal, Cumbria LA8 8BB Tel (015395) 68397

Tullythwaite House, a Grade II listed Regency house, is set in one acre of flower-filled gardens in the beautiful and tranquil Lyth Valley. Our bedrooms have lovely views, en-suite bathrooms, fresh flowers and antiques. Breakfast is served in the elegant dining room overlooking the unspoilt countryside. Dinner is optional, but we are renowned for excellent home cooking. Foremost a family home, the warmest of welcomes is assured. Winner of the Cumbria Tourist Board 'Bed & Breakfast of the Year' Award 1997.

Bed & Breakfast per night: single occupancy from £25.00–£28.00; double room £50.00
Dinner, Bed & Breakfast per person, per night: £40.00
Evening meal 1930 (pre-booking necessary)

Bedrooms: 2 double, 1 twin
Bathrooms: 3 en-suite
Parking for 8
Open: February–November

43 MIDDLE ORD MANOR HOUSE

 DE LUXE

Middle Ord Farm, Berwick-upon-Tweed, Northumberland TD15 2XQ Tel (01289) 306323 Fax (01289) 308423

Feeling stressed, want to unwind, or are you just wanting to indulge yourselves? Either way, why not visit our award-winning home and experience the warmth and quality of gracious living in a secluded tranquil setting. Relax in our spacious en-suite rooms (four-poster if desired). Sorry, no children or pets. www.middleord.ntb.org.uk

Bed & Breakfast per night: double room from £54.00

Bedrooms: 2 double, 1 twin
Bathrooms: 3 en-suite, 1 public
Parking for 6
Open: April–October

44 THE COACH HOUSE

 HIGHLY COMMENDED

Crookham, Cornhill-on-Tweed, Northumberland TD12 4TD Tel (01890) 820293 or (01890) 820284 Fax (01890) 820284

The Coach House offers warm, spacious bedrooms surrounding a sunlit courtyard. The large lounge, with peach leather furniture and fine pictures, overlooks a west-facing terrace. A flock of Soay sheep graze beneath the damson trees. Food is fresh and varied, reflecting modern ideas on healthy eating, with some Mediterranean influence. Local fish, game and meat are used, organically-reared where possible. Special diets catered for. Excellent facilities for disabled guests. Lovingly renovated to a high standard.
&CATEGORY 1

Bed & Breakfast per night: single room from £23.00–£36.00; double room from £46.00–£72.00
Dinner, Bed & Breakfast per person, per night: £39.50–£52.50
Evening meal 1930

Bedrooms: 2 single, 2 double, 5 twin
Bathrooms: 7 en-suite, 2 public
Parking for 12
Open: March–October
Cards accepted: Mastercard, Visa

At-a-glance symbols are explained on the flap inside the back cover

45 WAREN HOUSE HOTEL

~~~~ ~~~~ ~~~~ ~~~~ HIGHLY COMMENDED

Waren Mill, Belford, Northumberland NE70 7EE Tel (01668) 214581 Fax (01668) 214484 E-mail enquiries@warenhousehotel.co.uk

A traditional 18th-century country house set in six acres of well-tended, wooded grounds and a walled garden, on the edge of Budle Bay overlooking Holy Island. Anita & Peter Laverack have created a haven of peace and tranquillity for adults who enjoy good food, wine and excellent accommodation. The magnificent spacious dining room overlooks Lindisfarne, while the drawing room looks over the Cheviot Hills. The service from local staff is friendly, efficient and discreet.

Bed & Breakfast per night: single occupancy from £57.50–£85.00; double room from £115.00–£135.00
Dinner, Bed & Breakfast per person, per night: £57.00–£74.50
Evening meal 1900 (last orders 2030)

Bedrooms: 7 double, 3 twin
Bathrooms: 10 en-suite
Parking for 15
Cards accepted: Mastercard, Visa, Diners, Amex, Switch/Delta

Chillingham White Cattle

Many visitors to Chillingham, Northumberland, come to see its splendid castle (tel: 01668 215359), set imposingly above the River Till, and complete with dungeons, torture chambers and a spine-tingling assortment of lurid ghost stories. But also at Chillingham is a 600-acre (243-hectare) park, managed separately from the castle, which for over 700 years has been home to a herd of wild white cattle, now the only pure-bred herd of its type in the world.

The 40 or so animals that roam freely within the confines of the walled park are thought to be descendants of the wild oxen which inhabited Britain in pre-historic times. Too savage to be tamed, they wandered at will across vast tracts of land foraging for food. In the 13th century, Chillingham Park was enclosed by a wall and a herd of these cattle confined within it. Because of their aggressive natures, they were quite safe from cattle rustlers, and remained here, undisturbed, through seven centuries.

The cows are creamy white with long, black-tipped horns. The herd is ruled by a 'king' bull, which sires all the calves, until challenged by a rival male. The competing bulls attack each other head to head in a series of short 'rounds' until one is deemed victorious, and allowed to take his place as king. Calves are born away from the herd and are kept hidden by their mothers in hollows in the bracken. If touched by human hand they are abandoned and will certainly die.

Because the cattle are so wild, it is impossible to assist them in any way if they are ill, injured or having calving difficulties. Even in hard winters when food is scarce, they will eat only meadow hay, refusing other food even when the alternative is starvation. In the severe winter of 1947, 20 of Chillingham's 33 animals died and it was feared that the breed might become extinct. Gradually the numbers increased to previous levels, but, as a precaution, a reserve herd was established in Scotland.

Once the private property of the Lords Tankerville of Chillingham Castle, the herd is now owned by the Chillingham Wild Cattle Association, which allows viewings of the cattle in the company of a warden (tel: 01668 215250 for details of viewing times; not advisable for visitors with disabilities). Binoculars are recommended as it is not possible to approach these dangerous but fascinating beasts.

Glyn Satterley

46 LOW DOVER BEADNELL BAY

〰️ HIGHLY COMMENDED

Harbour Road, Beadnell, Chathill, Northumberland NE67 5BJ Tel (01665) 720291 or (07971) 444070 E-mail KathandBob@lowdover.demon.co.uk

Kath and Bob warmly invite you to relax in our luxurious beachside home which has an atmosphere of serene peace and tranquillity. Feel special in our superior, elegant, ground-floor suites, each with patio doors and lounges. Enjoy a hearty home-cooked breakfast with panoramic views across Beadnell Bay and over to the Cheviot Hills. Sit in our beautiful gardens, admire the many hanging baskets or stroll fifty yards down to the golden beach and beyond. Spectacular scenery surrounds us, surrender to the charm of Northumberland. Three miles to the Farne Islands. Private parking. Free brochure. www.lowdover.demon.co.uk

Bed & Breakfast per night: double room from £50.00–£56.00 (min 2 nights, 2 sharing)

Bedrooms: 1 double, 1 triple
Bathrooms: 2 en-suite
Parking for 4

47 DUKES RYDE

〰️〰️ HIGHLY COMMENDED

Longhoughton Road, Lesbury, Alnwick, Northumberland NE66 3AT Tel (01665) 830855 Fax (01665) 830855

Dukes Ryde is a detached house standing in lovely gardens on the outskirts of the peaceful village of Lesbury. It is furnished with interesting antiques, and all rooms have tea/coffee-making facilities, colour televisions and views over the gardens. One room has a four-poster bed. It is an ideal base from which to explore magnificent sandy beaches, castles, bird sanctuaries and golf courses.

Bed & Breakfast per night: double room from £49.00–£50.00

Bedrooms: 1 double, 2 twin
Bathrooms: 2 en-suite, 2 private
Parking for 6

48 HAWKHILL FARMHOUSE

〰️〰️ HIGHLY COMMENDED

Lesbury, Alnwick, Northumberland NE66 3PG Tel (01665) 830380 Fax (01665) 830380

Relax and enjoy the friendly atmosphere of our spacious farmhouse with its magnificent views over lovely countryside. Only two miles from the coast and glorious sandy beaches. Elegant dining room and large sitting room with access to lawns and grounds. All bedrooms are en-suite with full central heating, television and tea/coffee-making facilities. Ideal for relaxing, birdwatching, walking, golfing and visiting historic sites.

Bed & Breakfast per night: double room from £45.00–£50.00

Bedrooms: 1 double, 2 twin
Bathrooms: 3 en-suite
Parking for 10
Open: April–end October

At-a-glance symbols are explained on the flap inside the back cover

49 LOW STEAD

 HIGHLY COMMENDED

Wark, Hexham, Northumberland NE48 3DP Tel (01434) 230352 E-mail peel@lowstead.freeserve.co.uk

Low Stead was formerly a 16th-century bastle house (fortified farmhouse) and is now a haven of peace set deep in unspoilt countryside in the National Park, between Hadrian's Wall and Kielder. Imaginatively-produced meals are served in the oak-beamed dining room. The call of the curlew and the sheep on the fells are the loudest sounds to be heard. Solitude, history and comfort combine to create Low Stead's unique atmosphere. Packed lunches available. A no smoking house.

Bed & Breakfast per night: double room £53.00
Dinner, Bed & Breakfast per person, per night:
£42.00–£47.00
Evening meal 1900 (last orders 2000)

Bedrooms: 1 double, 1 twin
Bathrooms: 2 en-suite
Parking for 6
Open: March–October

50 GRAND HOTEL

 HIGHLY COMMENDED

Grand Parade, Tynemouth, North Shields, Tyne and Wear NE30 4ER Tel (0191) 293 6666 Fax (0191) 293 6665

High on the cliffs overlooking beautiful Long Sands beach, this imposing Victorian building was the seaside home of the Duchess of Northumberland and has now been completely modernised to offer every comfort.

Bed & Breakfast per night: single occupancy from
£65.00–£120.00; double room from £70.00–£150.00
Dinner, Bed & Breakfast per person, per night:
£80.00–£115.00
Lunch available: 1200–1430

Evening meal 1830 (last orders 2200)
Bedrooms: 32 double, 2 twin, 9 triple, 2 family rooms
Bathrooms: 45 en-suite   Parking for 30
Cards accepted: Mastercard, Visa, Diners, Amex,
Switch/Delta

51 BEE COTTAGE FARM

 HIGHLY COMMENDED

Castleside, Consett, Co Durham DH8 9HW Tel (01207) 508224

A working farm set in peaceful surroundings with access to quiet pleasant walks with unspoilt views. The farm is ideally situated for visits to Beamish Museum, Durham Cathedral, Hadrian's Wall or as an overnight break in a long journey. There are some ground floor rooms, a tearoom open daily between 1300 and 1800, and an evening meal is available. No smoking. Dogs by arrangement. You will be made very welcome.

Bed & Breakfast per night: single room from
£28.00–£35.00; double room from £44.00–£70.00
Evening meal 1900 (last orders 2000)

Bedrooms: 1 single, 3 double, 3 twin, 1 triple, 1 family
room
Bathrooms: 4 en-suite, 2 public
Parking for 20

52 BRUNSWICK HOUSE

〰〰〰 HIGHLY COMMENDED

55 Market Place, Middleton-in-Teesdale, Barnard Castle, CoDurham DL12 0QH Tel (01833) 640393 Fax (01833) 640393 E-mail brunswickhouse@onyxnet.co.uk

Situated in unspoilt Teesdale, our guest house provides the perfect centre for those seeking to enjoy the delights of unspoilt countryside, quiet roads, flower-filled meadows and gentle strolls through the breathtaking scenery of the North Pennines. Our reputation is built on outstanding home cooking using, wherever possible, only fresh and local produce. The house, dating from 1760, retains great charm with beamed ceilings and original fireplaces, thoughtfully combined with all modern comforts.

Bed & Breakfast per night: single occupancy max £30.00; double room max £45.00
Dinner, Bed & Breakfast per person, per night: max £38.50
Evening meal 1930 (last bookings 1900)

Bedrooms: 3 double, 2 twin
Bathrooms: 5 en-suite
Parking for 5
Cards accepted: Mastercard, Visa, Amex

The Angel of the North

In February 1998, something remarkable happened on the southern edge of Gateshead, one of England's erstwhile industrial centres. Here, on a hilltop visible from both the A1 and the main London–Newcastle railway, a winged figure was sighted. No ordinary angel, this, for reports spoke of it being as high as four double-decker buses and with a span as wide as a jumbo jet. It stood with wings outstretched, suggesting welcome and embrace. Word got out, cameras arrived and a website was devoted to it (www.gatesheadmbc.gov.uk). More remarkably still, all these reports turned out to be entirely true.

The Angel of the North, to give it its full name, is almost certainly England's most high-profile work of art. The creation of sculptor Antony Gormley, it towers 65ft (20m) above its site at the head of the Team Valley – and is set to become as much a symbol of the North-East as the Tyne Bridge. Its history, though, begins back in 1989, when the former bath block at the Team Colliery was reclaimed. This, Gateshead Council decided, would be an ideal location for a 'landmark sculpture'. Once the site had been landscaped, the council asked a shortlist of international artists to pitch for the commission, a competition won in January 1994 by Gormley.

The scale of the design clearly called for considerable funding, but the expense – about £800,000 all told – was met without any contributions from the local council tax. Both the size and the exposed position meant that the 200-ton angel would have to be enormously strong to cope with winds of up to 100mph (160kph). The engineering firm of Ove Arup was called in to advise and, after close consultation with the sculptor, fabrication began at nearby Hartlepool. By September 1997, vast sections of the sculpture, made from a weather-resistant steel designed to mellow to a rich red-brown, were arriving at Team Valley under police escort.

Thanks to its lofty position – it reminds the sculptor of a megalithic mound – more than one person every second will see the angel. This, in theory, works out at 33 million a year. Given that it is thought it will have a life of a hundred years or more, a lot of people are going to witness this arresting apparition.

Colin Cuthbert

53 HORSLEY HALL

 HIGHLY COMMENDED

Eastgate, Stanhope, Bishop Auckland, Co Durham DL13 2LJ Tel (01388) 517239 or 0802 327106 Fax (01388) 517608 E-mail horsleyhall@compuserve.com

The Hall is an elegant three-storey manor house dating back to the 17th century, situated in the heart of picturesque Weardale, an area of outstanding natural beauty. Whatever your interests – walking, cycling, fishing, painting, or relaxing by the fireside – all can be accommodated in this tranquil setting. The Hall has been recently fully refurbished, offering all modern amenities for the discerning guest, and we offer a varied choice of menu with cuisine prepared to a high standard.

Bed & Breakfast per night: single room max £46.75; double room max £60.50
Dinner, Bed & Breakfast per person, per night: £52.25–£68.75
Evening meal 1900 (last orders 2030)

Bedrooms: 1 single, 4 double, 1 twin
Bathrooms: 6 en-suite
Parking for 60

54 GREENHEAD COUNTRY HOUSE HOTEL

 HIGHLY COMMENDED

Fir Tree, Crook, Co Durham DL15 8BL Tel (01388) 763143 Fax (01388) 763143

Greenhead Hotel is perfectly situated at the centre of rural Durham countryside at the foot of Weardale, just fifteen minutes from Durham city, surrounded by open fields and woodlands. The tranquillity of Greenhead is complemented by the fact that only residential guests are catered for (no public bars or discos). The accolades, describing why Greenhead offers something special in the way of service and accommodation, can be seen in our full colour brochure.

Bed & Breakfast per night: single room from £40.00–£45.00; double room from £50.00–£60.00

Bedrooms: 1 single, 3 double, 2 twin
Bathrooms: 5 en-suite, 1 public
Parking for 15
Cards accepted: Mastercard, Visa

55 ELDON HOUSE

 HIGHLY COMMENDED

East Green, Heighington, Darlington, Co Durham DL5 6PP Tel (01325) 312270 Fax (01325) 315580

This is a 17th-century house with spacious bedrooms, overlooking the village green, with a large garden and tennis court. There is ample parking. Easy to find and convenient, it is situated six miles from Darlington railway station, twelve miles from Teesside Airport, three miles from A1(M), and three miles from Newton Aycliffe.

Bed & Breakfast per night: single occupancy from £30.00–£35.00; double room from £45.00–£50.00

Bedrooms: 3 twin
Bathrooms: 1 en-suite, 2 private
Parking for 6

Entries are cross referenced by number to the maps on pages 18–19

56 JERSEY FARM HOTEL

HIGHLY COMMENDED

Darlington Road, Barnard Castle, Co Durham DL12 8TA Tel (01833) 638223 Fax (01833) 631988 E-mail jerseyfarmhotel@infinet

Situated one mile east of Barnard Castle in an area of outstanding natural beauty. The Watsons created the hotel in 1978 after previously farming the land. All en-suite, comfortable rooms with panoramic views. The Carvery Restaurant is famous for home cooking and plenty of it! Alternative menu available. Residents' lounge, bar and conservatory are all tastefully decorated. Spacious surroundings to meet the animals down on the farm.

Bed & Breakfast per night: single room from £55.00–£63.00; double room from £70.00–£82.00
Lunch available: 1200–1400 Tuesday–Friday; 1200–1500 Sunday
Evening meal 1900 (last orders 2100)

Bedrooms: 1 single, 8 double, 6 twin, 4 triple, 1 family room
Bathrooms: 20 en-suite
Parking for 100
Cards accepted: Mastercard, Visa, Switch/Delta

57 SIMONSTONE HALL

HIGHLY COMMENDED

Hawes, North Yorkshire DL8 3LY Tel (01969) 667255 Fax (01969) 667741 E-mail email@simonstonehall.demon.co.uk

With magnificent views over Upper Wensleydale, this impressive 17th-century former shooting lodge is a haven of peace and tranquillity. Simonstone Hall has an atmosphere of relaxed, warm friendliness, with attention to detail its guiding principle. All eighteen bedrooms are extremely elegant, en-suite, have four-poster or French sleigh beds, and are individually furnished with antiques. Simonstone Hall is ideal for a sporting break or simply getting away from it all, shedding the cares of modern-day living, and enjoying some of the luxuries of life we can offer. AA Rosette award 1998.

Bed & Breakfast per night: single occupancy from £37.50–£70.00; double room from £75.00–£140.00
Dinner, Bed & Breakfast per person, per night: £57.50–£90.00
Lunch available: 1200–1400

Evening meal 1900 (last orders 2100)
Bedrooms: 14 double, 4 twin
Bathrooms: 18 en-suite
Parking for 48
Cards accepted: Mastercard, Visa, Amex, Switch/Delta

58 HELM

HIGHLY COMMENDED

Askrigg, Leyburn, North Yorkshire DL8 3JF Tel (01969) 650443 Fax (01969) 650443 E-mail drewhelm@compuserve.com

Idyllically situated with 'the finest view in Wensleydale'. Experience the comfort, peace and quiet of our 17th-century hillside Dales farmhouse. Each charmingly furnished bedroom has en-suite facilities and many special little touches. Period furniture, oak beams and log fires create the ideal atmosphere in which to relax and share our passion for really good food. We offer a superb choice of breakfasts, home-made bread and preserves, exceptionally good dinners and an inspired selection of wines. Totally non-smoking.

Bed & Breakfast per night: double room from £58.00–£72.00
Dinner, Bed & Breakfast per person, per night: £45.50 (3 nights or more) – £52.50 (1 night)
Evening meal 1900

Bedrooms: 2 double, 1 twin
Bathrooms: 3 en-suite
Parking for 5
Open: January–November
Cards accepted: Mastercard, Visa

At-a-glance symbols are explained on the flap inside the back cover

59 WENSLEYDALE HEIFER INN

〰〰〰〰 HIGHLY COMMENDED

West Witton, Wensleydale, North Yorkshire DL8 4LS Tel (01969) 622322 Fax (01969) 624183 E-mail heifer@dalenet.co.uk

17th-century country inn located in the Yorkshire Dales National Park, amidst glorious and unspoilt countryside. Ideal for visits to historic castles, National Trust properties and Middleham Racing Stables. Superbly placed for walking in the Dales. All bedrooms recently refurbished. Log fires burn when necessary. Four-posters available for that special occasion. Rustic country cooking. AA Rosette award-winning food. Pets most welcome!

Bed & Breakfast per night: single occupancy from £49.00–£55.00; double room from £70.00–£95.00 Dinner, Bed & Breakfast per person, per night: £55.00–£70.00 (min 2 nights) Lunch available: 1130–1400

Evening meal 1900 (last orders 2130) Bedrooms: 8 double, 5 twin, 1 triple, 1 family room Bathrooms: 15 en-suite   Parking for 40 Cards accepted: Mastercard, Visa, Diners, Amex, Switch/Delta

Yorkshire Dales Barns

THE BEAUTY OF THE YORKSHIRE DALES derives in large part from the natural magnificence of the landscape: nature generously gave this central stretch of the Pennine chain dramatic limestone outcrops and clear, fast-running rivers. But man, too, has added to the splendour of the Dales. The trees may have been cleared long ago, but in their stead on the lower slopes came hay-meadows full of as many as 40 species of herb, bounded by drystone walls of simple beauty. In the northern Dales such as Swaledale and Arkengarthdale, almost every field has its own barn, each one adding to the glorious impression these valleys create.

These barns – it is estimated that there are over a thousand in Swaledale and Arkengarthdale alone – are a sign of a vanishing form of agriculture. In the 17th-, 18th- and 19th-centuries, when most of these barns were built, farms were small and numerous. Many who tended the land also worked in the local lead and coal mines, and so had little time to devote to farming. The summer harvest of the hay crop was the most labour-intensive time of year, and the hard-pressed farmers evolved an agricultural system which allowed a more even spread of work. They built their barns – almost all using the drystone method of construction with stones sloping outwards to take the rain away – in the fields where the hay was growing. Storing the hay in the nearby barns was therefore a simple task. Since the cows spent the winter in the same barn as their foodstuff, it was easy both to feed the cattle and to fertilise the same field with their manure. The *quid pro quo* was that the farmer had to walk to each of his barns in the winter months – not too arduous if there were only a few barns on the round.

Modern employment practices and the quest for efficiency have meant that farms are now few and large. This no longer fits in with the traditional system, and many outlying field barns have become redundant. In Swaledale and Arkengarthdale a conservation scheme run by the national park has saved countless from dereliction; some are still used by their owners while others have found new life as 'bunkhouse barns'. These offer basic accommodation to walkers and are often on or near long-distance footpaths. At Hazel Brow, Low Row, visitors may go inside a traditional Dales barn as part of the open farm scheme (tel: 01748 886224 for more details).

60 MILLERS HOUSE HOTEL

HIGHLY COMMENDED

Middleham, Wensleydale, North Yorkshire DL8 4NR   Tel (01969) 622630 Fax (01969) 623570 E-mail hotel@millershouse.demon.co.uk

An award-winning luxury hotel set in the historic village of Middleham in the heart of Herriot's Yorkshire Dales where the owners emphasise personal care and attention to detail. The renowned restaurant (AA Rosette) uses quality local produce, including homegrown herbs and vegetables, and provides an original selection of dishes, including vegetarian choices. Elegant, individually-furnished en-suite rooms, including a luxury four-poster, are decorated in keeping with the Georgian period. Gourmet Wine Weekends, Racing Breaks, and Christmas and New Year celebrations are a must. Yorkshire & Humberside Tourist Board 'Hotel of the Year' runner-up.

Bed & Breakfast per night: single room from
£38.00–£40.00; double room from £76.00–£94.00
Dinner, Bed & Breakfast per person, per night:
£45.50–£65.50
Evening meal 1900 (last orders 2030)

Bedrooms: 1 single, 3 double, 3 twin
Bathrooms: 6 en-suite, 1 private
Parking for 8
Open: February–December
Cards accepted: Mastercard, Visa, Switch/Delta

61 MANOR HOUSE FARM

HIGHLY COMMENDED

Ingleby Greenhow, Great Ayton, North Yorkshire TS9 6RB   Tel (01642) 722384 E-mail mbloom@globalnet.co.uk

A charming old farm (part c1760) set idyllically in 168 acres of parkland and woodland at the foot of the Cleveland Hills in the North York Moors National Park. Wildlife surrounds the farmhouse. The environment is tranquil and secluded, and the accommodation is warm and welcoming. Guests have their own entrance, dining room and lounge with library. Evening dinners are prepared meticulously and the hosts are proud of their reputation for fine food and wines.

Dinner, Bed & Breakfast per person, per night:
£42.50–£47.50 (2 sharing)
Evening meal 1900 (last bookings 1600)

Bedrooms: 1 double, 2 twin
Bathrooms: 1 en-suite, 2 private
Parking for 66
Cards accepted: Mastercard, Visa, Switch/Delta

62 ACACIA LODGE

HIGHLY COMMENDED

21 Ripon Road, Harrogate, North Yorkshire HG1 2JL   Tel (01423) 560752 Fax (01423) 503725

Acacia Lodge is a warm, lovingly-restored and charming small family-run hotel with pretty gardens in a select, central conservation area, just a short stroll from Harrogate's fashionable shops, many restaurants and attractions. It retains all of its original character, with fine furnishings, beautiful antiques and old paintings. All bedrooms are en-suite and luxuriously furnished with every comfort to accommodate the most discerning guest. Award-winning breakfasts are served in the oak-furnished dining room and guests can relax in the beautiful lounge, which has an open fire and a library of books. Private floodlit parking for all. A non-smoking establishment.

Bed & Breakfast per night: single occupancy from
£44.00–£58.00; double room from £54.00–£68.00

Bedrooms: 1 double, 2 twin, 2 triple, 1 family room
Bathrooms: 6 en-suite
Parking for 8

63 RUSKIN HOTEL AND RESTAURANT

 HIGHLY COMMENDED

1 Swan Road, Harrogate, North Yorkshire HG1 2SS Tel (01423) 502045 Fax (01423) 506131 E-mail ruskin.hotel@virgin.net

A truly outstanding small Victorian hotel set in lovely mature gardens in a quiet conservation area, only five minutes' stroll from the town, magnificent gardens and conference/exhibition halls. Beautifully appointed and decorated, antique furnished en-suite bedrooms, including a four-poster room. Gracious and relaxing drawing room with fine antiques, open fire and interesting books. Renowned for superb breakfasts and excellent English cuisine served in the delightful Victorian-style restaurant with bar. Our warmth and hospitality ensure your stay is 'something special'. Private floodlit car park.

Bed & Breakfast per night: single room from £55.00–£69.00; double room from £80.00–£110.00
Dinner, Bed & Breakfast per person, per night: £50.00–£60.00 (min 2 nights)
Evening meal 1900 (last orders 2030)

Bedrooms: 2 single, 3 double, 1 triple
Bathrooms: 6 en-suite
Parking for 10
Cards accepted: Mastercard, Visa, Amex

64 VILLAGE FARM HOLIDAYS

 HIGHLY COMMENDED

Cherry Tree Avenue, Newton-on-Ouse, York, North Yorkshire YO30 2BN Tel (01347) 848064 Fax (01347) 848065

Situated between York and Easingwold, in a peaceful location close to Beningborough Hall, Village Farm Holidays is the perfect retreat for those who appreciate the tranquillity of rural life in accommodation that offers guests an irresistible combination of discreet hospitality, antique tradition and modern comforts in a 200-year-old former Georgian farmhouse. There is a guest snooker room and, for the more energetic, the Yoredale Way Walk and National Cycle Route No. 65 pass through the village, which has two excellent public houses offering fine cuisine. This is the ideal place for the discerning guest to stay.

Bed & Breakfast per night: single occupancy from £16.00–£25.00; double room from £32.00–£50.00

Bedrooms: 1 double, 1 twin
Bathrooms: 2 en-suite
Parking for 8

65 HAZLEWOOD CASTLE

 DE LUXE

Paradise Lane, Hazlewood, Tadcaster, North Yorkshire LS24 9NJ Tel (01937) 535353 Fax (01937) 530630

Set in seventy seven acres of delightful parkland and landscaped grounds, this fortified knights' residence offers an idyllic rural location only twenty minutes from York or Harrogate. Twenty one luxurious bedrooms with views of the estate. Three public rooms – the State Drawing Room, the Victoria Room and the Library – are warm and spacious. Two restaurants – the first a café bar which is full of character, offering honest cuisine at friendly prices, and Restaurant 1086, with a light and airy atmosphere, serving serious food in style.

Bed & Breakfast per night: single occupancy from £95.00–£125.00; double room from £125.00–£300.00
Dinner, Bed & Breakfast per person, per night: £75.00–£95.00 (1–3 nights, 2 sharing)
Lunch available: 1086, 1200–1400 Tuesday–Friday

Evening meal: 1086, 1800–2145 Monday–Saturday
Café open daily, 1100–2300
Bedrooms: 4 double, 17 twin/double
Bathrooms: 21 en-suite   Parking for 170
Cards accepted: Mastercard, Visa, Diners, Amex, Switch/Delta

66 THE MANOR COUNTRY HOUSE

HIGHLY COMMENDED

Acaster Malbis, York YO2 1UL Tel (01904) 706723 Fax (01904) 706723

Family-run manor house in rural tranquillity, with private lake, set in five and a half acres of beautiful mature grounds on the banks of the River Ouse. Fish in the lake, cycle or walk. Close to race-course and only a ten-minute car journey from the city – or take the leisurely river bus from Bishopthorpe (Easter to October). Conveniently situated to take advantage of the Dales, Moors, Wolds and splendid coastline. Cosy lounge and licensed lounge bar with open fire. Conservatory breakfast room with Aga-cooked food.

Bed & Breakfast per night: single room from £38.00–£42.00; double room from £50.00–£68.00

Bedrooms: 1 single, 4 double, 2 twin, 3 triple
Bathrooms: 10 en-suite
Parking for 15
Cards accepted: Mastercard, Visa

67 SOUTHLANDS BED AND BREAKFAST

HIGHLY COMMENDED

Huntington Road, Huntington, York YO3 9PX Tel (01904) 766796 Fax (01904) 764536

Avoid the hustle and bustle of York and stay in Southlands – a large detached house, with private parking, in attractive gardens on the edge of the city. A regular five-minute bus journey takes you to the city centre two miles away. Convenient for visiting all of Yorkshire, with superb scenery and other attractions. From Huntington/Strensall roundabout on the A1237, head for York/Huntington, and the house is one and a quarter miles on the left.

Bed & Breakfast per night: single occupancy from £26.00–£28.00; double room from £34.00–£40.00

Bedrooms: 1 double, 2 twin
Bathrooms: 3 en-suite
Parking for 4

68 DEAN COURT HOTEL

HIGHLY COMMENDED

Duncombe Place, York YO1 2EF Tel (01904) 625082 Fax (01904) 620305 E-mail deancourt-york@btconnect.com

Superbly situated in the shadow of York Minster, the hotel has an unrivalled position in the heart of York. This historic city's main attractions are within walking distance and tours to Castle Howard, the Moors and Dales can be arranged. Renowned for very friendly service, it boasts an elegant restaurant (AA Rosette and RAC awards 1998) offering excellent modern food and a delightful café/conservatory as well as comfortable lounges. Secure car park with valet parking service. De luxe and superior rooms are now available. www.deancourtyork.co.uk

Bed & Breakfast per night: single room from £69.00–£80.00; double room from £105.00–£160.00
Dinner, Bed & Breakfast per person, per night: £67.50–£75.00 (min 2 nights)
Lunch available: 1230–1400

Evening meal 1900 (last orders 2130)
Bedrooms: 9 single, 21 double, 7 twin, 2 family rooms
Bathrooms: 39 en-suite   Parking for 30
Cards accepted: Mastercard, Visa, Diners, Amex, Switch/Delta

69 AMBASSADOR

〰〰〰〰 HIGHLY COMMENDED

123-125 The Mount, York YO2 2DA Tel (01904) 641316 Fax (01904) 640259

The Ambassador Hotel is a fine example of a Georgian town house with beautiful mature gardens – and just an easy walk from the city and the racecourse. Built in 1842, The Ambassador has been carefully created without sacrificing the building's Georgian style and elegance, and still retains the feeling of a much loved home. Enjoy a candlelit dinner in our AA Rosette award-winning restaurant.

Bed & Breakfast per night: single occupancy from £98.00; double room from £118.00
Dinner, Bed & Breakfast per person, per night: £66.00–£70.00
Evening meal 1830 (last orders 2130)

Bedrooms: 19 double, 6 twin
Bathrooms: 25 en-suite
Parking for 38
Cards accepted: Mastercard, Visa, Amex, Switch/Delta

70 HOLMWOOD HOUSE HOTEL

〰〰 HIGHLY COMMENDED

112-114 Holgate Road, York YO2 4BB Tel (01904) 626183 Fax (01904) 670899 E-mail holmwood.house@dial.pipex.com

Close to the city walls, an elegant listed Victorian town house offering a feeling of home with a touch of luxury. All the en-suite bedrooms are different in size and decoration, some with four-poster beds and one has a spa bath; all rooms are non-smoking. Imaginative breakfasts are served to the sound of gentle classical music. The inviting sitting room, with its open fire, highlights the period style of the house. Car park. On the A59. www.smoothound.co.uk/hotels/holmwood.html

Bed & Breakfast per night: single occupancy from £35.00–£60.00; double room from £55.00–£75.00

Bedrooms: 8 double, 2 twin, 1 triple
Bathrooms: 11 en-suite
Parking for 9
Cards accepted: Mastercard, Visa, Amex, Switch/Delta

71 EASTONS

〰〰 HIGHLY COMMENDED

90 Bishopthorpe Road, York YO23 1JS Tel (01904) 626646 Fax (01904) 626165

A former Victorian wine merchant's residence, ideally located three hundred yards from the city walls. William Morris decor, period furniture, marble fireplaces, original paintings, imaginative and generous 'Victorian sideboard' breakfast menu – kippers, kidneys, kedgeree and more. Fully equipped en-suite bedrooms. Eastons provides a standard of style and comfort not normally associated with bed and breakfast, but which is in accord with the standard of excellence that the owners strive for. Yorkshire & Humberside Tourist Board 'Bed & Breakfast of the Year' Winner, 1996.

Bed & Breakfast per night: single occupancy from £35.00–£60.00; double room from £49.00–£69.00

Bedrooms: 7 double, 2 twin, 1 triple
Bathrooms: 10 en-suite
Parking for 8

72 NEWSTEAD GRANGE

 HIGHLY COMMENDED

Norton, Malton, North Yorkshire YO17 9PJ Tel (01653) 692502 Fax (01653) 696951

The Grange is an elegant Georgian country house set in two and a half acres of gardens and grounds with delightful views of the North Yorkshire Moors and Wolds. The style of the house is tastefully enhanced by antique furniture, open log fires burn in cooler weather and the bedrooms are individually furnished. The proprietors personally prepare the meals with produce from the organic kitchen garden and fresh local produce to a high standard (AA Rosette award for fine food). Totally non-smoking.

Bed & Breakfast per night: single occupancy from £38.00–£44.00; double room from £59.00–£75.00 Dinner, Bed & Breakfast per person, per night: £44.00–£59.00 (depending on length of stay) Evening meal 1930 (last bookings 1900)

Bedrooms: 4 double, 4 twin
Bathrooms: 8 en-suite
Parking for 15
Open: late March–mid October
Cards accepted: Mastercard, Visa

73 THE WOLD COTTAGE

HIGHLY COMMENDED

Wold Newton, Driffield, East Riding of Yorkshire YO25 3HL Tel (01262) 470696 Fax (01262) 470696

"Just what you always hope to find." Spacious Georgian farmhouse set in its own grounds which was once a city gentleman's country retreat. Being situated away from roads, we can offer you peace and tranquillity. Overlooking new and mature woodlands and continuous wold land. Come and relax and forget the pressures of everyday life. Stroll around our field margins and observe the wildlife and history, or explore the wonders of the east coast, York and the moors. No smoking.

Bed & Breakfast per night: single occupancy from £25.00–£31.00; double room from £40.00–£52.00 Dinner, Bed & Breakfast per person, per night: £32.00–£38.00 Evening meal 1900

Bedrooms: 2 double, 1 twin
Bathrooms: 3 en-suite
Parking for 8

74 BURTON LODGE HOTEL

HIGHLY COMMENDED

Brandesburton, Driffield, East Yorkshire YO25 8RU Tel (01964) 542847 Fax (01964) 542847

Standing in over two acres of grounds this delightful hotel lies in rural surroundings adjoining an 18-hole parkland golf course (reduced green fees for guests). The ten bedrooms are all en-suite with a television, telephone and tea/coffee-making facilities. There is a comfortable cocktail lounge with an open fire and a charming dining room offering fine English cooking and a carefully chosen wine list. The hotel lies at the southern edge of the village of Brandesburton on the A165, eight miles from Beverley. Tennis court.

Bed & Breakfast per night: single room from £35.00–£40.00; double room from £48.00–£52.00 Dinner, Bed & Breakfast per person, per night: £37.50–£40.00 (1–3 nights) Evening meal 1900 (last orders 2100)

Bedrooms: 2 single, 2 double, 3 twin, 1 triple, 2 family rooms
Bathrooms: 9 en-suite
Parking for 15
Cards accepted: Mastercard, Visa, Amex, Switch/Delta

At-a-glance symbols are explained on the flap inside the back cover

75 MANOR HOUSE

≋ ≋ ≋ HIGHLY COMMENDED

Newbald Road, Northlands, Walkington, Beverley, East Riding of Yorkshire HU17 8RT Tel (01482) 881645 Fax (01482) 866501

The Manor House is set amidst rolling countryside and landscaped gardens within easy reach of Beverley. Serious 'foodie' restaurant with friendly, efficient service. The area is surrounded by historic houses, local museums and many other tourist attractions, with Scarborough and York being easily accessible.

Bed & Breakfast per night: single occupancy from £70.00–£80.00; double room from £85.00–£117.00
Dinner, Bed & Breakfast per person, per night: £53.50–£73.50
Evening meal 1930 (last orders 2115)

Bedrooms: 6 double, 1 family room
Bathrooms: 7 en-suite
Parking for 50

76 BRIGGATE LODGE INN

≋ ≋ ≋ ≋ ≋ HIGHLY COMMENDED

Ermine Street, Broughton, Brigg, Scunthorpe, North Lincolnshire DN20 0NQ Tel (01652) 650770 Fax (01652) 650495

Superbly located for all business and pleasure needs. Nestling amid an idyllic landscape of two hundred acres of wooded parkland, the hotel is a haven for those who enjoy being pampered. Easily accessible from the motorway system, Lincoln, Hull and York are within easy reach. International cuisine is served in the elegant Beech Tree Restaurant. Extensive table d'hôte and à la carte menus are available daily. For those who prefer more casual dining, the Buttery and Grill is open all day, every day, for drinks and bar meals. Forest Pines, an award-winning 27 hole championship golf course provides the perfect venue for golfing breaks. A new leisure centre will open in spring 1999.

Bed & Breakfast per night: single occupancy from £61.00; double room from £72.00
Dinner, Bed & Breakfast per person, per night: £55.50
Lunch available: all day
Evening meal 1900 (last orders 2200)

Bedrooms: 37 double, 49 twin
Bathrooms: 86 en-suite
Parking for 300
Cards accepted: Mastercard, Visa, Diners, Amex, Switch/Delta

77 WENTBRIDGE HOUSE HOTEL

≋ ≋ ≋ ≋ HIGHLY COMMENDED

Wentbridge, Pontefract, West Yorkshire WF8 3JJ Tel (01977) 620444 Fax (01977) 620148

Dating from 1700 and situated in twenty acres of the beautiful Went Valley among century-old trees, Wentbridge House is within easy reach of the M62 and A1. A traditional open fireplace and a fine collection of Meissen porcelain welcome you to the cocktail bar. The Fleur de Lys Restaurant, with its international ambience and AA Rosette award, attracts cosmopolitan lovers of food and wine. Individually furnished bedrooms include the Oakroom with its Mouseman four-poster bed.

Bed & Breakfast per night: single room from £58.00–£95.00; double room from £68.00–£105.00
Dinner, Bed & Breakfast per person, per night: £79.00–£120.00
Lunch available: 1200–1400

Evening meal 1930 (last orders 2130)
Bedrooms: 1 single, 14 double, 4 twin
Bathrooms: 19 en-suite   Parking for 100
Cards accepted: Mastercard, Visa, Diners, Amex, Switch/Delta

78 WHITLEY HALL HOTEL

≈≈≈ ≈≈≈ ≈≈≈ ≈≈≈ HIGHLY COMMENDED

Elliott Lane, Grenoside, Sheffield, South Yorkshire S35 8NR Tel (0114) 245 4444 Fax (0114) 245 5414

Whitley Hall dates from the 16th century and is a lovely country house standing in its own thirty acres of gardens, woodland and lakes. Privately owned as a hotel for over twenty five years, we offer accommodation, food and service of the highest quality and in the best English tradition. This popular country hotel is ideally situated between the Yorkshire Dales and Derbyshire Peak District and only a few minutes from Sheffield's theatres, sports facilities and magnificent Meadowhall shopping complex.

Bed & Breakfast per night: single room from £67.00–£78.00; double room from £88.00–£102.00
Dinner, Bed & Breakfast per person, per night: £64.00–£98.00
Lunch available: 1145–1345

Evening meal 1900 (last orders 2130)
Bedrooms: 2 single, 10 double, 6 twin, 1 family room
Bathrooms: 19 en-suite   Parking for 100
Cards accepted: Mastercard, Visa, Diners, Amex, Switch/Delta

Wakefield Rhubarb

IN SPRING, SUPERMARKETS throughout the country are stocked with a crop which was once the pride of many a cottage garden and is now undergoing something of a renaissance in restaurant popularity – rhubarb. The chances are that the succulent pink stalks which end up in your shopping basket were pulled from a plant growing somewhere near Wakefield, for this is where a large proportion of the country's rhubarb is grown.

A hundred years ago an area stretching between Wakefield, Leeds and Morley, often known as the 'rhubarb triangle', was the world centre of rhubarb growing. At the height of its popularity in the 1930s over 4,000 acres were under cultivation. Today that figure is only 750 acres, but Wakefield still prides itself on being the country's rhubarb capital. The national rhubarb collection is kept just north of 'the triangle' at the Harlow Carr Botanic Gardens, near Harrogate, and consists of 150 or so different varieties.

Although regarded as one of the most English of desserts, rhubarb probably originated in China, where it has been used for medicinal purposes for almost 5,000 years. Its purgative properties are well-known, but it has also been claimed as a miracle cure for a whole variety of other ailments, from poisonous animal bites to venereal disease. It only took off as a culinary delicacy in England in the early 19th century.

Rhubarb is technically a vegetable rather than a fruit in that, like celery, the stalks of the plant are consumed. The first, tender shoots of the spring have the sweetest flavour and so the practice has developed of covering the plants in winter and surrounding them with warm straw to 'force' them into early growth. Much of Wakefield's rhubarb is grown in forcing sheds, now artificially heated to bring the crops to fruition as early as Christmas. Some growers still insist on picking by candle light to ensure maximum darkness for the crop.

It is possible to arrange group tours of the rhubarb growing areas and forcing sheds by calling 01924 305841. The dedicated horticulturalist may inspect the national rhubarb collection at Harlow Carr Gardens (tel: 01423 565418) while the acres of plants growing to the north of Wakefield, fleshy leaves dark, glossy and shoulder-high by late spring, are visible for all to see.

79 HEATH COTTAGE HOTEL & RESTAURANT

 HIGHLY COMMENDED

Wakefield Road, Dewsbury, West Yorkshire WF12 8ET Tel (01924) 465399 Fax (01924) 459405

Heath Cottage Hotel is a substantial stone-built Victorian residence standing in approximately one acre of grounds. The renovated stable block is full of character, with original exposed roof timbers on the upper floor. These rooms are most popular for honeymoons and weekend breaks. There are twenty nine bedrooms in total, some of which are non-smoking rooms. The well-appointed restaurant provides freshly-prepared ingredients cooked with flair and imagination. Ample car parking is available.

Bed & Breakfast per night: single room from £42.00–£55.00; double room from £65.00–£75.00
Lunch available: 1200–1400
Evening meal 1830 (last orders 2130)

Bedrooms: 7 single, 18 double, 1 twin, 3 triple
Bathrooms: 29 en-suite
Parking for 65
Cards accepted: Mastercard, Visa, Switch/Delta

80 CHEVIN LODGE COUNTRY PARK HOTEL

 HIGHLY COMMENDED

Yorkgate, Otley, West Yorkshire LS21 3NU Tel (01943) 467818 Fax (01943) 850335

A superb hotel situated in fifty acres of woodland and lakes. The lakeside restaurant offers both English and French cuisine of the highest standard, together with an extensive wine list. The hotel is well positioned for visiting many lovely beauty spots – the Dales, Brontë country, York, Harrogate, Yorkshire Abbeys and museums. There is an excellent leisure club. A tennis court and mountain bikes are available.

Bed & Breakfast per night: single room from £60.00–£104.00; double room from £97.00–£114.00
Dinner, Bed & Breakfast per person, per night: from £62.50 (min 2 nights)
Lunch available: 1230–1430

Evening meal 1930 (last orders 2130)
Bedrooms: 15 single, 26 double, 2 twin, 2 triple, 5 family rooms
Bathrooms: 50 en-suite   Parking for 100
Cards accepted: Mastercard, Visa, Amex, Switch/Delta

81 ROMBALDS HOTEL AND RESTAURANT

 HIGHLY COMMENDED

West View, Wells Road, Ilkley, West Yorkshire LS29 9JG Tel (01943) 603201 Fax (01943) 816586 E-mail reception@rombalds.demon.co.uk

Located on the edge of the famous Ilkley Moor, yet within walking distance of the centre of the beautiful Victorian spa town of Ilkley, this elegant Georgian hotel is run by the resident proprietors, Jo and Colin Clarkson. The award-winning restaurant is well known for its cuisine and friendly service. The hotel is the ideal location for touring the North of England, with York, the Lakes and Peak District all approximately one hour's drive away.

Bed & Breakfast per night: single room from £55.00–£99.50; double room from £75.00–£120.00
Dinner, Bed & Breakfast per person, per night: £50.00–£90.00
Lunch available: 1200–1400

Evening meal 1830 (last orders 2130)
Bedrooms: 3 single, 9 double, 2 twin, 1 triple
Bathrooms: 15 en-suite   Parking for 22
Cards accepted: Mastercard, Visa, Diners, Amex, Switch/Delta

82 FIVE RISE LOCKS HOTEL

〰〰〰 HIGHLY COMMENDED

Beck Lane, Bingley, West Yorkshire BD16 4DD Tel (01274) 565296 Fax (01274) 568828 E-mail 101731.2134@compuserve.com

Built for a wealthy Victorian mill owner, the house stands in mature gardens overlooking the Aire valley, yet is only a few minutes' walk away from the Five Rise Locks and Bingley town centre. Each en-suite bedroom has a unique view and has been individually designed and furnished. Enjoy home cooking prepared with intelligence and imagination and wines from a well-chosen list in elegant, yet comfortable, surroundings. Experience Haworth – the Brontës, Esholt village, steam trains, museums and tranquil, vast open spaces.

Bed & Breakfast per night: single room from £32.50–£47.00; double room from £50.00–£60.00
Dinner, Bed & Breakfast per person, per night: £46.50–£51.00
Evening meal 1930 (last orders 2100)

Bedrooms: 1 single, 5 double, 3 twin
Bathrooms: 9 en-suite
Parking for 15
Cards accepted: Mastercard, Visa, Switch/Delta

83 REDACRE MILL

〰〰〰 HIGHLY COMMENDED

Redacre, Mytholmroyd, Hebden Bridge, West Yorkshire HX7 5DQ Tel (01422) 885563 Fax (01422) 885563

Experience true Yorkshire hospitality in our beautifully restored waterside mill. Relax in one-and-a-half acres of peaceful gardens, only minutes from the main routes and the Mytholmroyd railway station. Visit Brontë country and the wild South Pennines of 'Summer Wine' fame. Enjoy good food, wine and personal service in the welcoming comfort of Redacre Mill. All the rooms are en-suite. Private parking. Licensed. Please phone or fax for a brochure.

Bed & Breakfast per night: single occupancy £39.00; double room £58.00
5-course Dinner, Bed & Breakfast per person, per night: £46.50–£56.50
Evening meal 1930

Bedrooms: 2 double, 2 twin
Bathrooms: 4 en-suite
Parking for 8
Cards accepted: Mastercard, Visa

84 YORK HOUSE HOTEL

〰〰〰〰 HIGHLY COMMENDED

York Place, Off Richmond Street, Ashton-under-Lyne, Lancashire OL6 7TT Tel (0161) 330 9000 Fax (0161) 343 1613

Situated in a peaceful tree-lined cul-de-sac, close to the A635/A6107 junction, this very well maintained family-run hotel has thirty four well-kept en-suite bedrooms set around a courtyard and an award-winning garden. The hotel's restaurant has an excellent reputation. Keith Absolom has owned the hotel for over twenty five years and the care and attention to his guests is to be found throughout the hotel.

Bed & Breakfast per night: single room from £54.00–£65.00; double room from £84.00–£87.00
Lunch available: 1200–1400
Evening meal 1900 (last orders 2130)

Bedrooms: 9 single, 18 double, 5 twin, 2 triple
Bathrooms: 34 en-suite
Parking for 36
Cards accepted: Diners, Amex

85 CORNERSTONES

HIGHLY COMMENDED

230 Washway Road, Sale, Cheshire M33 4RA Tel (0161) 283 6909 or (0161) 881 0901 Fax (0161) 283 6909

Cornerstones is located on the main A56 road into the city centre. The building is Victorian – built by Sir William Cunliff Brooks, a banker and Lord of the Manor. A total refurbishment was carried out in 1985, reproducing the splendour of the Victorian era. Brookland Metro station is less than five minutes' walk away, and on the fifteen minute journey into the city you will pass Manchester United Football Club, Lancashire County Cricket Club and the G-Mex. At your journey's end you will find an abundance of shops, theatres, museums and art galleries.

Bed & Breakfast per night: single room from £25.00–£29.37; double room from £50.00–£58.75
Dinner, Bed & Breakfast per person, per night: £40.00–£52.50
Evening meal 1930

Bedrooms: 3 single, 4 double, 2 twin
Bathrooms: 6 en-suite, 3 private showers
Parking for 10
Cards accepted: Mastercard, Visa, Switch/Delta

Lowry's Lancashire

THE LANCASHIRE ARTIST Laurence Stephen Lowry (1887–1976) has become immortalised as the painter of matchstick men. He did indeed paint figures in a stylised, rather stick-like manner, but he painted much more besides. Above all he was a painter of the industrial scene, realising early in his career that no other artist in the world had seen this as a fit subject for serious art, and tackling it in his own inimitable and very distinctive style.

Lowry lived all his life in the industrial north, never moving far from Manchester, and living longest at Pendlebury on the city's north-western fringe. He was an enigmatic, reclusive character, living with his parents until they died, and maintaining a close secrecy in artistic circles about his working life as a clerk and rent collector. As Lowry said of himself and his family, 'We were cold fish'. Lowry showed little interest in art as a boy, but from the age of 18 took evening classes at the Manchester Municipal College where his drawing skills soon attracted attention.

From the start he drew his subject matter from his immediate environment: his family and home, holidays at the seaside with his parents, and above all his local area. Pendlebury was a district of looming coal mines and cotton mills which swallowed workers at the start of each day and spat them out at the end. At first repulsed by these scenes, Lowry eventually became fascinated by them. His most famous paintings are often composites of places he knew: factory gates, belching chimneys, towering mills, all populated by workers reduced and dehumanised into tiny stylised figures, dwarfed by the vast industrial monuments around them.

By the 1920s Lowry's paintings were attracting critical acclaim from an art establishment who found them a refreshing alternative to abstraction. One of the first galleries to appreciate his talent was close to home, at Salford. As his success grew it frequently exhibited his work and over the years the Salford Art Gallery (tel: 0161 736 2649) bought many of his paintings and drawings. He donated still more, and today the Salford collection is the best in the world. Over 150 of his works are on permanent display there, and together they convey the great range of his work, from early art-school drawings to the lesser known seascapes and 'lonely landscapes' of his later years.

86 PYMGATE LODGE HOTEL

 HIGHLY COMMENDED

147 Styal Road, Gatley, Cheadle, Cheshire SK8 3TG Tel (0161) 436 4103 Fax (0161) 499 9171

Within two miles of Manchester Airport. Every bedroom overlooks garden or open fields. Decorated to an exceptionally high standard. A non-smoking establishment.

Bed & Breakfast per night: single occupancy from £42.50–£45.00; double room from £48.50–£51.00
Evening meal 1800 (last orders 2130)

Bedrooms: 2 double, 4 twin, 2 triple
Bathrooms: 6 en-suite, 2 public
Parking for 14
Cards accepted: Mastercard, Visa, Amex

87 THE ALDERLEY EDGE HOTEL

 HIGHLY COMMENDED

Macclesfield Road, Alderley Edge, Cheshire SK9 7BJ Tel (01625) 583033 Fax (01625) 586343

Originally a mill owner's private residence, this country house hotel is set in its own grounds with breathtaking views over the surrounding Cheshire countryside, yet just a matter of minutes from major air, road and rail links. The most recent additions, following extensive refurbishment, are a further twelve bedrooms, bringing the total to forty four, plus the bridal and presidential suites. Deservedly recognised for excellent food, service and beautifully appointed facilities. ☆CATEGORY 3

Bed & Breakfast per night: single occupancy from £40.00; double room from £80.00
Lunch available: 1200–1430
Evening meal 1900 (last orders 2200)

Bedrooms: 35 double, 11 twin
Bathrooms: 46 en-suite
Parking for 90
Cards accepted: Mastercard, Diners, Amex, Switch/Delta

88 THE WHITE HOUSE MANOR

HIGHLY COMMENDED

The Village, Prestbury, Macclesfield, Cheshire SK10 4HP Tel (01625) 829376 Fax (01625) 828627

18th-century manor house in picturesque Prestbury, 20 minutes from Manchester Airport, offering luxurious accommodation with each room stylishly themed. The Crystal Room has a four-poster bed and jacuzzi bath, while Millennium has glass bed and minimalist bathroom with a Turkish steam room. The AA 2 Rosette White House Restaurant, a short stroll away, is under the personal supervision of proprietors Ryland and Judith Wakeham, and offers award-winning contemporary British cuisine, with Cornish fish, duck and local cheeses a speciality. ☆CATEGORY 3

Bed & Breakfast per night: single room from £45.00–£103.50; double room from £80.00–£137.00
Dinner, Bed & Breakfast per person, per night: £62.95–£121.45
Lunch available: 1200–1400

Evening meal 1900 (last orders 2200)
Bedrooms: 3 single, 7 double, 1 twin
Bathrooms: 11 en-suite
Parking for 11
Cards accepted: Mastercard, Visa, Diners, Amex

At-a-glance symbols are explained on the flap inside the back cover

89 MANOR FARM

〰〰 HIGHLY COMMENDED

Cliff Road, Acton Bridge, Northwich, Cheshire CW8 3QP Tel (01606) 853181 Fax (01606) 853181

Peaceful, rural, elegantly-furnished traditional country house with open views from all rooms. Situated away from roads down a long private drive, above the banks of the River Weaver. A large garden provides access to a private path through our woodland into the picturesque valley. In the heart of Cheshire, we are an ideal location for business or pleasure, within easy reach of Chester, Merseyside and the motorway network. Ample safe parking.

Bed & Breakfast per night: single room from
£20.00–£25.00; double room from £40.00–£50.00

Bedrooms: 1 single, 2 twin
Bathrooms: 1 en-suite, 3 private
Parking for 14

90 THE PARK ROYAL INTERNATIONAL HOTEL, HEALTH AND LEISURE SPA

 〰〰〰〰 HIGHLY COMMENDED

Stretton Road, Stretton WA4 4NS Tel (01925) 730706 Fax (01925) 730740

Ideally situated within easy access to historic Chester, Manchester's Granada Studios and Liverpool's Albert Dock. Set in its own breathtaking gardens, the hotel has 140 de luxe bedrooms, an AA Rosette award-winning restaurant, comfortable lounges and a superb health and leisure spa, offering the ultimate in fitness and beauty. Facilities include a 22 metre swimming pool, sauna, steam room, whirlpool, gymnasium, dance studio, tennis courts and The Retreat beauty suites, making it an ideal setting for that special weekend break. 🚶 CATEGORY 3

Bed & Breakfast per night: single room from
£73.00–£111.50; double room from £93.00–£121.50
Dinner, Bed & Breakfast per person, per night:
£59.00–£131.20
Lunch available: 1200–1400

Evening meal 1900 (last orders 2200)
Bedrooms: 1 single, 84 double, 40 twin, 15 triple
Bathrooms: 140 en-suite   Parking for 400
Cards accepted: Mastercard, Visa, Diners, Amex,
Switch/Delta

91 GROVE HOUSE

〰〰 HIGHLY COMMENDED

Holme Street, Tarvin, Cheshire CH3 8EQ Tel (01829) 740893 Fax (01829) 741769

A warm welcome awaits you in a relaxing, spacious, comfortable home with a long-established Cheshire family. Ideal situation for Chester, Oulton Park, North Wales, Liverpool, the Potteries and Manchester Airport (where guests can be met by prior arrangement). Hosts happy to help with sight-seeing suggestions. Attractive walled garden, listed trees and ample off-road parking. Traditional English breakfast served in family dining room. In winter an open coal fire burns in the elegant drawing room. Excellent evening meals available within two miles. North West Tourist Board 'Place to Stay' Award and last year's runner-up for B&B of the Year.

Bed & Breakfast per night: single room from
£23.00–£35.00; double room from £40.00–£56.00

Bedrooms: 1 single, 1 double, 1 twin
Bathrooms: 2 en-suite, 1 private
Parking for 8

92 CRABWALL MANOR HOTEL AND RESTAURANT

 HIGHLY COMMENDED

Parkgate Road, Mollington, Chester, Cheshire CH1 6NE Tel (01244) 851666 Fax (01244) 851400 E-mail sales@crabwall.u-net.com

Crabwall Manor Hotel and Restaurant is a country house hotel situated just two miles from the historic Roman city of Chester, set in eleven acres of wooded parkland and private gardens. Forty eight bedrooms/suites, each individually designed, with bathrobes and sherry among the many extras to be found. We also boast an AA 3 Rosette award-winning conservatory restaurant where our chef introduces a classic French influence to traditional English dishes.

Bed & Breakfast per night: single occupancy from £105.00–£130.00; double room from £130.00–£150.00; Dinner, Bed & Breakfast per person, per night: £85.00–£110.00 (min 2 nights, 2 sharing)
Lunch available: 1200-1400

Evening meal 1900 (last orders 2130)
Bedrooms: 48 single/double/twin
Bathrooms: 48 en-suite
Parking for 120
Cards accepted: Mastercard, Diners, Amex, Switch/Delta

Cheshire Salt

Workers clogs and mine bucket at the Lion Salt Works

EVERYONE KNOWS that coal – in the main – comes from the North, while tin comes from Cornwall, but what about salt? The answer is the Cheshire Plain, that area of flat, fertile farmland between Chester and Macclesfield. Most of us may not know, for example, that one mine at Winsford supplies all the salt used to clear snow and ice from the United Kingdom's roads. But the Romans, those industrious plunderers of England's natural resources, knew all about the estimated 400 billion tons of salt lying beneath the rich soil – and they were here almost 2,000 years ago to tap the wealth of the area. Indeed the Latin name for Middlewich, 'Salinae', can be roughly translated as 'saltworks'.

The Cheshire Plain, 200 million years ago, was at the bottom of a shallow, salty sea. As the water evaporated, the salt formed into vast deposits of solid sodium chloride – or rock salt. Water flowing through this layer of rock salt reaches the surface as brine, and it was these brine springs that attracted the Romans.

In the 17th century coal began to be used to evaporate the brine in large iron pans, and the efficiency of salt production was hugely improved. The biggest headache then became transport, of coal to the works and salt from them. To this end the navigable stretch of the River Weaver was increased to Winsford, and the Trent and Mersey Canal completed in 1777, allowing salt works to open at Northwich, Middlewich, Wheelock and Lawton. Larger, deeper salt beds were soon discovered, and by the late 19th century over 1 million tons of white salt were sailing down the Weaver Navigation each year.

Today there are three commercial plants producing white salt for a range of uses (from food storage to soap and plastic manufacture). These (and others) adopted the 'vacuum evaporation process' at the turn of the century, but one, the Lion Salt Works at Marston, near Northwich, stuck with the traditional 'open pan' system of evaporation, largely unchanged since Roman times. In 1986 it eventually closed, but the local council bought the fascinating site, now open to the public in the afternoons (tel: 01606 41823). Together with the Salt Museum in the old Northwich Workhouse (tel: 01606 41331), it makes an intriguing exploration of Cheshire's industrial past – although perhaps the most fascinating site of all is the Anderton Boat Lift, a vast monument to the engineering achievements of the Victorian era. For over a century this 'wonder of the waterways' just north of Northwich, built in 1875, hauled boats from the Weaver Navigation up 50ft and into the Trent and Mersey Canal above. Closed in 1982, the Boat Lift may yet work again if a local restoration group is successful.

93 ALDEN COTTAGE

Listed HIGHLY COMMENDED

Kemple End, Birdy Brow, Stonyhurst, Clitheroe, Lancashire BB7 9QY Tel (01254) 826468

Luxury accommodation in an idyllic 17th-century beamed cottage, situated in an area of outstanding natural beauty overlooking the Ribble and Hodder valleys. Charming, individually furnished rooms with all modern comforts and fresh flowers. Private facilities, including jacuzzi bath. Perfect for a peaceful and relaxing stay away from it all. Ribble Valley Civic Design and Conservation award winner.

Bed & Breakfast per night: single occupancy from £21.00–£22.00; double room from £42.00–£44.00

Bedrooms: 2 double, 1 twin
Bathrooms: 1 public
Parking for 6

94 NORTHCOTE MANOR HOTEL

 HIGHLY COMMENDED

Northcote Road, Langho, Blackburn BB6 8BE Tel (01254) 240555 Fax (01254) 246568

Northcote Manor is a small, privately owned and managed hotel with fourteen en-suite bedrooms. Lovingly cared for, it is situated in the Ribble Valley, one of the least known and most beautiful parts of the country. The manor is best known for its excellent restaurant which has won many awards. Gourmet One-Night Breaks are available all year round and include champagne aperitif and a five-course gourmet meal, prepared individually for each guest.

Bed & Breakfast per night: single occupancy from £90.00–£110.00; double room from £110.00–£130.00
Dinner, Bed & Breakfast per person, per night: from £82.50
Lunch available: 1200–1330

Evening meal 1900 (last orders 2130)
Bedrooms: 10 double, 4 twin
Bathrooms: 14 en-suite
Parking for 50
Cards accepted: Mastercard, Diners, Amex, Switch/Delta

Key to Symbols

For ease of use, the key to symbols appears on the back of the cover flap and can be folded out while consulting individual entries. The symbols which appear at the end of each entry are designed to enable you to see at a glance what's on offer, and whether any particular requirements you have can be met. Most of the symbols are clear, simple icons and few require any further explanation, but the following points may be useful:

ALCOHOLIC DRINKS: Alcoholic drinks are available at all types of accommodation listed in the guide unless the symbol [UL] (unlicensed) appears. However, even in licensed premises there may be some restrictions on the serving of drinks, such as being available to diners only.

SMOKING: Some establishments prefer not to accommodate smokers, and if this is the case it will be indicated by the symbol ✕. Other establishments may offer facilities for non-smokers such as no-smoking bedrooms and parts of communal rooms set aside for non-smokers. Please check at the time of booking if the non-smoking symbol does not appear.

PETS: The symbol 🐕 is used to show that dogs are not accepted in any circumstances. Some establishments will accept pets, but we advise you to check this at the time of booking and to enquire as to whether any additional charge will be made to accommodate them.

Entries are cross referenced by number to the maps on pages 18–19

England's Heartland

Rutland Water

▶ Kilpeck

At Kilpeck, eight miles (13km) south-west of Hereford, is the tiny sandstone church of Sts Mary and David. Its size may be modest, but its stone-carvings are the most glorious example of the exuberant work of the 12th-century Herefordshire School of stonemasons. The south door in particular, long protected by a wooden porch, displays a magnificent array of carvings – of beasts, fishes, foliage, fruit – in an almost pristine state. Similar work may be found in churches at Fownhope and Rowlstone (both in Herefordshire) and at Ruardean in the Forest of Dean, all set in glorious countryside.

▶ Blue John

Near Castleton in Derbyshire, two cave systems, Treak Cliff Cavern (tel: 01433 620571) and Blue John Cavern (tel: 01433 620638), contain deposits of a rare blue-veined fluorspar found nowhere else. Known as blue john, it was mined extensively in the 18th century, but now only about half a ton is produced annually, mostly carved into small decorative items sold in Castleton's souvenir shops. Tours of the caverns provide an intriguing insight into a unique Peak District industry, while the superb stalactites cannot fail to impress.

Away from the throng

From East Anglia's fertile plains to the rugged border country of the Welsh Marches, from the Home Counties' prosperous market towns to the dark, stone-built communities of the Peaks, the great swathe of counties that forms England's heartlands has it all. And for the most part you can have the elegance, the savage beauty, the culture and the history to yourself. Yes, the Peak District National Park is deservedly popular and yes, Stratford-upon-Avon is rightly a stop on most visitors' itineraries. But choose your moment wisely and even these can be enjoyed at a leisurely pace, the madding crowd left far behind.

In the steps of literary giants

Whatever your particular bent, there's ample opportunity to indulge it. Keen to follow in the footsteps of the famous? Try Lichfield, whose sons include three major figures from the 18th-century flowering of the arts: Joseph Addison, David Garrick and Dr Johnson. The last has his own museum, based in the house of his birth in Breadmarket Street. Other places of literary pilgrimage are D H Lawrence's Eastwood and Lord Byron's gothic Newstead Abbey (both Nottinghamshire, though at opposite ends of the social scale), Shaw's comfortable Corner in Ayot St Lawrence (Hertfordshire), A E Housman's much wilder Wenlock Edge (Shropshire) and Samuel Pepys's urbane Brampton (Cambridgeshire).

Lanes for walking, cycling or pootling

But if meandering lazily along English backwaters on a limpid afternoon is more your taste, consider a few of the following. Add a couple more ingredients – a half-decent road map and nothing to hurry back for – and you are guaranteed some perfect pootling. Almost anywhere away from the big towns will reward an adventurous spirit, but these are an eclectic assortment of suggested starting points. Try the warren of lanes switchbacking around the Golden Valley in the shadow of the Black Mountains. Or the northern reaches of the Cotswolds, whose vistas stretch to the Malverns, the Vale of Evesham and Stratford-upon-Avon. There's the little-known but savagely beautiful countryside around the Clee Hills south and west of Bridgnorth, or the gentler, undulating farmland of Suffolk between Diss and Southwold. Norfolk's north coast offers sleepy villages – a pair are appropriately called Little and Great Snoring – and unspoilt coastline. And there are the Lincolnshire Wolds west of Louth, where few visitors discover the distinct charms of Bag Enderby or Normanby le Wold.

Striking out

But if the narrowest of lanes still has too much of the hurly-burly, swap the car for a pair of boots, the road atlas for a walking map. Strike out along the footpaths and bridleways. A good place to start is on one of England's many long-distance paths. Almost all have circular walks of anything from two to 20 miles (3–32km) sharing their waymarks, so don't be put off by the "long-distance" bit. Running down the western edge of the region, and criss-crossing in and out of Wales is Offa's Dyke Path, which roughly follows the route of the 8th-century earthwork constructed by the Mercian king to keep the Welsh at bay. Also oriented north–south but stretching from Staffordshire to the Cotswolds is the Heart of England Way. Rural in character for most of its length, it follows the Birmingham and Fazeley Canal to the east of the city, before dropping down to Chipping Campden (where it joins the Cotswold Way) and skirting the oriental splendour of Sezincote (see below). Two more long-distance paths explore East Anglia's many sandy beaches. The first, the Peddars Way and Norfolk Coast Path, was, as its name suggests, once two separate routes. It starts in the flinty fields near Thetford and follows the course of a Roman road (the Peddars Way) till it reaches the coast near Holme. From here until Cromer – the Norfolk Coast Path – you will have as company the varied birdlife that throngs the dunes and marshes. The Suffolk Coast Path between Lowestoft and Felixstowe involves a couple of ferries, and skirts the cliffs that once supported the lost medieval village of Dunwich.

Art for all

One highlight of the Suffolk Coast path is Snape Maltings, home of the Aldeburgh Festival (June), devoted in part to the music of Sir Benjamin Britten. The welcome proliferation of literary and musical festivals ensures a huge number of events, catering for every taste. By way of a small sample, you can now choose your venue from: Cheltenham (jazz in April, music – and cricket – in July, literature in October), Chelmsford Cathedral (jazz, classical and art exhibitions, May), Solihull (folk music, May), Thaxted (classical and jazz, weekends in June and July), Ludlow (music, drama and dance, June), Warwick and Leamington Spa (classical music, July), Ledbury (poetry, July), Oundle (organ recitals, July), Buxton (opera, July), Three Choirs Festival (held in Worcester in August 1999) and Ross-on-Wye (dance, comedy and theatre, August).

Narrow streets and imposing townhouses

Most such events are understandably based in attractive, historical market towns, the sort of town that specialises in medieval higgledy-piggledyness, Elizabethan and Jacobean sturdiness, Georgian elegance or a combination of these and countless other architectural styles. Some are well-known, others less so. Tewkesbury, for example, is a fine medieval town that has long been blessed by – and suffered from – its position at the confluence of the rivers Severn and Avon. A magnificent row of 15th-century shops and the intriguingly named House of the Nodding Gables are a couple of venerable survivors of the regular flooding. Bewdley is a thoroughly gracious former river port higher up the Severn. Since 1798, the centrepiece has been Thomas Telford's elegant bridge, but as well as the

► **Birmingham Pre-Raphaelites**

Birmingham's City Museum and Art Gallery (tel: 0121 303 2834) houses the largest (and arguably finest) collection of Pre-Raphaelite art in the world, including Holman Hunt's *The Last of England*, *The Blind Girl* by Millais and Rossetti's *Beata Beatrix*, together with a vast number of other paintings, drawings and crafts. Near by, Wightwick Manor, just outside Wolverhampton (tel: 01902 761108) is entirely furnished and decorated by some of the most prominent Pre-Raphaelite artists, while in Birmingham Cathedral may be found some superb stained-glass designed by Edward Burne-Jones, pre-Raphaelite and native of the city.

► **Westonbirt**

Robert Holford was just 21 when he began the outstanding collection of tree specimens that now forms Westonbirt Arboretum. Almost 170 years later, visitors can see the spectacular culmination of his life's work. The arboretum covers 600 acres (242.5 hectares) of woodland with 17 miles (27km) of paths and 18,000 listed specimens of plants. Some 4,000 species flourish here, many as exotic as the Chilean firebush or the handkerchief tree, all arranged in a landscape of great beauty (tel: 01666 880220).

▶ Slimbridge

When the naturalist and painter Peter Scott founded the Wildfowl & Wetlands Trust at Slimbridge, Gloucestershire, in 1946, he operated from two derelict cottages and used wartime pill-boxes as hides. Today the organisation is internationally recognised for its research into wetland conservation, and, at Slimbridge, offers visitors a superb opportunity to watch a vast range of birds. In winter up to 8,000 migrants fly in to the 800-acre (323-hectare) reserve, forming possibly the world's largest collection of ducks, geese and swans. Slimbridge is also the only place in Europe where all six species of flamingo can be seen!

▶ Dunmow Flitch

The once-common phrase 'to eat Dunmow bacon' means to live in conjugal bliss, and refers to an ancient custom still practised in Great Dunmow, near Bishop's Stortford in Essex. In order to win a flitch (or side) of bacon, a couple must prove that in the first twelve months and a day of their marriage they have not exchanged a word of anger, and certainly never repented of the day they wed. The trial, held every four years before a bewigged judge, is conducted with the utmost (mock) seriousness.

myriad streets ideal for strolling, there is a station on the scenic Severn Valley Railway. Bromyard, by contrast, has a striking hill setting, two old coaching inns and a clutch of timber-framed houses, not to mention sweeping views from the nearby Bromyard Downs. Uppingham is crammed full of 17th-, 18th- and 19th-century buildings all made from the glorious, mellow Rutland stone of the area. Southwold has the pleasing air of a town ignored by most aspects of the 20th century. The Suffolk port enjoyed something of a renaissance when it became fashionable with Victorian holidaymakers, but otherwise just the right amount of nothing has entertained locals and visitors ever since the bustling medieval harbour silted up. Melton Mowbray's cattle market was established over 900 years ago. Not much in the town is quite as old, but 14th-century Anne of Cleves' House is about to see its eighth century.

Pies and produce

Melton's real fame derives from its associations with pork pies and Stilton cheese, both of which are still made and sold here. Bakewell, in Derbyshire, is synonymous with a delicious upside-down jam tart, widely available in the area, but the town is also worth visiting for an agricultural show in August and its fine stone architecture. Heacham, in Norfolk has long been the English headquarters of lavender growing; tours are available. Spalding, over the border into Lincolnshire, draws thousands in early May to its annual flower parade, while asparagus takes centre stage at the Fleece Inn at Bretforton in Worcestershire. The ancient pub, owned by the National Trust, runs an auction devoted to asparagus on the evening of the last Sunday in May.

Homes and gardens

The Trust owns and manages a vast range of properties throughout the region, from Mr Straw's House in Worksop – a modest turn-of-the-century semi – to the working Theatre Royal in Bury St Edmunds. A random sample of other historic houses – most still privately owned – includes: Weston Park (Palladian mansion with gardens by 'Capability' Brown, Staffordshire); Eastnor Castle (Georgian castle with Gothic interiors, Ledbury, Herefordshire); Woburn Abbey (18th-century mansion with considerable art collection, Bedfordshire); Audley End (17th-century house with Adam touches, Essex); Stanford Hall (riverside William and Mary house with notable ballroom, Swinford, Leicestershire); Sezincote (reputedly the inspiration for the Indian-style Brighton Pavilion, Moreton-in-Marsh, Gloucestershire); Burghley House (Elizabethan palace with baroque interiors, Stamford, Lincolnshire); Kentwell Hall (Tudor mansion with garden maze, Long Melford, Suffolk); and Sulgrave Manor (ancestral home of George Washington, Northamptonshire). All these properties run special events of one form or another in high season.

Look east

The region's coastline runs from Essex to Lincolnshire. Essex has a mixture of lonely marsh and fine beach, while Suffolk alternates sand and shingle. Norfolk's golden shores, though, stretch for mile after mile, and Lincolnshire – after a marshy section around the Wash – boasts more excellent beaches. Naturally, there are the famous seaside resorts, with their quintessentially English attractions and their cheerful brashness, but there is another side to the coastline. For a quieter maritime excursion try Frinton (Essex), Covehithe (Suffolk), Happisburgh – pronounced 'Haysborough' – Holkham and Hunstanton (all Norfolk) and Anderby Creek (Lincolnshire). Unique amongst East-coast resorts, Hunstanton has the distinction of facing west. Watch the sun go down over the waves in the knowledge that no one else within 150 or so miles (240km) is doing the same…

Divine inspiration

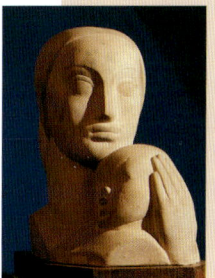

And, of course, there are the region's countless churches. The medieval stone-carvers of Herefordshire honed their skills to perfection at Kilpeck. Distinctive round towers stand out against the gentle Norfolk landscape, as at Sedgeford. The warm, honey-coloured stone that characterises so many of the unsung Northamptonshire villages was used on consecrated ground, too; Brixworth is a marvellous Saxon church in an imposing setting. In Suffolk and northern Essex, the locally abundant flint was the main material in such opulent churches as Long Melford and Dedham, both villages of remarkable beauty aside from their churches.

Contact numbers

Samuel Johnson Birthplace Museum, Lichfield (tel: 01543 264972)
D H Lawrence Birthplace, Eastwood (tel: 01773 763312)
Newstead Abbey, Newstead (tel: 01623 793557)
Shaw's Corner, Ayot St Lawrence (tel: 01438 820307)
Aldeburgh Festival of Music and the Arts (tel: 01728 452935)
Cheltenham International Jazz Festival (tel: 01242 237377)
Cheltenham Festival of Literature (tel: 01242 521621)
Cheltenham International Festival of Music (tel: 01242 521621)
Solihull Festival (tel: 01676 535818)
Thaxted Festival (tel: 01371 831421)
Warwick and Leamington Festival (tel: 01926 410747)
Ledbury Poetry Festival (tel: 01531 634156)
Oundle Festival (tel: 01832 272026)
Buxton Festival (tel: 01298 70395)
Three Choirs Festival (tel: 01905 616200)
Ross-on-Wye Festival (tel: 01594 544446)
Bakewell Agricultural Show (tel: 01629 813227)
Norfolk Lavender, Heacham (tel: 01485 570384)
Spalding Flower Parade (tel: 01775 724843)
Fleece Inn, Bretforton (tel: 01386 831173)
Mr Straw's House, Worksop (tel: 01909 482380)
Theatre Royal, Bury St Edmunds (tel: 01284 706035)
Weston Park, Shifnal (tel: 01952 850207)
Eastnor Castle, Ledbury (tel: 01531 633160)
Woburn Abbey (tel: 01525 290666)
Audley End (tel: 01799 522399)
Stanford Hall, Swinford (tel: 01788 860250)
Burghley House, Stamford (tel: 01780 52451)
Kentwell Hall, Long Melford (tel: 01787 310207)
Sulgrave Manor (tel: 01295 760205)

▶ Garman Ryan Collection

Ask where you can see works by Van Gogh, Turner, Picasso, Constable, Cézanne, Gainsborough, Titian, Reynolds and Gauguin outside London, and few would suggest Walsall. But the Garman Ryan collection at the Walsall Museum and Art Gallery boasts some 353 works by these and other artists. Their presence here is due to Kathleen Garman, wife of the renowned English sculptor, Sir Jacob Epstein, who, together with American sculptress Sally Ryan, Epstein's lifelong admirer, amassed this superb collection. After Ryan's death, Garman, who was born at Wednesbury, near Walsall, donated the collection to the town.

▶ Bakewell puddings

The story of Bakewell's famous puddings is one of triumph over adversity. In 1860 a cook at the White Horse Inn (now the Rutland Arms) preparing a strawberry tart for some dignitaries mistakenly placed egg mixture intended for the pastry base on top of the jam. The resulting 'disaster' was nevertheless

cooked up and promptly declared a culinary masterpiece. The puddings (those in the know never call them 'tarts') have been served in the town ever since.

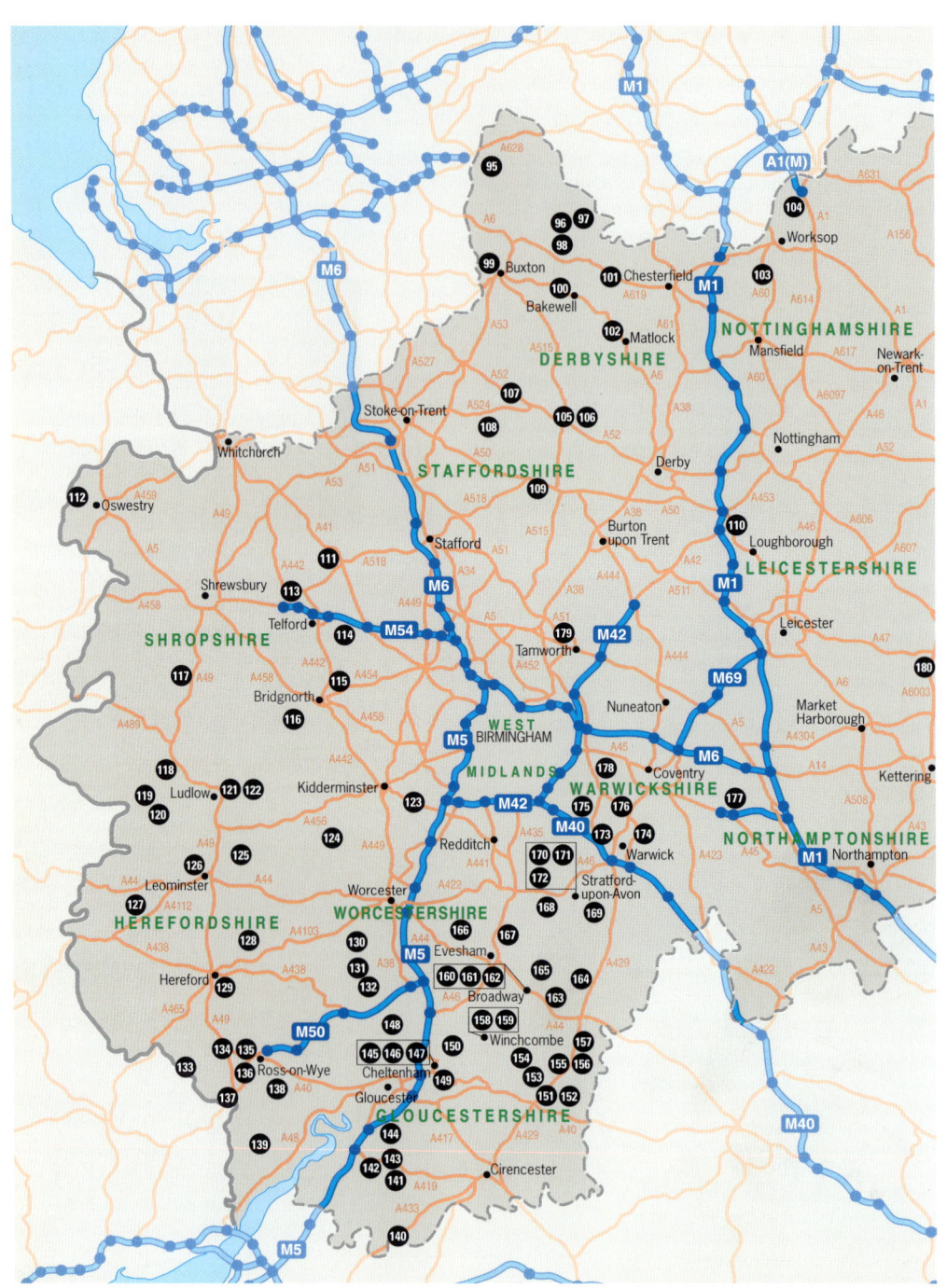

Colin Earl Cartography

95 WIND IN THE WILLOWS HOTEL

HIGHLY COMMENDED

Derbyshire Level, off Sheffield Road (A57), Glossop, Derbyshire SK13 7PT Tel (01457) 868001 Fax (01457) 853354

"Not so much an hotel, more a delightful experience" as someone said. A delightful combination of antiques, wood panelling, log fires and homely atmosphere, but with true professionalism. All rooms are individual and have en-suite facilities of the highest standard. Some half-tester beds, four-poster and brass beds, all of which are antiques. The dining room offers fine English food, all freshly prepared.

Bed & Breakfast per night: single occupancy from £70.00–£90.00; double room from £88.00–£115.00
Evening meal 1930 (last bookings 1600)

Bedrooms: 9 double, 3 twin
Bathrooms: 12 en-suite
Parking for 20
Cards accepted: Mastercard, Visa, Diners, Amex, Switch/Delta

Eyam and the plague

THE VILLAGE OF EYAM (pronounced 'Eem'), 800ft (244m) up in the Derbyshire hills, is like many another in the Peak: pretty old stone buildings against a backdrop of wild, mountainous terrain. But Eyam has a dark past which singles it out from any other village in the country, a tale of shared human misery which, though experienced over 300 years ago, has never been forgotten.

In September 1665, George Viccars, a journeyman tailor lodging in a cottage near the church, opened a parcel of cloth sent from London where bubonic plague was then raging. Within four days he was dead, his body marked with the tell-tale purple rings which characterised the disease. Plague had descended on Eyam, and, though many must have been tempted to flee, the young rector of Eyam, William Mompesson, realising that this would immediately spread the disease, persuaded the whole village to make a courageous act of self-sacrifice. Eyam was sealed off from the outside world: no-one could enter it, and no-one could leave. The Lord of the Manor, the Earl of Devonshire, arranged for vital supplies to be left at isolated spots around the village boundary, such as Mompesson's Well, and

money, dipped in vinegar to disinfect it, was returned as payment. Eyam paid dearly for its bravery: out of an estimated population of 350, some 250 died, almost three in every four villagers. The self-imposed quarantine lasted a year, before the plague finally ran its course in October 1666.

Today, it is hard to imagine the horror which once pervaded Eyam's quiet streets, but there are many reminders. Viccars' lodging (now called Plague Cottage) still stands, as do many other houses where victims died, now marked by neatly painted signs. In the churchyard are the graves of plague victims, including that of Mompesson's wife, Katherine. In a field about half-a-mile from the village, just off the Grindleford Road, are the Riley Graves, poignant memorials to a father, three sons and three daughters, all of whom died in the space of eight days in August 1666. Mompesson took to preaching in a limestone cavern known as Cucklet Church, where on the last Sunday each August, an annual commemorative service is held. An exhibition in Eyam church recounts the full story of the plague year. Information on Eyam is available from Bakewell's Tourist Information Centre (tel: 01629 813227).

Eyam Museum Limited

96 UNDERLEIGH HOUSE

HIGHLY COMMENDED

Edale Road, Hope, Hope Valley, Derbyshire S33 6RF Tel (01433) 621372 or (01433) 621324 Fax (01433) 621324 E-mail Underleigh.house@btinternet.com

A 19th-century, farmhouse-styled home with countryside views, privately situated one and a half miles from the village centre. Stone-flagged floors and oak beams, along with quality furnishings, create the ambience, and each excellent en-suite room and new suite has many extras including a resident teddy bear. Renowned for hearty breakfasts and gourmet houseparty dinners cooked by the owner/chef. Winner of national garden competition. Underleigh is ideally situated for exploring the area on foot or by car. No children under 12 yrs. Sorry, no pets – we have our own!!

Bed & Breakfast per night: single occupancy from £45.00–£60.00; double room from £65.00–£95.00
Dinner, Bed & Breakfast per person, per night: £95.00–£125.00 (min 2 nights)
Evening meal 1930 (last bookings 1200)

Bedrooms: 4 double, 2 twin
Bathrooms: 6 en-suite
Parking for 6
Cards accepted: Mastercard, Visa, Switch/Delta

97 PIONEER HOUSE

HIGHLY COMMENDED

Station Road, Bamford, Derbyshire S33 0BN Tel (01433) 650638

Our friendly and comfortable period home is the ideal base for your visit to the Peak District. Relax in our tastefully furnished en-suite rooms, each with colour television and well-stocked beverage tray. Sportsmen will enjoy the nearby golf, fishing and cycle ways; the less active will delight in the many nearby stately homes and museums. For walkers, we offer complimentary chauffeur-driven transport to the start of your route.

Bed & Breakfast per night: double room from £36.00–£44.00

Bedrooms: 2 double, 1 twin
Bathrooms: 2 en-suite, 1 private
Parking for 6

98 MAYNARD ARMS HOTEL

HIGHLY COMMENDED

Main Road, Grindleford, Derbyshire S32 2HE Tel (01433) 630321 Fax (01433) 630445

Established in 1898 in the heart of the Peak National Park, the Maynard Arms is an idyllic location for pleasure or business. Superior bedrooms have views over the Derwent Valley. The best local produce is served for both lunch (1200–1400) and dinner (1900–2130) accompanied by our extensive wine list, in the Padley Restaurant overlooking the hotel gardens. The Longshaw Bar satisfies the heartiest of appetites between 1200–1400 and 1900–2130, also serving traditional hand-pulled beers.

Bed & Breakfast per night: single occupancy from £67.00–£87.00; double room from £77.00–£97.00
Dinner, Bed & Breakfast per person, per night: £48.50–£58.50 (min 2 nights)
Lunch available: 1200–1400

Evening meal 1900 (last orders 2130)
Bedrooms: 8 double, 2 twin
Bathrooms: 10 en-suite
Parking for 60
Cards accepted: Mastercard, Visa, Amex, Switch/Delta

At-a-glance symbols are explained on the flap inside the back cover

99 CONINGSBY

 DE LUXE

6 Macclesfield Road, Buxton, Derbyshire SK17 9AH Tel (01298) 26735

We take great pleasure in welcoming guests to our Victorian home where we try to add those special touches that make all the difference when staying away from home. Our guests are assured superior accommodation, good food and impeccable cleanliness in a relaxed atmosphere where the hosts care and have time to talk. If you would like more details we would be pleased to send you our colour brochure upon request. Please, no smoking, children or pets.

Bed & Breakfast per night: double room from
£55.00–£70.00
Evening meal 1900 (last bookings 1600)

Bedrooms: 3 double
Bathrooms: 3 en-suite
Parking for 6
Open: February–October

100 RIVERSIDE HOUSE HOTEL

HIGHLY COMMENDED

Fennel Street, Ashford in the Water, Bakewell, Derbyshire DE4 1QF Tel (01629) 814275 Fax (01629) 812873

Located in the heart of the Peak District by the tranquil banks of the Wye, Riverside House is a discovery to thrill you. You'll find a period country retreat perfectly in tune with the best traditions of hospitality, charming yet informal, professional yet intimate. With just fifteen elegantly furnished bedrooms, one can savour the relaxed and private house party atmosphere, while, as with any good host, there's a high importance placed on all things culinary. The restaurant boasts top honours for its distinctive brand of modern English cooking – and it does a mean afternoon tea too! So seek, find and enjoy!

Bed & Breakfast per night: single occupancy from
£85.00–£105.00; double room from £110.00–£150.00
Dinner, Bed & Breakfast per person, per night: from
£85.00 (min 2 nights, 2 sharing)
Lunch available: 1200–1400 (Buttery Bar open all day)

Evening meal 1900 (last orders 2130)
Bedrooms: 10 double, 5 twin
Bathrooms: 15 en-suite   Parking for 25
Cards accepted: Mastercard, Visa, Diners, Amex,
Switch/Delta

101 THE OLD STABLES

Listed HIGHLY COMMENDED

Calver Road, Baslow, Bakewell, Derbyshire DE45 1RP Tel (01246) 582409

A warm welcome awaits you at our 260 year old barn conversion set on the River Derwent. Situated in the Peak District National Park, on the A623, 100 yards from Baslow Church, The Old Stables is ideally placed for exploring this beautiful part of Derbyshire. Close by are the stately homes of Chatsworth House and Haddon Hall. Within walking distance are numerous hotels, pubs and restaurants for dining out.

Bed & Breakfast per night: single occupancy from
£35.00; double room from £40.00–£45.00

Bedrooms: 1 twin
Bathrooms: 1 en-suite
Parking for 4

102 RIBER HALL

🌊🌊🌊🌊 HIGHLY COMMENDED

Matlock, Derbyshire DE4 5JU Tel (01629) 582795 Fax (01629) 580475 E-mail info@riber-hall.co.uk

Relax in the peaceful and picturesque setting of this historic Derbyshire country house and stroll in the old walled garden and orchard. Enjoy our superb cuisine and sit by the log fire or in the conservatory for our excellent afternoon tea. AA 2 Rosettes.

Bed & Breakfast per night: single occupancy from
£89.75–£104.00; double room from £115.00–£157.00
Dinner, Bed & Breakfast per person, per night:
£116.75–£121.75
Lunch available: 1200–1330 (last orders)

Evening meal 1900 (last orders 2130)
Bedrooms: 12 double, 2 twin
Bathrooms: 14 en-suite   Parking for 50
Cards accepted: Mastercard, Visa, Diners, Amex,
Switch/Delta

103 BROWNS

Listed HIGHLY COMMENDED

The Old Orchard Cottage, Holbeck, Worksop, Nottinghamshire S80 3NF Tel (01909) 720659 Fax (01909) 720659

ETB England for Excellence Silver Award 1998. Winner of four awards including joint winner of the Heart of England Tourist Board 'Bed & Breakfast of the Year' 1998. 'Cross over the ford and discover somewhere special'. 1730 stone country cottage in a picturesque one acre garden, set in a quiet, peaceful hamlet on the Welbeck Country Estate in the heart of Sherwood Forest. Two en-suite garden lodges providing maximum privacy. Breakfast served in the elegant dining room of the cottage. Chauffeur service available for dinner at a nearby Egon Ronay recommended country house restaurant.

Bed & Breakfast per night: single occupancy from
£35.00–£35.00; double room from £44.00–£48.00

Bedrooms: 1 double, 1 family room
Bathrooms: 2 en-suite
Parking for 6

104 THE CHARNWOOD HOTEL

🌊🌊🌊🌊 HIGHLY COMMENDED

Sheffield Road, Blyth, Worksop, Nottinghamshire S81 8HF Tel (01909) 591610 Fax (01909) 591429

Centrally placed near to the heart of England, The Charnwood Hotel is set in extensive landscaped gardens and offers an ideal choice for both business and pleasure. Whether your requirements are for a wedding reception, business conference, relaxing accommodation, a bar snack from our extensive menu, a meal in our renowned Lantern Restaurant or just a drink from the bar, you can be assured of a warm welcome from this family-owned and managed hotel.

Bed & Breakfast per night: single room from
£50.00–£65.00; double room from £65.00–£90.00
Dinner, Bed & Breakfast per person, per night:
£68.00–£83.00
Lunch available: 1200–1400

Evening meal 1900 (last orders 2145)
Bedrooms: 2 single, 23 double, 9 twin
Bathrooms: 34 en-suite   Parking for 75
Cards accepted: Mastercard, Visa, Diners, Amex,
Switch/Delta

105 THE COACH HOUSE

Listed DE LUXE

The Firs, Ashbourne, Derbyshire DE6 1HF Tel (01335) 300145 Fax (01335) 300958

A private house, formerly a Victorian coach house, nestling amongst mature trees in a quiet location near Ashbourne town centre. Our rooms are very different, each one special in its own way: Oriens – a room with every facility and many, many pictures, and the superb bathroom has a bath big enough for two! Occidens – enter into your own sitting room, then climb the stairs to a romantic hideaway bedroom. Meridies – a sumptuous, panelled room with a hand-crafted, fully draped four-poster bed.

Bed & Breakfast per night: double room £60.00
Dinner, Bed & Breakfast per person, per night: £47.50
Evening meal by arrangement

Bedrooms: 3 double
Bathrooms: 3 en-suite
Parking for 3
Cards accepted: Mastercard, Visa, Switch/Delta

106 STANSHOPE HALL

HIGHLY COMMENDED

Stanshope, Ashbourne, Derbyshire DE6 2AD   Tel (01335) 310278 Fax (01335) 310470

Seven miles from Ashbourne, between Dovedale and the Manifold Valley in the southern Peak District, Stanshope Hall offers peace and quiet, comfortable licensed en-suite accommodation and home cooking. The rooms have been decorated by theatre artists and the result is a mixture of the theatrical, the humorous and the indulgent. Fruit and vegetables served at dinner are, whenever possible, from our own kitchen garden.

Bed & Breakfast per night: single occupancy from £25.00–£40.00; double room from £50.00–£80.00
Dinner, Bed & Breakfast per person, per night: £44.00–£59.00
Evening meal 1900 (last orders 2000)

Bedrooms: 2 double, 1 twin
Bathrooms: 3 en-suite
Parking for 3
Cards accepted: Mastercard, Visa, Switch/Delta

107 LEE HOUSE FARM

HIGHLY COMMENDED

Leek Road, Waterhouses, Stoke-on-Trent, Staffordshire ST10 3HW Tel (01538) 308439

A charming 18th-century house in the centre of a picturesque village in the Peak District National Park. Lee House is full of character: all bedrooms are non-smoking, centrally heated and en-suite, with colour TV and tea/coffee-making facilities. Ideally situated for walking and cycling in the Manifold Valley, visiting stately homes, touring the Staffordshire moorlands, the Peak District and the famous Potteries. Waterhouses is midway between Leek and Ashbourne on the A523. 6 miles from Alton Towers.

Bed & Breakfast per night: single occupancy from £25.00–£35.00; double room from £40.00–£50.00

Bedrooms: 2 double, 1 twin
Bathrooms: 3 en-suite
Parking for 4
Open: all year except Christmas

108 BANK HOUSE

HIGHLY COMMENDED

Farley Road, Oakamoor, Stoke-on-Trent, Staffordshire ST10 3BD Tel (01538) 702810 Fax (01538) 702810 E-mail john.orme@dial.pipex.com

A luxurious, elegant and peaceful licensed country home offering the highest standards of food and comfort, a third of a mile south of the village. Each en-suite or private-bath bedroom has a beautiful view of the picturesque Churnet Valley, England's little Rhineland. Within the Staffordshire moorlands, next to the National Park, one mile from Alton Towers, and amidst superb countryside for walking, it is also convenient for visiting the Potteries, Derbyshire Dales, numerous great houses, gardens and other attractions.

Bed & Breakfast per night: single occupancy from £41.00–£51.00; double room from £54.00–£74.00 Dinner, Bed & Breakfast per person, per night: £48.00–£58.00 Evening meal 1930 (last orders 2130)

Bedrooms: 1 double, 2 twin Bathrooms: 2 en-suite, 1 private Parking for 8 Cards accepted: Mastercard, Visa

109 THE BEECHES FARMHOUSE

HIGHLY COMMENDED

Waldley, Doveridge, Nr Ashbourne, Derbyshire DE6 5LR Tel (01889) 590288 Fax (01889) 590559 E-mail beechesfa@aol.com

Relax and unwind in our rural farm retreat after exploring the Derbyshire Dales or the thrills of Alton Towers. Dine in our AA 2 Rosette, award-winning, 18th-century licensed farmhouse restaurant on fresh English food and home-made desserts. Guests are invited to meet the Shetland pony, pigs, dogs, rabbits and kittens, whilst enjoying the freedom of the gardens, fields and the beautiful countryside.

Bed & Breakfast per night: single occupancy from £42.00–£45.00; double room from £56.00–£66.00 Dinner, Bed & Breakfast per person, per night: £41.50–£57.00 (min 2 nights at weekends during peak periods) Lunch available: 1200-1400

Evening meal 1830 (last orders 2030) Bedrooms: 2 double, 1 twin, 7 family rooms Bathrooms: 10 en-suite Parking for 30 Cards accepted: Mastercard, Visa, Amex, Switch/Delta

110 KEGWORTH HOUSE

HIGHLY COMMENDED

42 High Street, Kegworth, Derby, Derbyshire DE74 2DA Tel (01509) 672575 Fax (01509) 670645 E-mail kegworthhouse@mcmail.com

Set in the heart of England with access to the M1, M42, A50, East Midlands airport and Donington race circuit five minutes away; Nottingham, Derby, Leicester and Birmingham within thirty minutes. We welcome the discerning traveller to stay in our 17th-century home. Luxurious accommodation. Fine English cooking with fresh vegetables from our own walled garden. Secure, private parking. Stay and be pampered in a warm and friendly atmosphere: a unique experience! "Unforgettable..." "Simply the best..."

Bed & Breakfast per night: single occupancy from £57.58–£64.63; double room from £81.00–£94.00 Dinner, Bed & Breakfast per person, per night: £55.80–£68.15 Evening meal 1800 (last orders 2000)

Bedrooms: 5 double Bathrooms: 5 en-suite Parking for 10 Cards accepted: Mastercard, Visa, Diners, Amex, Switch/Delta

111 THE GRANGE

 HIGHLY COMMENDED

Sutton, Newport, Shropshire TF10 8DD Tel (01952) 812232 or (0468) 946299 Fax (01952) 812232

The Grange is a delightful, friendly, family-run country house set in three acres, overlooking the beautiful, sleepy Meese valley. All our spacious, en-suite rooms have high-standard, individually coordinated decor and furnishings, including one room with a king-size antique brass bed for that extra romantic feeling. Our varied breakfast menu uses best quality local produce, combined with superb home cooking. We are perfectly situated to explore the history, culture and diversity of Staffordshire and Shropshire.

Bed & Breakfast per night: single room from £24.50–£34.50; double room from £39.00–£49.00

Bedrooms: 1 single, 3 double, 1 twin, 1 family room
Bathrooms: 6 en-suite, 1 public
Parking for 15
Cards accepted: Mastercard, Visa

112 PEN-Y-DYFFRYN COUNTRY HOTEL

 HIGHLY COMMENDED

Rhyd-y-Croesau, Oswestry, Shropshire SY10 7DT Tel (01691) 653700 Fax (01691) 653700

Once a Georgian rectory, now an award-winning country hotel in the most peaceful of situations in the lovely Shropshire Hills, midway between Shrewsbury and Chester. Full of character with a delightfully informal atmosphere, the hotel has ten bedrooms (including one on the ground floor), all with lovely hill views and en-suite bathrooms. The renowned restaurant, with its AA Rosette food award, is fully licensed and utilises the best local produce. Several National Trust castles nearby. Guests return again and again.

Bed & Breakfast per night: single room from £53.00–£56.00; double room from £66.00–£88.00
Dinner, Bed & Breakfast per person, per night: £49.00–£60.00 (min 2 nights)
Evening meal 1900 (last orders 2100)

Bedrooms: 1 single, 4 double, 4 twin, 1 triple
Bathrooms: 10 en-suite
Parking for 38
Cards accepted: Mastercard, Visa, Amex, Switch/Delta

113 BUCKATREE HALL HOTEL

 HIGHLY COMMENDED

The Wrekin, Wellington, Telford, Shropshire TF6 5AL Tel (01952) 641821 Fax (01952) 247540

A country house hotel nestling at the foot of the famous Wrekin Hill, three miles from Ironbridge and one mile from Junction 7/ M54. Many of the 62 bedrooms have balconies overlooking either an ornamental lake or gardens. Some have been specifically designed with lady travellers in mind: security spy holes, vanity mirror/hair dryer and ironing facilities. Terrace Restaurant overlooking patio and gardens. Liszt Lounge and Bar. Penthouse suite with a crown-tester bed and black and gold bathroom with whirlpool. Special weekend break: half-board from £49.50 pppn.

Bed & Breakfast per night: single room from £109.00–£129.00; double room from £129.00–£149.00
Dinner, Bed & Breakfast per person, per night: £49.50–£79.50 (weekend rates)
Lunch available: 1230–1400

Evening meal 1900 (last orders 2200)
Bedrooms: 2 single, 42 double, 18 twin
Bathrooms: 62 private   Parking for 120
Cards accepted: Access, Visa, Diners, Amex, Switch/Delta

114 HUNDRED HOUSE HOTEL RESTAURANT AND INN · HIGHLY COMMENDED

Bridgnorth Road, A442, Norton, Shifnal, Telford, Shropshire TF11 9EE Tel (01952) 730353 Fax (01952) 730355

Delightfully situated in the beautiful village of Norton, the Hundred House Hotel epitomizes the tradition and charm of rural England. The hotel cuisine uses the finest local ingredients and is both imaginative and wonderfully presented. This fine food can be enjoyed in the Jacobean style dining room or in the more informal setting of the hotel bars. Individually styled bedrooms, some including swings suspended from the beams, and extensive gardens make any visit truly memorable.

Bed & Breakfast per night: single room from £69.00–£85.00; double room from £89.00–£110.00
Lunch available: 1200–1430
Evening meal 1800 (last orders 2200)

Bedrooms: 2 single, 2 double, 1 twin, 5 triple
Bathrooms: 10 en-suite
Parking for 30
Cards accepted: Mastercard, Visa, Amex, Switch/Delta

The Shropshire Hills

THE 'SHROPSHIRE ALPS' and 'Little Switzerland' are not altogether fanciful names for that dramatically hilly part of the county sandwiched between the Welsh border and the River Severn. Here, ancient earth movements have tilted up great layers of different rock strata, each now forming its own ridge of hills stretching in a roughly south-westerly to north-easterly direction.

Most easterly of the ridges are the Clee Hills, formed of rich red sandstone, topped with basalt, and consisting of two separate ridges, Brown Clee Hill (1,792ft - 546m) and Titterstone Clee Hill (1,749ft - 533m). To their west the River Corve flows through a gentle wooded valley, before the land rises again to Wenlock Edge, a well-defined and steep-sided ridge of limestone flanked with trees. West of the Edge the hump of Caer Caradoc (1,506ft - 459m) dominates the Caradoc Hills around Church Stretton, and beyond rises the forbidding plateau of the Long Mynd (1,696ft - 517m). This 10-mile ridge of moorland, composed of heather-covered grit and shale, is a favourite launch point for gliders, and also provides some of the best walking country in Shropshire. An ancient path of unknown age, the Port Way, runs the entire length of the crest, commanding magnificent views of the Wrekin (1,335ft - 407m), which protrudes dramatically from the Shropshire Plain, its volcanic rocks the oldest in England. The eastern flank of the Long Mynd is eroded by streams into a series of deep ravines, of which the popular Carding Mill Valley (shown right) is considered the most beautiful; two others are Callow Hollow and Ashes Hollow. Westward again are

Heart of England Tourist Board

the Stiperstones, a sombre rocky outcrop where devils are believed to gather on Midwinter Night and, at 1,731ft (528m), a dramatic vantage point.

Aside from its superb scenery the area is rich in other attractions, with appealing towns, such as Shrewsbury, Bridgnorth, Bewdley and Ludlow all within easy reach. It boasts a string of impressive castles and fortified manors (Ludlow, Clun, Stokesay are three of many), some fine ecclesiastical ruins (Buildwas and Wenlock), and a fascinating industrial heritage (Ironbridge). At the heart of the hills is Church Stretton, an appealing little town which became something of a land-locked resort in the 19th century, a perfect base, then and now, from which to explore the slopes. Contact Church Stretton Tourist Information Centre (tel: 01694 723133) for details of sights and walks (guided hikes are available) throughout the region.

At-a-glance symbols are explained on the flap inside the back cover

115 OLD VICARAGE HOTEL

〰〰〰〰 DE LUXE

Worfield, Bridgnorth, Shropshire WV15 5JZ Tel (01746) 716497 Fax (01746) 716552

An Edwardian vicarage set in two acres of grounds on the edge of a conservation village in glorious Shropshire countryside, close to Ironbridge Gorge, Severn Valley Railway and Welsh border towns. With an award-winning (AA 3 Rosettes) dining room and cellar, the Old Vicarage is personally run by Peter and Christine Iles. Two-night leisure breaks available at any time of the year which include free admission to Attingham Park (National Trust). &
CATEGORY 2

Bed & Breakfast per night: single occupancy from £70.00–£100.00; double room from £107.50–£160.00
Dinner, Bed & Breakfast per person, per night: £95.00–£125.00
Lunch available: 1200–1400 (except Saturday)

Evening meal 1900 (last orders 2100)
Bedrooms: 8 double, 5 twin, 1 triple
Bathrooms: 14 en-suite
Parking for 30
Cards accepted: Mastercard, Visa, Diners, Amex

116 MIDDLETON LODGE

〰〰 HIGHLY COMMENDED

Middleton Priors, Bridgnorth, Shropshire WV16 6UR Tel (01746) 712228 Fax (01746) 712675

An imposing stone building in a one-acre garden with spacious bedrooms overlooking Brown Clee Hill, Middleton Lodge is within easy reach of many places of interest, including Severn Valley Railway, Ironbridge, and the historic towns of Ludlow, Shrewsbury, Much Wenlock, Bridgnorth and Church Stretton.

Bed & Breakfast per night: single occupancy from £30.00–£35.00; double room from £45.00–£55.00

Bedrooms: 2 double, 1 twin
Bathrooms: 2 en-suite, 2 private
Parking for 4

117 JINLYE

〰〰〰 HIGHLY COMMENDED

Castle Hill, All Stretton, Church Stretton, Shropshire SY6 6JP Tel (01694) 723243 Fax (01694) 723243

Heart of England Tourist Board 'Bed & Breakfast of the Year' 1997, ETB England for Excellence Silver Award. A beautifully situated country guest house set amidst the lovely Shropshire Highlands. A stroll from the house can provide some of the most stunning views in England. Delightfully furnished in period decor, Jinlye offers peaceful and luxurious accommodation. All of our spacious en-suite rooms have magnificent views. For a romantic interlude, our Wedding Suite is furnished around a splendidly carved 17th-century French wedding bed. The cottage gardens abound with rare plants and we are renowned for our excellent home cooking and home-from-home atmosphere. ⚡CATEGORY 3

Bed & Breakfast per night: single occupancy from £42.00–£55.00; double room from £54.00–£80.00
Dinner, Bed & Breakfast per person, per night: £45.00–£60.00
Evening meal 1900 (last bookings 1200)

Bedrooms: 4 double, 4 twin
Bathrooms: 7 en-suite, 1 private
Parking for 10

118 KNOCK HUNDRED COTTAGE

HIGHLY COMMENDED

Abcott, Clungunford, Craven Arms, Shropshire SY7 0PX Tel (01588) 660594 Fax (01588) 660594

Situated in the scenic Clun valley, Knock Hundred Cottage is believed to originate from the 16th century and enjoys an open aspect with extensive views. Many places of interest are within easy reach, including National Trust and English Heritage properties and gardens, the Heart of Wales Railway and the Ironbridge museums. There are also historic towns to visit and an abundance of walks to enjoy. Guests are promised a warm and friendly welcome.

Bed & Breakfast per night: double room £45.00
Evening meal 1930 (last orders 1930)

Bedrooms: 1 double, 1 twin
Bathrooms: 1 en-suite, 1 private
Parking for 2

119 LOWER HOUSE

HIGHLY COMMENDED

Adforton, Leintwardine, Craven Arms, Shropshire SY7 0NF Tel (01568) 770223 Fax (01568) 770592 E-mail cutler@globalnet.co.uk

Lower House originates from the early 17th century and is situated in North Herefordshire in the Welsh Marches. There is excellent walking in the surrounding hills and the area is quiet and unspoilt. There are many castles, gardens and National Trust properties within an easy drive. We offer first class, home-cooked food served in our elegant dining room. We are unlicensed, but guests are welcome to bring their own wine. www.stargate-uk.co.uk/lower-house

Bed & Breakfast per night: single occupancy from £25.00–£28.00; double room from £50.00–£56.00
Dinner, Bed & Breakfast per person, per night: £42.00–£45.00
Evening meal 1900

Bedrooms: 2 double, 2 twin
Bathrooms: 3 en-suite, 2 private
Parking for 10

120 THE BRAKES

HIGHLY COMMENDED

Downton, Ludlow, Shropshire SY8 2LF Tel (01584) 856485 Fax (01584) 856485

In the heart of beautiful rolling countryside, only five miles from the historic town of Ludlow, The Brakes offers delightful accommodation with excellent cuisine. A period farmhouse, tastefully furnished, with central heating throughout, standing in three acres of grounds with a beautiful garden. Bedrooms are en-suite, with TV, and there is a charming lounge with a log fire for chilly evenings. Licensed; dinner at 19.15. Excellent walking country, including Offa's Dyke and the Long Mynd. Golf, riding and fishing available. Steeped in history, with many places of interest nearby.

Bed & Breakfast per night: single occupancy from £30.00–£35.00; double room from £50.00–£60.00
Dinner, Bed & Breakfast per person, per night: £44.00–£49.00
Evening meal 1915 (last orders 2015)

Bedrooms: 1 double, 2 twin
Bathrooms: 3 en-suite
Parking for 8
Open: March–October

121 BROMFIELD MANOR

〰〰 HIGHLY COMMENDED

Bromfield, Ludlow, Shropshire SY8 2JU Tel (01584) 856536 or 0850 713340 Fax (01584) 856536

Relax in the informal, friendly atmosphere of a house with character while enjoying the personal attention of the owners. Bromfield Manor is a stone-built Grade II listed building situated in the village of Bromfield, two miles north of Ludlow. Gardens of one acre have views of the surrounding hills. Bedrooms and drawing room enjoy a south facing vista to the Whitcliffe beauty spot. Get a taste of country house living – you may like it.

Bed & Breakfast per night: double room from £50.00
Evening meal by prior arrangement

Bedrooms: 1 double, 1 twin
Bathrooms: 2 private
Parking for 10
Open: March–December

122 NUMBER TWENTY EIGHT

〰〰〰〰 HIGHLY COMMENDED

28 Lower Broad Street, Ludlow, Shropshire SY8 1PQ Tel (01584) 876996 Fax (01584) 876860 E-mail ross.no28@btinternet.com

This listed town house of charm and character, with its secluded walled garden, is situated close to the river in this 'most lovely of English towns'. We welcome you to our home, where there is generous hospitality and a quiet, relaxed atmosphere. Abounding with pictures, prints and book-lined walls – all adding to your enjoyment. All bedrooms are charmingly individual and en-suite, with every comfort and 'many thoughtful extras'. Lovely woodland and riverside walks, with castles and antique shops galore.

Bed & Breakfast per night: single occupancy from
£40.00–£65.00; double room from £60.00–£75.00

Bedrooms: 4 double, 2 twin
Bathrooms: 6 en-suite, 1 public
Cards accepted: Mastercard, Visa, Amex

123 BROCKENCOTE HALL

〰〰〰〰 DE LUXE

Chaddesley Corbett, Kidderminster, Worcestershire DY10 4PY Tel (01562) 777876 Fax (01562) 777872

Nestling in the heart of the Worcestershire countryside, Brockencote Hall is set in seventy acres of private parkland with its own lake. It is the perfect place for relaxation. Proprietors Alison and Joseph Petitjean have created a charming Gallic oasis in the heart of England, combining traditional French comfort and friendliness with superb French cuisine. The hotel offers a choice of seventeen magnificent en-suite bedrooms, including one that has been especially designed to make stays comfortable for disabled guests.

Bed & Breakfast per night: single occupancy from
£97.00–£112.00; double room from £120.00–£145.00
Dinner, Bed & Breakfast per person, per night:
£83.50–£121.50
Lunch available: 1200–1330

Evening meal 1900 (last orders 2130)
Bedrooms: 13 double, 3 twin, 1 triple
Bathrooms: 17 en-suite
Parking for 50
Cards accepted: Mastercard, Diners, Amex, Switch/Delta

124 HOME FARM

Listed HIGHLY COMMENDED

reat Witley, Worcester, Worcestershire WR6 6JJ Tel (01299) 896825

Home Farm offers a warm welcome to all its guests. It is a Grade II* Listed moated farmhouse, surrounded by beautiful gardens, with breathtaking views of Worcestershire. Each bedroom has a character of its own, being spacious and individually decorated, with many 'personal' touches. Breakfast incorporates a large choice of local and seasonal produce to suit all tastes. Enjoy a relaxing, peaceful stay and visit the many nearby places of interest.

ed & Breakfast per night: single room from £22.00;
ouble room from £44.00–£50.00

Bedrooms: 1 single, 2 twin
Bathrooms: 1 en-suite, 1 public
Parking for 12

125 THE HILLS FARM

HIGHLY COMMENDED

eysters, Leominster, Herefordshire HR6 0HP Tel (01568) 750205 Fax (01568) 750205

We offer stunning views, scrumptious food and charming bedrooms. The Hills stands on high ground amidst 120 arable acres, complete with a two-mile farm walk. Three of our bedrooms are in lovingly converted barns, each completely self-contained and so offering the ultimate in seclusion and privacy. To round the day off – delicious home-cooked dinners complete with a vegetarian choice if required. No smoking. Brochure available.

ed & Breakfast per night: single occupancy from
34.00–£37.00; double room from £48.00–£54.00
inner, Bed & Breakfast per person, per night:
41.00–£44.00 (min 2 nights)
vening meal 1900 (last bookings 1700)

Bedrooms: 3 double, 2 twin
Bathrooms: 4 en-suite, 2 private
Parking for 5
Open: March–October
Cards accepted: Mastercard, Visa, Switch/Delta

126 THE PADDOCK

HIGHLY COMMENDED

hobdon, Leominster, Herefordshire HR6 9NQ Tel (01568) 708176

Situated in idyllic countryside bordering Wales, The Paddock offers a warm welcome, wonderful service and delightful en-suite accommodation. All the well-equipped rooms are on the ground floor and include a mechanical ventilation system and underfloor central heating. Guests have their own entrance, a comfortable lounge with satellite television, and a large garden and patio. We serve a substantial breakfast and offer a delicious three-course dinner. Visit The Paddock for a truly relaxing break.

ed & Breakfast per night: single occupancy £25.00;
ouble room from £40.00–£44.00
inner, Bed & Breakfast per person, per night:
34.00–£36.00 (2 sharing)
vening meal 1900

Bedrooms: 4 double, 1 twin
Bathrooms: 5 en-suite
Parking for 10

127 BROXWOOD COURT

 HIGHLY COMMENDED

Broxwood, Leominster, Herefordshire HR6 9JJ Tel (01544) 340245 Fax (01544) 340573

This beautiful home, with its sweeping lawns where peacocks roam, magnificent trees and lake, and uninterrupted views of the Black Mountains, offers an atmosphere of peace and tranquillity. Relax in the cosy library, enjoy the views from the drawing room, play tennis on the all-weather court, swim in the pool, or walk in the lovely thirty-acre garden. Mike and Anne are a relaxed and well-travelled couple who will give you a very warm welcome.

Bed & Breakfast per night: single occupancy from £40.00–£50.00; double room from £66.00–£76.00
Dinner, Bed & Breakfast per person, per night: £53.00–£58.00 (2 sharing)
Evening meal 2000

Bedrooms: 1 double, 2 twin
Bathrooms: 2 en-suite, 1 private
Parking for 15
Cards accepted: Mastercard, Visa

128 THE STEPPES

HIGHLY COMMENDED

Ullingswick, Hereford HR1 3JG Tel (01432) 820424 Fax (01432) 820042

This award-winning country-house hotel with an intimate atmosphere abounds in antique furniture, inglenook fireplaces, oak beams and flag-stoned floors. The old dairy now houses a magnificent cobbled bar with Dickensian atmosphere, and a restored timber-framed barn and converted stable accommodate six large luxury en-suite bedrooms. Outstanding cordon bleu cuisine (AA 2 Rosettes) is served by candle light, and highly praised breakfasts come with an imaginative selection.

Bed & Breakfast per night: single occupancy from £40.00–£45.00; double room from £80.00–£90.00
Dinner, Bed & Breakfast per person, per night: £68.00–£75.00
Evening meal 1930 (last orders 2030)

Bedrooms: 4 double, 2 twin
Bathrooms: 6 en-suite
Parking for 8
Open: February–November and Christmas
Cards accepted: Mastercard, Visa, Amex, Switch/Delta

129 AYLESTONE COURT HOTEL

HIGHLY COMMENDED

Aylestone Hill, Hereford HR1 1HS Tel (01432) 341891 or (01432) 359342 Fax (01432) 267691

For those who appreciate the finer things in life and enjoy being looked after with care and courtesy. The three-storey Georgian building has been tastefully renovated throughout, with spacious, comfortable public rooms, elegant Louis IV-style dining room, and orangery breakfast room extending into the private, mature gardens with extensive lawns and fruit trees. All nine en-suite bedrooms are individually designed and furnished with home comforts. Situated on the A4103, four minutes' walk from Hereford city centre.

Bed & Breakfast per night: single occupancy from £45.00–£55.00; double room from £60.00–£75.00
Dinner, Bed & Breakfast per person, per night: £57.50–£79.95

Evening meal 1900 (last orders 2100)
Bedrooms: 6 double, 3 twin
Bathrooms: 9 en-suite Parking for 18
Cards accepted: Mastercard, Visa, Diners, Amex, Switch/Delta

Entries are cross referenced by number to the maps on pages 62–63

130 WYCHE KEEP COUNTRY HOUSE

 HIGHLY COMMENDED

22 Wyche Road, Malvern, Worcestershire WR14 4EG Tel (01684) 567018 Fax (01684) 892304

Wyche Keep is a stunning arts and crafts style house, perched high on the Malvern Hills, built by the family of Sir Stanley Baldwin, Prime Minister, to enjoy the spectacular sixty-mile views, and having a long history of elegant entertaining. Three large luxury double suites, including a four-poster. Traditional English cooking is a speciality and guests can savour memorable four-course candlelit dinners. Fully licensed. Magical setting with private parking. A no smoking establishment.

Bed & Breakfast per night: single occupancy from £35.00–£40.00; double room from £50.00–£60.00
Dinner, Bed & Breakfast per person, per night: £43.00–£48.00
Evening meal 1930 (last orders 2000)

Bedrooms: 1 double, 2 twin
Bathrooms: 3 en-suite
Parking for 6

The Malvern Hills

SOME OF ENGLAND'S oldest rocks push their way up through the geological strata to reach fresh air a few miles south-west of Worcester. Looking from the east, the Malverns, rising sheer from the Severn Plain, seem to belie their modest height. The 17th-century traveller Celia Fiennes may have described them as being 'at least 2 or 3 miles up and... in a Pirramidy fashion on the top', but in reality they can claim no more than 1,394ft (425m) at their highest point, Worcestershire Beacon. What they lack in altitude, however, they more than make up for in age, beauty and the panoramas they offer.

Only experienced geologists may recognise the clues which reveal that the Malverns are, in the main, made up of pre-Cambrian rocks created about 600 million years ago. On a clear day, however, all visitors will stare in awe at a view which stretches to a far-distant horizon in all directions. The summit of Worcestershire Beacon has a toposcope – or direction indicator – which confirms that those pimples far to the south are indeed the Mendips of Somerset, that slight bump in the hazy east is Bardon Hill near Leicester, that craggy bulge to the north is the Wrekin, and that peak to the west is Plynlimmon, near the Welsh coast. To look down from the Beacon is also to look into England's history, for the battlefields of Evesham (1265), Shrewsbury (1403), Mortimer's Cross (1461), Tewkesbury (1471), Edge Hill (1642) and Worcester (1651) are all there. Closer to hand, toward the southern end of the Malvern ridge and across the old county boundary are remains of perhaps England's finest hillfort, the 32-acre (13 hectare) settlement on Herefordshire Beacon (1,115ft - 340m).

The best way to explore these glorious hills – they stretch roughly 8 miles (13km) in a north–south direction – is naturally on foot, but several roads cross the Malverns affording magnificent views for the less mobile. If you're not arriving by car, then follow in the footsteps of the Victorian visitors to Great Malvern. In the 19th century this attractive inland resort was almost as popular a spa as Cheltenham or Bath, with Malvern spring water the main draw. The town's prosperity ensured that an extravagantly ornate station was built – and it serves the town to this day. Great Malvern's architectural highlight is, however, its Priory Church of St Mary and St Michael. Inside the largely 15th-century building can be found a collection of medieval stained glass second only to that in York Minster. The town also makes the most of its considerable musical associations through its highly-regarded Elgar festival held in late May and early June.

131 THE COTTAGE IN THE WOOD HOTEL

 HIGHLY COMMENDED

Holywell Road, Malvern Wells, Malvern, Worcestershire WR14 4LG Tel (01684) 575859 Fax (01684) 560662

Stunningly set high on the Malvern Hills, looking across thirty miles of the Severn Plain to the horizon formed by the Cotswold Hills. Owned and run by the Pattin family for eleven years, the aim is to provide a relaxing and peaceful base from which to tour this area of outstanding natural beauty. The restaurant provides exceptional food backed by an extensive wine list of over five hundred bins. The daily half board price is based on a minimum two-night stay, and the weekly price offers seven nights for the price of six. Special breaks all week, all year. AA 2 Rosettes.

Bed & Breakfast per night: single occupancy from £72.00–£82.00; double room from £89.50–£139.00
Dinner, Bed & Breakfast per person, per night: £55.00–£91.00 (min 2 nights, 2 sharing)
Lunch available: 1230–1400

Evening meal 1900 (last orders 2100)
Bedrooms: 16 double, 4 twin
Bathrooms: 20 en-suite
Parking for 40
Cards accepted: Mastercard, Visa, Amex, Switch/Delta

132 HOLDFAST COTTAGE HOTEL

 HIGHLY COMMENDED

Marlbank Road, Little Malvern, Malvern, Worcestershire WR13 6NA Tel (01684) 310288 Fax (01684) 311117

Pretty wisteria-covered country house hotel, set in two acres of gardens and private woodland, tucked into the foot of the Malvern Hills. Highly recommended for its freshly-prepared menu which changes daily and uses the best local and seasonal produce. Delightful dining room and bar. Cosy lounge with log fire. Enchanting en-suite bedrooms are individually furnished. A personal welcome plus care and attention throughout your stay is assured by the resident proprietors, Stephen and Jane Knowles.

Bed & Breakfast per night: single room from £44.00–£45.00; double room from £85.00–£88.00
Dinner, Bed & Breakfast per person, per night: £58.00–£60.00 (min 2 nights)
Evening meal 1900 (last orders 2100)

Bedrooms: 1 single, 5 double, 2 twin
Bathrooms: 8 en-suite, 1 public
Parking for 20
Cards accepted: Mastercard, Visa, Switch/Delta

133 THE OLD RECTORY

HIGHLY COMMENDED

Garway, Hereford HR2 8RH Tel (01600) 750363 Fax (01600) 750364

Our home is Victorian, with a wonderfully welcoming atmosphere – the tick of the grandfather clock, the smell of log fires, arrangements of flowers and Aga cooking all combine to make you feel at home. The Blue Room has a double four-poster and the Pink Room has twin beds; both have handbasins and beautiful views of the countryside looking towards Wales. Private sitting room with colour TV. Peaceful garden with many birds.

Bed & Breakfast per night: double room from £40.00–£45.00
Dinner, Bed & Breakfast per person, per night: £36.00–£38.50 (2 sharing)
Evening meal 1900 (last orders 2030)

Bedrooms: 1 double, 1 twin
Bathrooms: 2 public
Parking for 4
Cards accepted: Mastercard

Entries are cross referenced by number to the maps on pages 62–63

134 GLEWSTONE COURT HOTEL

≈≈≈≈ HIGHLY COMMENDED

Glewstone, Ross-on-Wye, Herefordshire HR9 6AW Tel (01989) 770367 Fax (01989) 770282

Located in the heart of the Wye Valley, an area of outstanding natural beauty, Glewstone Court is a unique hotel where the priority is placed on making guests feel totally welcome. The style is relaxed country-house, with comfortable furnishings, period decor, open log fires and a warm, friendly ambience. Food is always prepared to a high standard using local produce – Hereford beef, Wye salmon and Welsh lamb are constantly on the menu. AA Rosette food award.

Bed & Breakfast per night: single room from £45.00–£70.00; double room from £70.00–£105.00
Dinner, Bed & Breakfast per person, per night: £55.00–£70.00 (min 2 nights)
Lunch available: 1200–1400

Evening meal 1900 (last orders 2130)
Bedrooms: 1 single, 6 double
Bathrooms: 7 en-suite
Parking for 20
Cards accepted: Mastercard, Visa, Amex, Switch/Delta

135 THE CHASE HOTEL

≈≈≈ HIGHLY COMMENDED

Gloucester Road, Ross-on-Wye, Herefordshire HR9 5LH Tel (01989) 763161 Fax (01989) 768330

A country house hotel set in 11 acres of gardens and grounds within close proximity of the town centre. All rooms have en-suite facilities, hair dryers, colour satellite televisions, radios and hospitality trays. The AA 2 Rosette award-winning restaurant provides excellence in food, service and cuisine. All public rooms overlook the gardens and, with ample parking, this hotel offers an ideal situation to enjoy a relaxing time while touring the area. Leisure breaks from £45 per person per night.

Bed & Breakfast per night: single occupancy from £60.00–£85.00; double room from £85.00–£100.00
Evening meal 1900 (last orders 2145)

Bedrooms: 17 double, 21 twin, 1 triple
Bathrooms: 39 en-suite
Parking for 200
Cards accepted: Mastercard, Visa, Diners, Amex, Switch/Delta

136 PENCRAIG COURT HOTEL

≈≈≈ HIGHLY COMMENDED

Pencraig, Ross-on-Wye, Herefordshire HR9 6HR Tel (01989) 770306 or (01989) 770416 Fax (01989) 770040 E-mail michael.cliffordf@rfdc.ac.uk

A fine Georgian house, full of character and elegance, set in three and a half acres of gardens and secluded woodland, high above the banks of the River Wye. All bedrooms have private bathrooms and are individually furnished. The food is prepared fresh to order and, when available, use is made of local beef, salmon and lamb. In season there are also vegetables and herbs from the kitchen garden. All of this is complemented by an excellent wine list.

Bed & Breakfast per night: single room from £45.00–£52.50; double room from £62.50–£75.00
Dinner, Bed & Breakfast per person, per night: £54.25–£60.50
Evening meal 1900 (last orders 2100)

Bedrooms: 1 single, 4 double, 4 twin, 2 triple
Bathrooms: 11 en-suite
Parking for 20
Cards accepted: Mastercard, Visa, Switch/Delta

137 NORTON HOUSE

🌊🌊 HIGHLY COMMENDED

Whitchurch, Ross-on-Wye, Herefordshire HR9 6DJ Tel (01600) 890046 Fax (01600) 890045 E-mail jackson@osconwhi.source.co.uk

A 17th-century Grade II Listed former farmhouse, which has been beautifully renovated with pine shutters and doors, oak beams, flagstone floors and inglenook fireplaces. It oozes old fashioned charm but offers all the modern comfort our guests could wish for. Delicious Aga-cooked meals served by candle light make for a romantic escape. Situated in the beautiful Wye Valley, a short walk from the River Wye and five minutes' drive from Yat Rock, making it an ideal touring centre.

Bed & Breakfast per night: single occupancy from £25.00–£30.00; double room from £40.00–£44.00
Dinner, Bed & Breakfast per person, per night: £29.50–£39.50
Evening meal 1930

Bedrooms: 2 double, 1 twin
Bathrooms: 3 en-suite
Parking for 3

138 SUTTON HOUSE

🌊 HIGHLY COMMENDED

Hope Mansell, Ross-on-Wye, Herefordshire HR9 5TJ Tel (01989) 750351 Fax (01989) 750351

If you are looking for peace and quiet, comfort, elegant surroundings, lovely views and fresh, well-prepared food, you will be very welcome at our carefully restored 18th-century house nestling in the tranquil, unspoilt valley of Hope Mansell. We are well positioned for walking, cycling, sight-seeing or just relaxing with a book from our well-stocked shelves. We will do our best to make your stay happy and memorable.

Bed & Breakfast per night: single occupancy from £25.00–£27.00; double room from £40.00–£44.00

Bedrooms: 2 double
Bathrooms: 1 en-suite, 1 public
Parking for 3

139 WYNDHAM ARMS

🌊🌊🌊🌊 HIGHLY COMMENDED

Clearwell, Coleford, Gloucestershire GL16 8JT Tel (01594) 833666 Fax (01594) 836450

A 14th-century village inn with 20th-century amenities. At the edge of the Royal Forest of Dean, just above the Wye Valley, the Wyndham Arms has been in the Stanford family's competent ownership since 1973. All bedrooms en-suite, award-winning restaurant, traditional beers, lots of different malt whiskies, and very pretty gardens. Just the place for a get-away weekend. Stay free on Sundays if you dine in the restaurant.

Bed & Breakfast per night: single room £56.50; double room from £80.00–£100.00
Dinner, Bed & Breakfast per person, per night: £50.00–£60.00
Lunch available: 1200–1400

Evening meal 1845 (last orders 2130)
Bedrooms: 2 single, 4 double, 9 twin, 2 triple
Bathrooms: 17 en-suite   Parking for 52
Cards accepted: Mastercard, Visa, Diners, Amex, Switch/Delta

150 CLEEVE HILL HOTEL

DE LUXE

Cleeve Hill, Cheltenham, Gloucestershire GL52 3PR Tel (01242) 672052 Fax (01242) 979969

This award-winning hotel, perched on the slopes of Cleeve Hill, the highest point in the Cotswolds, is a mere ten minute drive from the centre of Cheltenham. The immaculate Edwardian house is elegantly decorated with quality furnishings and fabrics and all of the bedrooms are equipped to a very high standard with all the little extras that make this a very special place to stay. The hotel upholds a strict 'No Smoking' policy.

Bed & Breakfast per night: single room from £50.00–£65.00; double room from £65.00–£80.00

Bedrooms: 1 single, 5 double, 2 twin, 1 family room
Bathrooms: 9 en-suite
Parking for 12
Cards accepted: Mastercard, Visa, Amex

151 COOMBE HOUSE

HIGHLY COMMENDED

Rissington Road, Bourton-on-the-Water, Gloucestershire GL54 2DT Tel (01451) 821966 Fax (01451) 810477

Quietly located just a river-side walk from the centre of this beautiful Cotswold Village, Coombe House offers a haven of cleanliness, comfort and personal attention from your hosts. Gentle elegance, charming bedrooms and reception rooms, and a delightful garden with unusual plants. Perfect central base for discovering the superb Cotswolds, gardens and castles. London 75 miles. Oxford/Stratford 26 miles. Assistance with routes, ideas and restaurants. No smoking. www.smoothhound.co.uk/hotels/coombeho.html

Bed & Breakfast per night: single occupancy from £42.00–£52.00; double room from £58.75–£75.00

Bedrooms: 4 double, 2 twin
Bathrooms: 6 en-suite
Parking for 6
Cards accepted: Mastercard, Visa

152 FARNCOMBE

HIGHLY COMMENDED

Clapton, Bourton-on-the-Water, Cheltenham, Gloucestershire GL54 2LG Tel (01451) 820120 or 0378 843123 Fax (01451) 820120

Farncombe provides peace and tranquillity, with superb views of the Windrush Valley, in Clapton-on-the-Hill, two and a half miles from Bourton-on-the-Water, in the centre of the Cotswolds. A comfortable, non-smoking, family Cotswold home set in large gardens. Two double rooms with showers and basins, and one en-suite twin room, each with hairdryer and radio. Large dining room with tea/coffee-making facilities. Television lounge.

Bed & Breakfast per night: double room from £39.00–£44.00

Bedrooms: 2 double, 1 twin
Bathrooms: 1 en-suite, 2 private showers
Parking for 3

153 LORDS OF THE MANOR HOTEL

〰〰〰〰 DE LUXE

Upper Slaughter, Bourton-on-the-Water, Cheltenham, Gloucestershire GL54 2JD Tel (01451) 820243 Fax (01451) 820696

In the heart of the Cotswolds, in one of England's most unspoilt and picturesque villages, stands the Lords of the Manor Hotel. Built in the 17th century of honeyed Cotswold stone, the house enjoys splendid views over the surrounding meadows, stream and parkland. The heart of this country house is the dining room where truly memorable dishes, made from the best local ingredients, are served. Nearby are Blenheim Palace, Warwick Castle and Shakespeare country.

Bed & Breakfast per night: single room from £98.00–£138.00; double room from £138.00–£295.00
Dinner, Bed & Breakfast per person, per night: £120.00–£340.00 (min 2 nights)
Lunch available: 1200–1430

Evening meal 1930 (last orders 2130)
Bedrooms: 2 single, 15 double, 10 twin
Bathrooms: 27 en-suite   Parking for 40
Cards accepted: Mastercard, Visa, Diners, Amex, Switch/Delta

154 GUITING GUESTHOUSE

〰〰 HIGHLY COMMENDED

Post Office Lane, Guiting Power, Cheltenham, Gloucestershire GL54 5TZ Tel (01451) 850470 Fax (01451) 850034 E-mail guiting.guest_house@virgin.net

The house is a delightful and carefully-restored 16th-century Cotswold stone farmhouse. Everywhere there are exposed beams, inglenook fireplaces, open fires and polished solid pine floors from the Wychwood forest. Three rooms have four-poster beds and are en-suite, whilst the other room has totally private facilities. Television and generously-filled hospitality tray in each room. Access to the guesthouse is available at all times. Delicious evening meals, served by candle light, are prepared and presented by the hosts (with the exception of Sunday and Monday).
www.freespace.virgin.net/guiting.guest_house/

Bed & Breakfast per night: single occupancy £30.00; double room from £50.00–£55.00
Dinner, Bed & Breakfast per person, per night: £40.00–£42.00
Evening meal 1845

Bedrooms: 3 double, 1 twin
Bathrooms: 3 en-suite, 2 private
Parking for 4
Cards accepted: Mastercard, Visa, Switch/Delta

155 GRAPEVINE HOTEL

〰〰〰〰 HIGHLY COMMENDED

Sheep Street, Stow-on-the-Wold, Gloucestershire GL54 1AU Tel (01451) 830344 Fax (01451) 832278 E-mail enquiries@vines.co.uk

An award-winning 17th-century market town hotel in the antiques centre of the Cotswolds. Romantic conservatory restaurant crowned by a magnificent historic vine and finely furnished Garden and Vine rooms. The outstanding personal service provided by a loyal team of staff is perhaps the secret of the hotel's success. This, along with the exceptionally high standard of overall comfort, hospitality and fine food with two AA Rosettes, has earned the Grapevine its many accolades. www.vines.co.uk

Bed & Breakfast per night: single room from £87.00–£107.00; double room from £134.00–£174.00
Dinner, Bed & Breakfast per person, per night: £72.00–£112.00
Lunch available: 1200–1400

Evening meal 1900 (last orders 2130)
Bedrooms: 3 single, 7 double, 10 twin, 2 triple
Bathrooms: 22 en-suite
Parking for 23
Cards accepted: Mastercard, Visa, Diners, Amex

Entries are cross referenced by number to the maps on pages 62–63

156 STOW LODGE HOTEL

≋≋≋ HIGHLY COMMENDED

The Square, Stow-on-the-Wold, Gloucestershire GL54 1AB Tel (01451) 830485 Fax (01451) 831671

Privately owned and family-run Cotswold Manor House Hotel set back in its own gardens in a secluded corner of the market square. Bedrooms are comfortably furnished with a private bathroom, and the no smoking restaurant offers excellent home cooking and an interesting extensive wine list. There are warm open fires for those cooler days in both the bar and residents' lounge. The hotel is ideal for those touring the Cotswolds and Shakespeare country and requiring a relaxing holiday.

Bed & Breakfast per night: single room from £45.00–£95.00; double room from £65.00–£110.00
Lunch available: 1200–1400
Evening meal 1900 (last orders 2100)

Bedrooms: 1 single, 9 double, 9 twin, 2 triple
Bathrooms: 21 en-suite
Parking for 30
Open: February–December
Cards accepted: Mastercard, Visa, Diners, Switch/Delta

157 COLLEGE HOUSE

≋≋ DE LUXE

Chapel Street, Broadwell, Moreton-in-Marsh, Gloucestershire GL56 OTW Tel (01451) 832351

College House is a 17th-century residence of great character located in a quiet and enchanting Cotswold village. It has superb bedrooms and luxurious bathrooms, of which two are en-suite, and a sitting-room with a large inglenook fireplace for exclusive guest use. Breakfast and, if desired, three-course dinners are served in the beamed dining-room. Broadwell is just two miles from Stow-on-the-Wold. Oxford, Cheltenham and Stratford-upon-Avon are all easily accessible.

Bed & Breakfast per night: double room from £55.00–£68.00
Dinner, Bed & Breakfast per person, per night: £46.00–£55.50
Evening meal 1800 (last bookings 1200)

Bedrooms: 3 double
Bathrooms: 2 en-suite, 2 private
Parking for 6

158 ISBOURNE MANOR HOUSE

≋≋ HIGHLY COMMENDED

Castle Street, Winchcombe, Cheltenham, Gloucestershire GL54 5JA Tel (01242) 602281 Fax (01242) 602281

This beautiful listed house is quietly situated within attractive gardens which are bordered by the River Isbourne. We are adjacent to the lovely grounds of Sudeley Castle and only two minutes' walk away from both stunning Cotswold countryside and the centre of historic Winchcombe. All rooms are decorated and furnished to the highest standard, combining modern comfort with family antiques and beautiful fabrics. Guests have the sole use of two elegant reception rooms, private parking and garden.

Bed & Breakfast per night: single occupancy from £40.00–£55.00; double room from £50.00–£70.00

Bedrooms: 2 double, 1 twin
Bathrooms: 2 en-suite, 2 private
Parking for 5

At-a-glance symbols are explained on the flap inside the back cover

159 SUDELEY HILL FARM

 HIGHLY COMMENDED

Winchcombe, Cheltenham, Gloucestershire GL54 5JB Tel (01242) 602344 Fax (01242) 602344

A friendly welcome awaits you on our eight hundred acre sheep and arable farm. The 15th-century listed farmhouse is situated above Sudeley Castle, with a large garden and panoramic views across the valley. A comfortable lounge, log fires, separate dining room, no smoking en-suite bedrooms with television and facilities for hot drinks. Central for exploring the Cotswolds. Good pub food in Winchcombe, half a mile away.

Bed & Breakfast per night: single occupancy from
£26.00–£30.00; double room from £44.00–£48.00

Bedrooms: 1 double, 2 triple
Bathrooms: 3 en-suite
Parking for 10

160 THE LYGON ARMS

DE LUXE

Broadway, Worcestershire WR12 7DU Tel (01386) 852255 Fax (01386) 858611 E-mail info@the-lygon-arms.co.uk

The 16th-century Lygon Arms is the centrepiece of Broadway, one of the Cotswolds' prettiest villages. Recently restored rooms and suites are furnished in country house style. The historic Great Hall combines the best traditional British foods with innovative modern cooking, whilst Oliver's Brasserie and the Patio Restaurant specialise in lighter fare. The adjoining Country Club boasts a magnificent galleried pool, and provides health and beauty treatments. The Inn provides the perfect base to explore the surrounding countryside.

Bed & Breakfast per night: single room from
£131.60–£168.03; double room from £205.63–£229.13
Dinner, Bed & Breakfast per person, per night:
£245.00–£270.00 (min 2 nights to include Saturday)
Lunch available 1230–1400

Evening meal 1930 (last orders 2115)
Bedrooms: 2 single, 48 double, 9 twin, 6 triple
Bathrooms: 65 en-suite   Parking for 153
Cards accepted: Mastercard, Visa, Diners, Amex,
Switch/Delta

161 DORMY HOUSE

HIGHLY COMMENDED

Willersey Hill, Broadway, Worcestershire WR12 7LF Tel (01386) 852711 Fax (01386) 858636 E-mail reservation@dormyhouse.co.uk

The 17th-century Dormy House is ideally located for visiting the picturesque villages of the Cotswolds as well as Shakespeare's Stratford-upon-Avon. Enjoy the beautifully appointed rooms, superb restaurant and high standard of cuisine and service. Our croquet lawn, putting green, sauna/steam room, gym, games room and nature trail offer the chance to combine leisure with pleasure. Pamper yourself with a Champagne Weekend or a carefree midweek break in the Heart of England.

Bed & Breakfast per night: single room from
£71.00–£95.00; double room from £142.00–£170.00
Dinner, Bed & Breakfast per person, per night:
£96.00–£106.00
Lunch available: 1230–1400 (except Saturday); bar meals daily

Evening meal 1900 (last orders 2130)
Bedrooms: 6 single, 16 double, 26 twin, 1 family room
Bathrooms: 49 en-suite   Parking for 90
Cards accepted: Mastercard, Visa, Diners, Amex,
Switch/Delta

162 TUDOR COTTAGE

 HIGHLY COMMENDED

High Street, Broadway, Worcestershire WR12 7DT Tel (01386) 852674

Situated on Broadway's famous High Street, this traditional 17th-century stone Cotswold cottage, full of character and charm, is an ideal location for touring the Cotswolds. All bedrooms are en-suite and have been tastefully decorated, furnished with style and equipped with modern comforts, including the four-poster bedroom which is ideal for a romantic weekend. Walks across open countryside lie within a few yards of the cottage. Or simply stroll the High Street with its interesting shops, pubs and restaurants.

Bed & Breakfast per night: single occupancy from £35.00–£40.00; double room from £50.00–£65.00

Bedrooms: 3 double, 1 twin
Bathrooms: 4 en-suite
Parking for 4

163 THE OLD BAKERY

 HIGHLY COMMENDED

High Street, Blockley, Moreton-in-Marsh, Gloucestershire GL56 9EU Tel (01386) 700408 Fax (01386) 700408

An early Victorian country guest house with a lovely cottage garden situated in one of the quiet and unspoilt Cotswold villages. There are three individually designed en-suite bedrooms and the house is furnished with antiques. Special features of a stay here are the excellent four-course dinners, prepared from local and fresh garden produce, and the carefully selected and interesting wine list, both served with the friendliest of welcomes by the proprietors.

Dinner, Bed & Breakfast per person, per night: £53.00–£63.00 (2 sharing)
Evening meal 1930 (last orders 2030)

Bedrooms: 2 double, 1 twin
Bathrooms: 3 en-suite
Parking for 3
Cards accepted: Mastercard, Visa, Amex, Switch/Delta

164 CHARINGWORTH MANOR

 DE LUXE

Charingworth, Chipping Campden, Gloucestershire GL55 6NS Tel (01386) 593555 Fax (01386) 593353 E-mail charingworthmanor@englishrosehotels.com

The Manor of Charingworth dates back to the 14th century and is set in beautiful gardens on a private 54-acre estate with panoramic views over the Cotswolds. This peaceful country house has twenty six de luxe bedrooms, a fine restaurant with two AA Rosettes, snug billiard room and welcoming lounges with log fires, beautiful furnishings and decor, and a quality of service which is second to none. De luxe Roman Leisure Spa with pool, sauna, steam room and solarium.

Bed & Breakfast per night: single occupancy from £105.00–£140.00; double room from £140.00–£240.00
Dinner, Bed & Breakfast per person, per night: £95.00–£150.00 (min 2 nights)
Lunch available: 1230–1400

Evening meal 1900 (last orders 2200)
Bedrooms: 15 double, 8 twin, 3 triple
Bathrooms: 26 en-suite   Parking for 30
Cards accepted: Mastercard, Visa, Diners, Amex, Switch/Delta

165 THE OLD RECTORY
🜲 DE LUXE

Church Street, Willersey, Broadway, Worcestershire WR12 7PN Tel (01386) 853729 Fax (01386) 858061 E-mail beauvoisin@btinternet.com

Built of Cotswold stone, the 17th-century Rectory is quietly tucked away opposite the church. Enclosed by its dry-stone wall, the garden with its ancient mulberry tree is truly idyllic. Superb breakfasts served in the elegant dining room (beside a log fire in winter). The Bell Inn, one minute walk away, offers excellent meals. The immaculate bedrooms, including four-posters, are furnished and decorated to a high standard and include all facilities. All rooms have their own bathroom with Crabtree & Evelyn toiletries. E-mail: if no reply, owners are away – please use fax.
www.homepages.tesco.net/~j.walker/

Bed & Breakfast per night: single occupancy from £45.00–£80.00; double room from £65.00–£98.00

Bedrooms: 5 double, 1 twin, 2 triple
Bathrooms: 6 en-suite, 2 private
Parking for 10
Cards accepted: Mastercard, Visa, Amex, Switch/Delta

---

166 ARBOUR HOUSE BED AND BREAKFAST
🜲🜲 HIGHLY COMMENDED

Main Road, Wyre Piddle, Pershore, Worcestershire WR10 2HU Tel (01386) 555833

Arbour House Bed and Breakfast is a charming old home with oak beams, real fires and flagstone floors, containing a fascinating collection of china and objets d'art. We offer beautifully prepared bedrooms with hospitality trays, a good selection of quality teas, fresh flowers, and many other personal touches that will make your stay thoroughly enjoyable. Situated in the vale of Evesham, there are several good hostelries here, and the Cotswolds, Stratford and Worcester are all nearby.

Bed & Breakfast per night: single occupancy from £25.00–£26.00; double room from £42.00–£44.00
Dinner, Bed & Breakfast per person, per night: £37.00–£40.00
Evening meal 1800 (by prior arrangement)

Bedrooms: 1 double, 2 twin
Bathrooms: 3 en-suite
Parking for 5

---

167 THE MILL AT HARVINGTON
 HIGHLY COMMENDED

Anchor Lane, Harvington, Evesham, Worcestershire WR11 5NR Tel (01386) 870688 Fax (01386) 870688

Friendly, owner-run hotel, sensitively converted from a beautiful Georgian house and former baking mill. Situated on the banks of the River Avon in acres of private parkland, our hotel offers peace, tranquillity and a view over the garden and river towards the morning sun from every bedroom. Find gentle elegance without formality, good food without fussiness (AA 2 Rosettes), and friendly staff who will help you relax immediately.

Bed & Breakfast per night: single occupancy from £61.00–£66.00; double room from £96.00–£112.00
Dinner, Bed & Breakfast per person, per night: £57.00–£66.00 (min 2 nights, 2 sharing)
Lunch available: 1145–1345

Evening meal 1900 (last orders 2045)
Bedrooms: 16 double, 5 twin
Bathrooms: 21 en-suite   Parking for 45
Cards accepted: Mastercard, Visa, Diners, Amex, Switch/Delta

168 GRAVELSIDE BARN

HIGHLY COMMENDED

Binton, Stratford-upon-Avon, Warwickshire CV37 9TU Tel (01789) 750502 or (01789) 297000 Fax (01789) 298056

Serenely situated on a hilltop in the middle of rolling Warwickshire farmland, with magnificent views of the surrounding countryside and Cotswold Hills, Gravelside Barn offers the discerning traveller all of today's modern conveniences and comforts in a stunning and tranquil setting. A great base for exploring Shakespeare country and the Heart of England, or simply a place to relax. Three and a half miles from Stratford and ten minutes from Junction 15/M40. Please ring for a brochure. Totally non-smoking. No extra charge for birdsong and fresh air!

Bed & Breakfast per night: single occupancy from £35.00–£40.00; double room from £50.00–£60.00

Bedrooms: 2 double, 1 twin
Bathrooms: 3 en-suite
Parking for 6

169 LOXLEY FARM

HIGHLY COMMENDED

Loxley, Warwick, Warwickshire CV35 9JN Tel (01789) 840265 Fax (01789) 840265

Picturesque thatched, half-timbered farmhouse and barn, surrounded by one and a half acres of garden and orchard, in a quiet village on the edge of the Cotswolds. Three and a half miles from Stratford-upon-Avon, seven miles from Warwick. Accommodation is in the recently restored single-storey barn, which has two private suites of rooms, one of which includes a small kitchen. Traditional English breakfasts are served in the farmhouse dining room. Mrs Horton is happy to book theatre tickets at no extra charge.

Bed & Breakfast per night: single occupancy from £35.00–£38.00; double room from £55.00–£60.00

Bedrooms: 2 double
Bathrooms: 2 en-suite
Parking for 10

170 STRATFORD COURT HOTEL

HIGHLY COMMENDED

Avenue Road, Stratford-upon-Avon, Warwickshire CV37 6UX Tel (01789) 297799 Fax (01789) 262449

This beautiful Edwardian residence is situated in one of Stratford's finest locations and is surrounded by an acre of walled gardens, providing a peaceful setting where our guests can relax and be looked after with care and courtesy. All our bedrooms are en-suite, having been refurbished to the highest standard in keeping with the style of the hotel. On the ground floor, antiques, oak and comfy sofas in both the garden bar and lounge ensure a warm and welcoming atmosphere.

Bed & Breakfast per night: single room from £55.00–£65.00; double room from £90.00–£150.00 Dinner, Bed & Breakfast per person, per night: from £72.00
Evening meal 1800 (last orders 2030)

Bedrooms: 4 single, 5 double, 2 twin, 2 triple
Bathrooms: 13 en-suite
Parking for 32
Cards accepted: Mastercard, Visa

At-a-glance symbols are explained on the flap inside the back cover

171 WELCOMBE HOTEL AND GOLF COURSE

 HIGHLY COMMENDED

Warwick Road, Stratford-upon-Avon, Warwickshire CV37 0NR Tel (01789) 295252 Fax (01789) 414666 E-mail sales@welcombe.co.uk

When you arrive at the Welcombe Hotel, the sweeping driveway leads you up past the 18-hole championship golf course to a spectacular listed 19th-century Jacobean style mansion with many original antiques which are listed at Sotheby's. Set within 157 acres of parkland with formal gardens, lakes and a waterfall – history is inscribed in the very atmosphere! 67 bedrooms, four-posters, suites and gallery rooms. AA 2 Rosette award-winning restaurant and bar. Hair, health and beauty salon. CATEGORY 3

Bed & Breakfast per night: single room from £110.00–£140.00; double room £175.00
Dinner, Bed & Breakfast per person, per night: £122.50–£175.00
Evening meal 1900 (last orders 2130)

Bedrooms: 1 single, 39 double, 27 twin
Bathrooms: 67 en-suite
Parking for 120
Cards accepted: Mastercard, Visa, Diners, Amex, Switch/Delta

172 STRATFORD MANOR HOTEL

 HIGHLY COMMENDED

Warwick Road, Stratford-upon-Avon, Warwickshire CV37 0PY Tel (01789) 731173 Fax (01789) 731131

Set in twenty one acres of beautiful countryside, superbly located just three miles from the centre of Stratford-upon-Avon, and a similar distance from Warwick and its superb castle. Stratford Manor is a modern hotel, attractively decorated with four murals depicting the seasons, with the theme carried through in the well-fitted bedrooms. Reflections Leisure Club has ample facilities, including a heated indoor pool, spa, sauna, plunge pool, gymnasium, fitness assessment and beauty treatments.

Bed & Breakfast per night: single occupancy from £104.00–£124.00; double room from £130.00–£170.00
Dinner, Bed & Breakfast per person, per night: £75.00–£95.00 (min 2 nights, 2 sharing)
Lunch available: 1230–1400

Evening meal 1900 (last orders 2130)
Bedrooms: 90 double, 13 twin
Bathrooms: 103 en-suite   Parking for 220
Cards accepted: Mastercard, Visa, Diners, Amex, Switch/Delta

173 NORTHLEIGH HOUSE

HIGHLY COMMENDED

Five Ways Road, Hatton, Warwick, Warwickshire CV35 7HZ Tel (01926) 484203 or 0374 101894 Fax (01926) 484006

A personal welcome, the individually-designed rooms with colour co-ordinated furnishings, en-suite bathrooms, television, fridge, kettle and many thoughtful extras make this the perfect hide-away in rural Warwickshire. A full English breakfast is freshly cooked to suit guests' individual tastes. Evening meals can be arranged, although there are excellent country pubs nearby, as well as the historic towns of Stratford-upon-Avon and Warwick, and the exhibition centres. Please call Sylvia Fenwick for brochures. No smoking.

Bed & Breakfast per night: single room from £33.00–£40.00; double room from £46.00–£58.00

Bedrooms: 1 single, 5 double, 1 twin
Bathrooms: 7 en-suite
Parking for 8
Open: February–November
Cards accepted: Mastercard, Visa

⟨174⟩ LANSDOWNE HOTEL

〰〰〰 HIGHLY COMMENDED

87 Clarendon Street, Leamington Spa, Warwickshire CV32 4PF Tel (01926) 450505 Fax (01926) 421313

An elegant Regency hotel, the Lansdowne offers a tranquil atmosphere. The comprehensive menus change daily, providing guests with a choice of freshly prepared dishes. David and Gillian Allen's personal selection of good quality wines underlines their policy of excellent value and complements the high standard of cuisine which is recognised by most discerning guides. Licensed bar, ample parking. Discount tickets to Warwick Castle. The Lansdowne is in the town centre, so easy for browsing round the shops. AA Rosette.

Bed & Breakfast per night: single room from £49.95–£56.95; double room from £59.90–£69.90
Dinner, Bed & Breakfast per person, per night: £42.50–£46.50 (4–2 nights, 2 sharing)
Evening meal 1830 (last orders 2130)

Bedrooms: 4 single, 5 double, 5 twin
Bathrooms: 14 en-suite, 1 public
Parking for 11
Cards accepted: Mastercard, Visa, Switch/Delta

Packwood Yew Garden

THERE IS SOMETHING rather surreal about the famous Yew Garden at Packwood House. On the manicured green lawn, smooth and flat as a billiard table, immaculately clipped yew bushes stand to attention. Seen from a distance they are strangely people-like, resembling a gathering of hooded figures, poised waiting, listening, ready to hurry off about their business. It is no wonder that a human symbolism has been attributed to them; the arrangement of trees with its single large yew 'the Master' standing atop a mound, surrounded by a 'multitude' of others, is said to represent the 'Sermon on the Mount'. Further refinements to the scheme include four large trees near the 'Master' known as 'the Apostles', and a row of twelve on a raised terrace called 'the Evangelists'.

Whether the original designer of the garden intended such a scheme is unknown, for references to the 'Sermon on the Mount' idea do not appear in documents until the late 19th century, some 200 years after the first trees were planted. All that is known about the origins of the Yew Garden is that John Fetherston, who inherited Packwood in 1634, laid out at least part of it between 1650 and 1670, but it is possible that many of the trees were planted some time later.

It was probably John Fetherston's father, another John, who began the fine timber-framed mansion which still forms the core of the present house. Though less famous than the garden, this too is of considerable interest. During the course of the Fetherston family's ownership the original Tudor building underwent considerable alterations, in particular the addition of fine stables and outbuildings in the 1670s. Packwood left the Fetherston family in 1869 and was eventually bought by Alfred Ash, a wealthy industrialist, in 1905. Ash's son, Graham Baron Ash, lavished meticulous care on it, restoring it to match his vision of the perfect Tudor mansion. He was a punctiliously correct and obsessively tidy man who kept everything, including the gardens, in perfect order. The restoration of his house became his passion – until he tired of it and bought a moated castle in Sussex. Donating Packwood to the National Trust, he hoped it would be kept forever as he created it, and so it has been. It remains the kind of museum piece it always was in his lifetime, a perfect monument to the Tudor age.

175 HIGH HOUSE

 HIGHLY COMMENDED

Old Warwick Road, Rowington, Warwick, Warwickshire CV35 7AA Tel (01926) 843270 or 0385 748134 Fax (01926) 843689

Beautiful country house built in 1690, having antique four-poster beds, beamed rooms and open fireplaces. Home produced bread, preserves, and eggs from genuine free-range hens – like everything else at High House, breakfasts are extra special. Perfectly positioned in a rural, secluded spot, ideal for visiting Warwick, Stratford, Birmingham's exhibition centres, National Trust houses and NAC Royal Showground. Many country pubs serving excellent food, all within two miles.

Bed & Breakfast per night: single occupancy from £28.00–£35.00; double room from £45.00–£60.00

Bedrooms: 2 double, 1 twin
Bathrooms: 3 en-suite
Parking for 20

176 VICTORIA LODGE HOTEL

 HIGHLY COMMENDED

180 Warwick Road, Kenilworth, Warwickshire CV8 1HU Tel (01926) 512020 Fax (01926) 858703

Victoria Lodge is a family-run hotel providing luxurious accommodation for those who appreciate the finer things in life and enjoy being looked after with care and courtesy. All the highly appointed bedrooms are en-suite. We have our own car park and a Victorian walled garden for guests' use. From its central Kenilworth location, the hotel is ideally situated for touring Shakespeare country and the Cotswolds. Victoria Lodge is a no smoking hotel.

Bed & Breakfast per night: single room from £39.00–£47.00; double room from £54.00–£59.00
Evening meal by prior arrangement

Bedrooms: 1 single, 7 double, 1 twin
Bathrooms: 9 en-suite
Parking for 11
Cards accepted: Mastercard, Visa, Amex, Switch/Delta

177 VILLAGE GREEN HOTEL

Listed HIGHLY COMMENDED

The Green, Dunchurch, Rugby, Warwickshire CV22 6NX Tel (01788) 813434 or (0410) 576867 Fax (01788) 814714 E-mail villagegreenhotel.rugby@btinternet.com

Situated in the centre of this historic and picturesque old coaching village in the heart of Shakespeare's county. The village has no less than five excellent eating houses all within one hundred yards of the hotel. Refurbished in 1997, our speciality is first class accommodation with bedrooms appointed to the highest specification, including our Princess Victoria room which has a four-poster bed. Complete your stay by enjoying one of our traditional English breakfasts.

Bed & Breakfast per night: single room from £35.00–£49.00; double room from £44.00–£69.00

Bedrooms: 4 single, 5 double, 1 twin
Bathrooms: 10 en-suite
Parking for 7
Cards accepted: Mastercard, Visa, Switch/Delta

178 NAILCOTE HALL HOTEL AND RESTAURANT

 HIGHLY COMMENDED

Nailcote Lane, Berkswell, West Midlands CV7 7DE Tel (01203) 466174 Fax (01203) 470720 E-mail info@nailcotehall.co.uk

Nailcote Hall is a charming Elizabethan country house hotel set in 15 acres of gardens and surrounded by Warwickshire countryside. Built in 1640, the house was used by Cromwell during the Civil War. Guests can enjoy the relaxing atmosphere of the Piano Bar Lounge and the intimate Tudor Oak Room restaurant or the lively Mediterranean style of Rick's Garden Café and Bar with a regular programme of live entertainment. Leisure facilities include a championship 9-hole par 3s golf course, a superb indoor leisure complex with Roman-style swimming pool, gymnasium, steam room, solarium, and health and beauty salon. www.nailcote.co.uk

Bed & Breakfast per night: single occupancy from £135.00; double room from £145.00–£225.00
Dinner, Bed & Breakfast per person, per night: £92.50 (2 sharing)
Lunch available: 1200–1400

Evening meal 1900 (last orders 2130)
Bedrooms: 25 double, 13 twin
Bathrooms: 38 en-suite   Parking for 130
Cards accepted: Mastercard, Visa, Diners, Amex, Switch/Delta

179 OAK TREE FARM

 HIGHLY COMMENDED

Hints Road, Hopwas, Tamworth, Staffordshire B78 3AA Tel (01827) 56807 or 0836 387887 Fax (01827) 56807

A country farmhouse with river frontage. Recently renovated to luxurious standards. Large, warm and welcoming bedrooms, all en-suite, with all comforts provided – sofas, courtesy tray, trouser press, hairdryer, iron, mineral water, etc. Set in the pretty village of Hopwas, between the River Tame and the Fazely Canal, Oak Tree Farm offers tranquil surroundings, but is very convenient for Tamworth, Lichfield, NEC and the airport.

Bed & Breakfast per night: single occupancy from £45.00; double room from £60.00

Bedrooms: 3 double, 1 twin, 2 triple
Bathrooms: 6 en-suite
Parking for 10

180 LAKE ISLE HOTEL

HIGHLY COMMENDED

16 High Street East, Uppingham, Oakham, Rutland LE15 9PZ Tel (01572) 822951 Fax (01572) 822951

The personal touch we provide will make your stay extra special, starting with a decanter of sherry, home-made biscuits and fresh fruit in your room. Our AA 2 Rosette restaurant menus, changed weekly, offer fresh produce and a list of over 300 wines, with special 'Wine Dinners' held throughout the year. Whirlpool baths and cottage suites are available. The shops of this sleepy market town surround us, yet we are within a short drive of Rutland Water, Burghley House and many pretty villages.

Bed & Breakfast per night: single room from £45.00–£62.00; double room from £65.00–£79.00
Dinner, Bed & Breakfast per person, per night: £54.00–£59.00 (2 sharing)
Lunch available: 1230–1345

Evening meal 1930 (last orders 2130)
Bedrooms: 1 single, 9 double, 2 twin
Bathrooms: 12 en-suite
Parking for 7
Cards accepted: Mastercard, Visa, Diners, Amex

At-a-glance symbols are explained on the flap inside the back cover

181 PIPWELL MANOR

 HIGHLY COMMENDED

Washway Road, Saracens Head, Holbeach, Spalding, Lincolnshire PE12 8AL Tel (01406) 423119

This handsome listed Georgian manor house, circa 1730, has many original features and is situated in a small village in the Lincolnshire Fens, in the midst of the flower-growing area. Guests are welcomed with afternoon tea in the comfortable sitting room, which has a log fire in winter. Traditional English breakfast is served in the elegant dining room and includes home-made preserves and home-produced fruit and eggs. Pipwell Manor is a lovely place to stay.

Bed & Breakfast per night: single room from £30.00; double room from £40.00

Bedrooms: 1 single, 2 double, 1 twin
Bathrooms: 2 en-suite, 3 private
Parking for 4

Norfolk Lavender

THE ROMANS USED lavender daily. They used it as a healing agent and as an insect repellent, in massage oils and to scent their bath water. Indeed, the name of the genus to which all species of lavender belong, Lavandula, derives from the Latin word meaning 'for washing'. Whether the Romans brought lavender to England or whether it was already growing here is uncertain, but Roman soldiers settling here would certainly have planted it as part of their herbal first-aid kit. Similarly, lavender was grown for medicinal uses in medieval monastic gardens. The dried flowers were used in Tudor times to scent chests and closets and to keep bedbugs at bay. Its cleansing properties were particularly valued during the plague of 1665, when the street cries of lavender sellers were part of everyday urban life. Victorian women used lavender perfume lavishly to scent themselves, their linen and their clothes.

In Victorian days there were a number of famous lavender fields in the south of England but in the early years of this century the bushes were attacked by a deadly disease, shab, and very little has been grown since. The only large-scale lavender farm left in England is that at Heacham in Norfolk, planted in 1932. Seven varieties of lavender are grown at Norfolk Lavender (tel: 01485 570384), five for distilling and two for drying. The fields are harvested – mechanically – from about mid-July, about one third of the crop being used as flowers for potpourris and sachets, two-thirds for distilling. The flowers for drying are packed loosely into sacks through which warm air is blown for several days. The flower heads are then removed from the stalks and sifted. The distilling process is an ancient one. Lavender's fragrance is contained in the oil stored in glands at the base of each floret and this oil is extracted by steam distillation. About 500lb (227kg) of flowers, stalks and all, are loaded into each still while one of the workers stands in it treading them down. Steam is then passed through the still and the mixture of steam and oil vapour passes to the condenser. The pure essential oil then collects in the separator and is drawn off, at the rate of about half a litre per still-load. The oil is matured for a year before being blended with other oils and fixatives.

182 CORFIELD HOUSE

 HIGHLY COMMENDED

Sporle, Swaffham, Norfolk PE32 2EA Tel (01760) 723636

Corfield House is an attractive brick-built house standing in half an acre of lawned gardens in the peaceful village of Sporle near Swaffham, an ideal base for touring Norfolk. Some of the comfortable en-suite bedrooms (one ground floor) have fine views across open fields and all have television, clock radio and a fact-file on places to visit. Good home-cooked food using excellent local produce. No smoking throughout.

Bed & Breakfast per night: single occupancy from £25.00–£35.00; double room from £37.00–£43.00
Dinner, Bed & Breakfast per person, per night: £31.00–£34.00 (2 sharing)
Evening meal 1900 (last bookings 1730)

Bedrooms: 2 double, 2 twin
Bathrooms: 4 en-suite
Parking for 5
Open: April–December
Cards accepted: Mastercard, Visa

 183 GREENBANKS COUNTRY HOTEL

 HIGHLY COMMENDED

Swaffham Road, Wendling, Dereham, Norfolk NR19 2AR Tel (01362) 687742

Charming 18th-century country hotel with delightful restaurant, superb cuisine and special diets catered for by the chef/proprietor. Greenbanks is situated in the heart of Norfolk and has eight acres of meadows, two private fishing lakes, a bog garden and wild flower walk. Luxury accommodation in four en-suite rooms and five double/treble units, all ground floor with patio garden seating. Ideal touring position for Norwich, Sandringham, the Broads and the Norfolk coast. Pets by arrangement.

Bed & Breakfast per night: single room from £36.00–£50.00; double from £52.00–£75.00
Evening meal 1900 (last orders 2130)

Bedrooms: 9
Bathrooms: 9 en-suite
Parking for 20

 184 FELBRIGG LODGE

 HIGHLY COMMENDED

Aylmerton, North Norfolk NR11 8RA Tel (01263) 837588 Fax (01263) 838012

Set in beautiful countryside two miles from the coast, Felbrigg Lodge is hidden in eight acres of spectacular woodland gardens. Time has stood still since Edwardian ladies came here in their carriages to take tea and play croquet. Great care has been taken to preserve this atmosphere with large comfortable en-suite rooms all luxuriously decorated and with every facility. This is a true haven of peace and tranquillity. A nature lover's paradise. Delicious candlelit dinners and copious breakfast. Indoor heated pool and gym.

Bed & Breakfast per night: single occupancy from £45.00–£65.00; double room from £60.00–£110.00
Dinner, Bed & Breakfast per person, per night: £54.50–£79.50
Packed lunches by arrangement

Evening meal 1945
Bedrooms: 3 double/twin
Bathrooms: 3 en-suite
Parking for 4

At-a-glance symbols are explained on the flap inside the back cover

185 THE OLD RECTORY

HIGHLY COMMENDED

103 Yarmouth Road, Thorpe St Andrew, Norwich, Norfolk NR7 0HF Tel (01603) 700772 Fax (01603) 300772 E-mail RectoryH@aol.com

Chris and Sally Entwistle invite you to relax and enjoy a friendly atmosphere and traditional hospitality in this charming Georgian house with its extensive gardens and sun terrace, delightful view over the Yare valley and heated outdoor swimming pool (spring and summer months only). Our intimate dining room (AA Rosette), where a freshly prepared four-course dinner menu is served each evening, is the perfect setting in which to celebrate your special occasion, whilst our spacious, individually furnished bedrooms offer you the highest standards of comfort and amenities.

Bed & Breakfast per night: single occupancy from £58.00–£68.00; double room from £75.00–£85.00 Dinner, Bed & Breakfast per person, per night: £49.00–£55.00 (2 sharing) Evening meal 1900 (last orders 2045)

Bedrooms: 7 double, 1 twin
Bathrooms: 8 en-suite
Parking for 18
Cards accepted: Amex

186 BEECHES HOTEL & VICTORIAN GARDENS

HIGHLY COMMENDED

4-6 Earlham Road, Norwich, Norfolk NR2 3DB Tel (01603) 621167 Fax (01603) 620151 E-mail beeches.reception@.co.uk

'An oasis in the heart of Norwich' with three acres of English Heritage Victorian garden to enjoy, this hotel provides a peaceful retreat from the bustle of the city, which is just ten minutes' walk away. Two listed Victorian houses and a modern annexe have been tastefully refurbished and extended to offer high standards of comfort in a relaxed, informal setting. Non-smoking bedrooms are individually designed, enhancing their own character and charm. Our licensed restaurant offers mouth-watering contemporary cuisine. The photograph shows Plantation House, which is part of the Beeches. CATEGORY 2

Bed & Breakfast per night: single room from £59.00–£64.00; double room from £76.00–£88.00 Dinner, Bed & Breakfast per person, per night: £51.00–£60.00 (min 2 nights, 2 sharing) Evening meal 1830 (last orders 2100)

Bedrooms: 8 single, 14 double, 3 twin
Bathrooms: 25 en-suite
Parking for 24
Cards accepted: Mastercard, Diners, Amex, Switch/Delta

187 IVY HOUSE FARM

HIGHLY COMMENDED

Ivy Lane, Oulton Broad, Lowestoft, Suffolk NR33 8HY Tel (01502) 501353 or (01502) 588144 Fax (01502) 501539

Often described as 'Oulton Broad's hidden oasis...', nestling beside Oulton Broad in the Broads National Park. Set in forty acres, we offer a tranquil, rural location, but with easy access to Norwich, the Broads and the Suffolk and Norfolk coasts. All rooms are individually decorated, many with views of the surrounding countryside or gardens. Delicious cuisine is served in the 18th-century, thatched Crooked Barn restaurant (AA Rosette). CATEGORY 1

Bed & Breakfast per night: single occupancy from £67.00–£69.00; double room from £89.00–£99.00 Dinner, Bed & Breakfast per person, per night: from £55.00 (min 2 nights, 2 sharing) Lunch available: 1200–1345

Evening meal 1900 (last orders 2130)
Bedrooms: 7 double, 3 twin, 1 triple, 1 family room
Bathrooms: 12 en-suite Parking for 50
Cards accepted: Mastercard, Visa, Diners, Amex, Switch/Delta

188 CHIPPENHALL HALL

🌊🌊🌊 HIGHLY COMMENDED

Fressingfield, Eye, Suffolk IP21 5TD Tel (01379) 588180 or (01379) 586733 Fax (01379) 586272

A listed Tudor manor of Saxon origin, recorded in the Domesday Book, enjoying total rural seclusion in seven acres of gardens with ponds, and a heated outdoor pool set in a rose-covered courtyard. The manor is heavily beamed with inglenook log fireplaces. For that special anniversary with friends, arrange for pre-dinner drinks served in the bar and fine food and wines served by candle light. Located one mile south of Fressingfield, B1116.

Bed & Breakfast per night: single occupancy from £62.00–£68.00; double room from £68.00–£72.00
Dinner, Bed & Breakfast per person, per night: £59.00–£61.00
Lunch available: 1215–1400

Evening meal 1930 (last bookings 1700)
Bedrooms: 3 double
Bathrooms: 3 en-suite
Parking for 12
Cards accepted: Mastercard, Visa

189 SECKFORD HALL HOTEL

🌊🌊🌊🌊 HIGHLY COMMENDED

Woodbridge, Suffolk IP13 6NU Tel (01394) 385678 Fax (01394) 380610 E-mail reception@seckford.co.uk

A romantic Elizabethan mansion set in 32 acres of landscaped gardens and woodlands. Personally supervised by the owners, Seckford Hall is a haven of seclusion and tranquillity. Oak panelling, beamed ceilings, antique furniture, four-poster bedrooms, suites, leisure club with indoor pool, gym and spa bath and adjacent 18-hole golf course. Two restaurants featuring fresh lobster and game from local farms, extensive wine cellar. Picturesque Woodbridge with its tide mill, antique shops and yacht harbour is a short walk away. 'Constable Country' and Suffolk coast nearby. www.seckford.co.uk

Bed & Breakfast per night: single room from £79.00–£125.00; double room from £115.00–£160.00
Lunch available: 1200–1400
Evening meal 1915 (last orders 2130)

Bedrooms: 3 single, 14 double, 10 twin, 1 triple, 4 family rooms
Bathrooms: 32 en-suite
Parking for 102
Cards accepted: Mastercard, Visa, Diners, Amex

190 HOCKLEY PLACE

🌊🌊 HIGHLY COMMENDED

Hockley Place, Frating, Colchester, Essex CO7 7HG Tel (01206) 251703 Fax (01206) 251578

Peace and tranquillity greet you at this country house built in the 'Lutyens' style. The individually designed bedrooms are en-suite, the standard of cuisine is high and guests eat in the beamed dining room. The outdoor swimming pool and gymnasium are open to guests throughout the day. The coastline of Frinton, Clacton and Brightlingsea, Beth Chatto's garden, Colchester's Roman castle and the picturesque countryside of Dedham and 'Constable Country' are all within easy reach.

Bed & Breakfast per night: single occupancy from £45.00–£50.00; double room from £70.00–£80.00
Dinner, Bed & Breakfast per person, per night: £55.00–£60.00

Bedrooms: 1 double, 2 twin
Bathrooms: 3 en-suite
Parking for 20
Cards accepted: Access, Visa, Switch/Delta

191 THE GREAT HOUSE RESTAURANT AND HOTEL 〰〰〰〰 HIGHLY COMMENDED

Market Place, Lavenham, Sudbury, Suffolk CO10 9QZ Tel (01787) 247431 Fax (01787) 248007 E-mail greathouse@surflink.co.uk

Ideally located on the Market Square of the beautiful medieval village of Lavenham, we are the perfect place for a relaxing get-away. Our spacious bedrooms offer the best comfort, with luxury bathrooms and sitting rooms or sitting areas. The creative French cuisine of our award-winning restaurant is complemented by excellent and friendly service from our professional staff. Choose from the daily menu or from the à la carte for that something 'special'. Special leisure breaks from Monday to Thursday.
www.lavenham.demon.co.uk

Bed & Breakfast per night: single occupancy from £55.00–£88.00; double room from £70.00–£102.00
Dinner, Bed & Breakfast per person, per night: £49.95–£56.95 (min 3 nights)
Lunch available: 1200–1430

Evening meal 1900 (last orders 2130)
Bedrooms: 3 double, 1 twin, 1 triple
Bathrooms: 5 en-suite
Parking for 10
Cards accepted: Mastercard, Visa, Amex, Switch/Delta

Audley End

AT THE DISSOLUTION of the Monasteries in 1536 Henry VIII gave the Benedictine Abbey of Walden to Lord Audley, who built himself a distinguished house in the grounds. This passed to Lord Howard of Walden, who in 1603 was created 1st Earl of Suffolk. Rather than enlarge the existing building, the Earl (who later became Lord High Treasurer) decided to construct a house which befitted his elevated status. Indeed the plans were on such a vast scale that James I tellingly declared it 'too big for a king, but might do for the Lord Treasurer'. When completed, Audley End had two enormous courts, built around the ruins of the Benedictine Abbey, and was one of the largest houses in the land.

In the early 1720s, the 5th Earl, keen to leave his mark on the building, called in the services of the talented Sir John Vanbrugh, playwright, society figure and architect of both Castle Howard and Blenheim Palace. Vanbrugh recommended that the outer court should be demolished, and also substantially altered the rest of the house, although he ensured that the Jacobean flavour of the exterior, with its balustraded roof and many turrets, was retained.

After a short period of neglect, the strangely named Sir John Griffin Griffin was the next to shape the look of Audley End. Sir John commissioned Robert Adam who, like his predecessor, Sir John Vanbrugh, kept the 17th-century façade but added many 18th-century devices to the interior, where his additions include the magnificent state rooms. Outside, Lancelot 'Capability' Brown set about turning the park into the 18th-century ideal of the picturesque, with a Palladian bridge-cum-summerhouse, Temple of Victory, and the Temple of Concord (1781), from where there is a particularly fine vista.

Other highlights include the Jacobean Hall (largely untouched by Vanbrugh and Adam), some superb plaster ceilings, a chapel in the 'Strawberry Hill gothick' (highly ornate) style and some contemporary furniture and paintings. Some idea of the size of the earlier buildings can be gauged from the fact that Audley End is roughly half the size of its early 17th-century incarnation. The house (tel: 01799 522399) and its estate village of Audley End are 1 mile (1.6km) west of Saffron Walden.

Audley End House and Palladian bridge

192 LAVENHAM PRIORY

 DE LUXE

Water Street, Lavenham, Sudbury, Suffolk CO10 9RW Tel (01787) 247404 Fax (01787) 248472 E-mail tim.pitt@btinternet.com

Benedictine monks originally owned this Grade I Listed house, one of Lavenham's finest. Bed chambers feature crown posts, Elizabethan wall paintings and oak floors, with four-poster, lit bateau and polonaise beds. Visitors can relax by inglenook fires in the 13th-century hall or sitting room. Breakfast and pre-dinner drinks can be enjoyed in the sheltered courtyard herb garden. Lavenham is often described as one of the finest medieval villages in England with its historic buildings and streets. A relaxed family atmosphere, good humour and a memorable visit are Gilli and Tim's objectives.

Bed & Breakfast per night: single occupancy from £50.00–£60.00; double room from £70.00–£90.00

Bedrooms: 2 double, 1 twin
Bathrooms: 3 en-suite
Parking for 8
Cards accepted: Mastercard, Visa, Switch/Delta

---

193 THE ANGEL HOTEL

 HIGHLY COMMENDED

Angel Hill, Bury St Edmunds, Suffolk IP33 1LT Tel (01284) 753926 Fax (01284) 750092

During the past 400 years, royal guests, artists and renowned writers have stayed at The Angel. Charles Dickens wrote part of the Pickwick Papers while in residence. This beautiful, historic coaching inn dates back to 1452 and has 42 bedrooms, including four four-posters and a suite, all individually decorated and with a private bathroom, colour TV, direct dial telephone and trouser press.

Bed & Breakfast per night: single room from £77.00; double room from £100.00–£170.00
Dinner, Bed & Breakfast per person, per night: £70.00–£90.00
Lunch available: 1230–1400

Evening meal 1900 (last orders 2200)
Bedrooms: 11 single, 19 double, 12 twin
Bathrooms: 42 en-suite   Parking for 58
Cards accepted: Mastercard, Visa, Diners, Amex, Switch/Delta

---

194 MARYGREEN MANOR HOTEL

 HIGHLY COMMENDED

London Road, Brentwood, Essex CM14 4NR Tel (01277) 225252 Fax (01277) 262809

16th-century timber-framed building, visited by King Henry VIII. Original Tudor bedrooms with four-poster beds (3). Garden rooms overlook olde-worlde garden. Restaurant with two AA Rosettes offers extensive à la carte or fixed price menus complemented by comprehensive award-winning wine list. Lunch served from 1230–1430, dinner served from 1915–2215. Two minutes from J28 on M25. Motorway links to the Channel Tunnel, Stansted, Gatwick and Heathrow Airports.

Bed & Breakfast per night: single occupancy from £122.00–£135.00; double room from £133.50–£140.00
Lunch available: 1230–1430
Evening meal 1915 (last orders 2215)

Bedrooms: 26 double, 17 twin
Bathrooms: 43 en-suite
Parking for 100
Cards accepted: Mastercard, Diners, Amex, Switch/Delta

At-a-glance symbols are explained on the flap inside the back cover

195 DOWN HALL COUNTRY HOUSE HOTEL

 HIGHLY COMMENDED

Hatfield Heath, Bishop's Stortford, Hertfordshire CM22 7AS Tel (01279) 731441 Fax (01279) 730416

Down Hall is a majestic Victorian mansion set in over one hundred acres of beautiful woodland, parkland and landscaped gardens in the Hertfordshire countryside. The luxurious bedrooms, choice of two restaurants and both indoor and outdoor leisure facilities means Down Hall combines the elegance of centuries with the excellence of today. The perfect venue for a carefree stay, with time to enjoy those finer things in life.

Bed & Breakfast per night: single room from £125.25–£146.25; double room from £171.50–£190.50
Dinner, Bed & Breakfast per person, per night: £83.00–£88.50 (min 2 nights)
Lunch available: 1230–1400

Evening meal 1900 (last orders 2130)
Bedrooms: 16 single, 76 double, 11 twin
Bathrooms: 103 en-suite
Parking for 130
Cards accepted: Diners, Amex

196 CANFIELD MOAT

 HIGHLY COMMENDED

High Cross Lane West, Little Canfield, Dunmow, Essex CM6 1TD Tel (01371) 872565 or (01385) 384648 Fax (01371) 876264 E-mail vfalk@compuserve.com

A peaceful Georgian rectory set among eight acres in the heart of the Essex countryside yet only ten minutes from the M11 and Stansted Airport and within easy reach of London, Cambridge, St Albans and 'Constable Country'. The large, elegant en-suite bedrooms are supplied with almost every conceivable luxury. Breakfasts include our own eggs and produce from our vegetable garden, and guests are welcome to use the tennis court, croquet lawn and, in season, heated outdoor swimming pool.

Bed & Breakfast per night: single occupancy from £33.00–£35.00; double room from £55.00–£60.00
Evening meal 1930 (last orders 2100)

Bedrooms: 1 double, 1 twin
Bathrooms: 2 en-suite
Parking for 10

197 TUDOR COTTAGE

Listed HIGHLY COMMENDED

Upwick Green, Albury, Ware, Hertfordshire SG11 2JX Tel (01279) 771440 or (0370) 898424

A delightfully spacious house of Tudor origin (Grade II Listed) situated in a beautiful landscaped garden. Complete seclusion and stunning panoramic views. Ideally situated for London/Cambridge and Stansted Airport. Ten minutes from the airport and the M11, yet not under flight paths. Ample parking. All rooms are elegantly furnished to a high standard. Excellent breakfasts served in the dining room or on the terrace. Simply savour the peace, or use the house as a base for further exploration.

Bed & Breakfast per night: single room £33.00; double room £55.00

Bedrooms: 2 single, 1 double, 1 twin
Bathrooms: 1 en-suite, 1 private, 1 public
Parking for 10

198 SOPWELL HOUSE HOTEL AND COUNTRY CLUB HIGHLY COMMENDED

Cottonmill Lane, Sopwell, St Albans, Hertfordshire AL1 2HQ Tel (01727) 864477 Fax (01727) 844741

Just minutes from four major motorways, half an hour from central London, Sopwell House stands in eleven acres of landscaped gardens and grounds amongst pleasant Hertfordshire countryside. An extensive refurbishment has further enhanced its country-style ambience. The Country Club and Spa, a haven for relaxation and pampering, features an ozone-treated indoor pool, jacuzzi, steam room and sauna, together with beauty and hairdressing salons, full-size snooker table and superbly-equipped fitness studio. Golf available nearby.

Bed & Breakfast per night: single room from
£83.45–£130.70; double room from £120.75–£186.00
Dinner, Bed & Breakfast per person, per night:
£117.40–£209.50
Lunch available: 1230–1400

Evening meal 1930 (last orders 2200)
Bedrooms: 12 single, 60 double, 20 twin
Bathrooms: 92 en-suite   Parking for 200
Cards accepted: Mastercard, Visa, Diners, Amex,
Switch/Delta

Hat-making in Luton

LUTON TOWN FOOTBALL CLUB has long been known as 'the Hatters', a name which reveals the town's importance as the centre of the English hat-making industry. The main reason for the Bedfordshire town's pre-eminent position is the quality of the surrounding soil, which allows wheat grown in nearby fields to reach a considerable height. The long stems (or straws), once plaited, were ideal for use in making straw hats. These, together with other straw goods such as corn dollies, were sold in the markets of 17th- and 18th-century Luton and Dunstable.

Special schools known as 'plait schools' appeared in the town as demand for the high-quality products increased. Plaited straws were also imported from the town of Livorno, on Italy's Tuscan coast. Indeed the Italian connection in the history of English hat-making is important, and the word 'millinery' comes from the placename Milan (even preserving the now lost pronunciation, 'Millen'). When the Napoleonic wars meant that Italian imports became scarce, the Luton hat-making industry took off.

Trade continued to grow throughout the 19th century, although cheaper plait from the Far East was bought in from the 1870s onwards. The area of Luton known as Plaiters' Lea (now a conservation area) was where the hat factories, with their newly installed and adapted sewing machines, congregated. These were usually tall, narrow buildings, with each floor dedicated to a separate process, such as blocking (stretching the materials over metal moulds),

machining, trimming, dyeing and so forth. Good examples of these factories can be seen in Bute and Guildford Streets.

The first half of this century saw continued prosperity in the hat trade, but in the 1960s the hat ceased to be an item of everyday wear and became instead an item of occasional wear. Nevertheless there are still almost 40 manufacturers in the town, and visitors can often view a working factory; check with the Tourist Information Centre (tel: 01582 401579) – itself housed in an old hat factory – for details. They also have leaflets about a millinery trail through Plaiters' Lea, while displays of past Luton-made hats (as well as occasional hat-making demonstrations) can be seen at the Luton Museum and Art Gallery (tel: 01582 36941).

199 THE CRICKETERS

 HIGHLY COMMENDED

Clavering, Saffron Walden, Essex CB11 4QT Tel (01799) 550442 Fax (01799) 550882

This popular and well-established 16th-century freehouse, which is situated in the Essex countryside, a mere ten minutes from Stansted Airport and the M11, has a reputation for good food in both the bar and the restaurant. Its delightful decor is reflected in the standard of the accommodation, which is immediately adjacent to the Cricketers and consists of six bedrooms, two with four-poster beds, all individually and tastefully decorated to a very high standard.

Bed & Breakfast per night: single occupancy £60.00; double room £80.00
Dinner, Bed & Breakfast per person, per night: £50.00–£83.00
Lunch available: 1200–1400

Evening meal 1900 (last orders 2200)
Bedrooms: 2 double, 4 twin
Bathrooms: 6 en-suite
Parking for 45
Cards accepted: Mastercard, Amex, Switch/Delta

200 WALLIS FARM

 HIGHLY COMMENDED

98 Main Street, Hardwick, Cambridge, Cambridgeshire CB3 7QU Tel (01954) 210347 Fax (01954) 210988

A warm welcome awaits you at our traditional Victorian farmhouse on our working farm in the picturesque village of Hardwick. We are seven miles from the university town of Cambridge and ideally situated for touring Cambridgeshire, Norfolk and Suffolk. All rooms are ground floor, en-suite, twin/double, with four in a recently-converted barn, furnished to a high standard. Large gardens and farmland which guests are welcome to use. All have colour TVs and tea/coffee-making facilities.

Bed & Breakfast per night: single occupancy from £30.00–£35.00; double room from £42.00–£46.00

Bedrooms: 2 double, 2 twin, 1 triple
Bathrooms: 5 en-suite
Parking for 8
Cards accepted: Diners

201 THE OLD BRIDGE HOTEL

 HIGHLY COMMENDED

1 High Street, Huntingdon, Cambridgeshire PE18 6TQ Tel (01480) 458410 Fax (01480) 411017

A handsome 18th-century building overlooking the River Ouse, and yet only 500 yards from the town centre. The atmosphere of a beautiful luxurious hotel, yet also a busy meeting place for the local community. All rooms are individually decorated, with satellite TVs and power showers – many with air conditioning and CD-stereos. An eclectic, modern menu (AA 2 Rosettes), winner of the AA Wine Award 1998 (for the UK's best wine list) and real ales highly acclaimed by CAMRA.

Bed & Breakfast per night: single room from £79.50–£99.50; double room from £89.50–£139.50
Lunch available: 1200–1430
Evening meal 1830 (last orders 2230)

Bedrooms: 5 single, 15 double, 4 twin
Bathrooms: 24 en-suite
Parking for 70
Cards accepted: Access, Visa, Diners, Amex, Switch/Delta

Entries are cross referenced by number to the maps on pages 62–63

England's West Country

Cornwall

Morwenstow, near Bude, was the home of Robert Stephen Hawker, a remarkable 19th-century parson and poet who left his whimsical mark upon the village. The vicarage chimneys are built to resemble the various churches with which he had been connected, while a capital on the village church displays the message 'This is the house of God' carved upside-down – for a celestial readership! High on the cliffs near by is a tiny driftwood hut, now owned by the National Trust, where, often in a fug of opium, he composed much of his poetry.

► **Wookey Hole**

Since the 15th century visitors have come to peer into the dark caverns and subterranean passages of Wookey Hole, near Wells. Today, dramatic electric lighting illuminates fantastic rock-formations and the glassy surface of an underground lake. There are a number of other attractions on offer too: paper-making demonstrations on the site of a 19th-century paper-mill; a collection of fairground art; a re-creation of Madame Tussaud's touring 'Cabinet of Curiosities'; and an exhibition of amusements from penny pier arcades. (Tel: 01749 672243.)

An unrivalled coastline

The very pace of life seems to slow as you head west. The counties of Cornwall, Devon, Dorset, Somerset and Wiltshire somehow conduct their various businesses at a more civilised speed. Wiltshire alone is land-locked, so perhaps the sea's proximity has a relaxing effect. The magnificent coastline certainly draws people, but its huge length – the South-West Coastal Path, hugging the foreshore from Minehead to Poole, is 613 miles (986km) long – ensures that even on the sunniest of days, many beaches remain uncrowded. As always, those further from car parks are the quietest, but have fewest facilities. The well-known resorts, such as Torquay, Newquay and Ilfracombe, cater for all tastes and depths of pocket. Quieter havens to consider include Ladram Bay (near Sidmouth), Soar (a tiny bay south-west of Salcombe), Crinnis Beach (near St Austell), Pendower Beach (east of St Mawes), Portheras (west of St Ives), Lee Bay (near Ilfracombe) and St Audrie's Bay (just east of Watchet). Five minutes with a detailed map, especially the superb southern coasts of Devon and Cornwall, will reveal countless other coves, bays and beaches, often with perfect sand.

Where the catch is landed

And if the weather is too cold for the beach, why not explore a Cornish or Devonian fishing village? These, as much a West Country speciality as Exmoor ponies or clotted cream, are one of the region's most engaging attractions. Some, such as Clovelly, on the northern coast of Devon, are justifiably famous. Tumbling in picturesque manner down the cliffs into the sea and with a main 'street' too steep and too narrow for cars, it nevertheless copes admirably with its visitors. Others – some popular, some little-known – to explore include Port Isaac (on the North Cornish coast and also without cars), Helford, Looe (both East and West), Gorran Haven, Gunwalloe, Porthcurno (all on the southern coast of Cornwall) and Beer (on Devon's southern shores).

Perfect bases for exploration

As the sumptuous fishing villages are mainly in the extreme south-west, so the historic towns and cities tend to be further east in Somerset, Dorset and Wiltshire. Here you can choose from the incomparable cities of Salisbury, Bath and Wells, each with a magnificent range of secular and ecclesiastical architecture. Sherborne, too, has a glorious abbey and many fine buildings dating from the 16th and 17th centuries, as well as two castles, one in ruins, the other home to a range of art treasures. Shaftesbury is the setting for one of England's best-loved views – the steep, cobbled Gold Hill was famously used for a bread commercial – but has other intriguing nooks and crannies. Marlborough's broad High Street is lined with substantial 18th-century houses, yet is only a mile from Savernake, England's largest privately owned forest, criss-crossed with footpaths. Ilchester dates from Roman times, but the town prospered in the medieval and Georgian periods; the houses round the green reveal the town's latter lineage. Looking further west, Salcombe, wonderfully situated on the Kingsbridge Estuary and enjoying the mildest of climates, became a resort in the 19th century. It has a gentle charm all its own, and is near Totnes, an appealing market town that has whole-heartedly embraced alternative culture. Just over the Tamar into Cornwall lies Launceston, a town of old-world character with two 16th-century bridges and a ruined medieval castle. Surrounded by unspoilt countryside, all make ideal bases for a long weekend's exploration.

Pasties, scrumpy and yarg

An important part of a weekend away is to indulge in local specialities. The West Country has its fair share, with few visitors able to resist the cream tea. Clotted cream, the essential ingredient, is widely available throughout the region. Cornwall has its pasty, now eaten the length and breadth of the land, but nowhere as good, so they say, as in its home. Somerset's many orchards have long produced cider and the earthier, more potent scrumpy. Many farms still produce – and a couple of museums at Dowlish Wake and Bradford-on-Tone celebrate – the heady brews. The name of Cheddar is synonymous with cheese, but there are many more beside, from Cornish yarg to Somerset brie. And throughout, sold in market, shop, pub and restaurant, are fresh fish of the finest quality. The West Country is a piscivore's paradise.

Getting away from it all

Few places in the West Country have an urban feel. Bristol and Plymouth are cities redolent of their maritime history yet remaining close to their rural hinterlands. Elsewhere, the predominant mood is of the country, and visitors are spoilt for choice when it comes to walking territory. The three moors – Bodmin, Exmoor and Dartmoor – are all wild enough to have challenging routes suitable for the experienced hiker only, but on their gentler fringes are endless, easier options that reveal some of England's most sublime countryside. The National Parks of Dartmoor and Exmoor have many suggestions for walks; outside these, areas particularly rewarding for exploration on foot include the Mendips in north Somerset, the Lizard in south-west Cornwall, the Marlborough Downs in north-east Wiltshire and the Quantock Hills just east of Exmoor. Thanks to the South-West Coastal Path, walking the coast is straightforward, though often strenuous. Other long-distance paths in

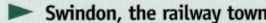

► **Swindon, the railway town**

In the hundred years between 1830 and 1930, Swindon's population increased from 1,740 to 65,000. The reason was the arrival of the Great Western Railway (GWR) and the setting up of its manufacturing works in the town. The company built a 'railway village' to house its growing workforce: no. 34 Faringdon Road is now a museum (tel: 01793 466553) furnished as it might have been in the late 19th century. The company's hostel for male workers is now the GWR museum (tel: 01793 466555), displaying locomotives and railway memorabilia.

► **Chesil Beach**

One of the stranger natural phenomena of the South Coast, Chesil Beach is a 16-mile (26km) strip of shingle running from the Dorset village of Abbotsbury to the Isle of Portland. Fashioned entirely by the sea to a height of some 30–40ft (9–12m), the bank forms a thin barrier between the Fleet, the largest lagoon in Britain, and the sea. Barely disturbed by mankind, the Fleet supports as many as 150 species of seaweed, as well as abundant fish and water-fowl. (Tel: 01305 760579.)

▶ Brunel's Bristol

The great engineer Isambard Kingdom Brunel was only 23 when he won a competition to design a bridge across the Avon Gorge at Bristol. This was the start of a long association with the city, one which produced its most famous landmarks. Brunel, chief engineer for the Great Western Railway, designed its splendid neo-Tudor station, Temple Meads, now a Grade I listed building. His great steam-ships SS *Great Western*, and SS *Great Britain* were built in Bristol: the latter, in the city docks, is now a museum (tel: 0117 926 0680).

▶ Lundy Island

Lundy is as remote an island as England has to offer and makes a magnificent day out from Ilfracombe and Bideford, both some 24 miles (38.5km) distant on the north Devon coast. The island, 3 miles (5km) long and never much more than half a mile (1km) wide, boasts some superb scenery, and there can be no better way of passing time here than strolling its gentle paths. The west coast is the highlight of the island: here Soay sheep and feral goats pick their way over stacks of granite tumbling hundreds of feet to the Atlantic while ravens wheel above.

the region include the Exe Valley Way (a 45-mile (72.5km), level route following the River Exe from Exmoor to its estuary), the West Devon Way, a shorter path that runs along Dartmoor's western edge from Plymouth to Okehampton, the Two Moors Way, a magnificent and demanding path extending over 100 miles (161km) and linking Dartmoor and Exmoor, the Liberty Trail, following the route taken by the Monmouth Rebellion through south Somerset and west Dorset, and The Saints Way, a 37-mile (59.5km) coast to coast route across Cornwall from Padstow to Fowey. Public transport links with many of these longer paths, allowing them to be walked in sections; most also have shorter, circular routes using part of their length. For the walker keen to get away from motor traffic, there is an alternative suggestion. The island of Lundy has a pub, church and shop but not a single road within 12 miles (19km). It also has spectacular cliff-top paths.

A celebration of words and music

Held annually in late May and early June, the Salisbury Festival presents both classical and jazz concerts, poetry and exhibitions, folk, circus and children's events. Further west, the Roman city of Bath hosts a festival of literature (February) and of music (May). The latter kicks off with opening-night celebrations featuring fireworks, and celebrates contemporary European jazz, early and classical music. On a smaller scale at roughly the same time of year, Chard, in southern Somerset, promotes music in a variety of styles composed by women. Held over six weeks or so in July and August, the Dartington Festival gives a series of concerts devoted to opera, dance and classical music in the medieval Dartington Hall and gardens. It is aimed as much at those who wish to partake as to listen. Also in July is the Exeter Festival, when the broad-ranging programme may include classical music in the Gothic cathedral, opera and fireworks, lectures, comedy, jazz, theatre and fringe events.

Houses of substance

The region's historic houses range from the large-scale – such as Longleat and Wilton House, both in Wiltshire – to the more compact Coleridge Cottage at Nether Stowey, where the eponymous poet found inspiration for *The Rime of the Ancient Mariner*. Little has changed in the two centuries since Coleridge moved in. Other remarkable – and visitable – residences of the region include Great Chalfield Manor (near Melksham), a 15th-century house of mellow stone with a fine great hall, and Forde Abbey, a former monastery near Chard now also known for its gardens. Not far away, in the sleepy countryside near Beaminster, is the Tudor mansion of Parnham, renowned for its furniture workshop. By contrast, Bristol and Bath each preserve a magnificent 18th-century townhouse: Bristol's is appropriately called The Georgian House, while Bath's proudly proclaims its address – No. 1 Royal Crescent. The latter was once the home of the Duke of York who famously marched his men up and down hills. Devon, meanwhile, invites you to a couple of castles a little out of the ordinary. Castle Drogo, perched above the River Teign near Drewsteignton is the work of Edwin Lutyens, and was not completed until the 1930s. Of more authentic age for a castle is Bickleigh, though it is in reality more fortified manor house than full-blooded medieval castle. One of its attractions is a display of gadgets used by Second World War spies. It is best to turn up at Pencarrow, a Georgian family home near Bodmin, in late spring or early summer when no fewer than 692 separate species of rhododendron welcome visitors, whether of a botanical bent or not. Trerice, a few miles south-east of Newquay, is a glorious Elizabethan house with unusual curved and scrolled gables. As well as an orchard of Cornish apple trees, there is a remarkable collection of lawn-mowers.

In search of St Hyacinth

Cornwall offers the church-hunter rich-pickings. There are superb buildings – such as Launcells Church, inland from Bude, little altered since its completion in the 15th century. There are incomparable settings: the churches of St Anthony-in-Meneage on the Helford River and St Just-in-Roseland are two of the best. And there are the wondrous names. Churches in Cornwall are dedicated to St Petroc, St Hyacinth, St Nonna, St Germans and St Winnow. Other consecrated buildings to seek out in the West Country include St Brannock's in Braunton and St Andrew's in Cullompton (both Devon), St Andrew's in Banwell (Somerset) and St Mary's in Lydiard Tregoze (near Swindon).

Contact phone numbers

Perry's Cider Mills, Dowlish Wake, Ilminster (tel: 01460 52681)
Sheppy's Farmhouse Cider, Bradford-on-Tone, Taunton (tel: 01823 461233)
Dartmoor National Park (tel: 01822 890414)
Exmoor National Park (tel: 01398 323665)
Salisbury Festival (tel: 01722 323883)
Bath Literature Festival (tel: 01225 463362)
Bath International Music Festival (tel: 01225 463362)
Chard Festival of Women in Music (tel: 01460 66115)
Dartington International Summer School (tel: 01803 865988)
Exeter Festival (tel: 01392 265118)
Longleat, Warminster (tel: 01985 844400)
Wilton House, Wilton (tel: 01722 743115)
Coleridge Cottage, Nether Stowey (tel: 01278 732662)
Great Chalfield Manor, Melksham (tel: 01985 843600)
Forde Abbey, Chard (tel: 01460 220231)
Parnham, Beaminster (tel: 01308 862204)
The Georgian House, Bristol (tel: 0117 921 1362)
No. 1 Royal Crescent, Bath (tel: 01225 428126)
Castle Drogo, Drewsteignton (tel: 01647 433306)
Bickleigh Castle, Tiverton (tel: 01884 855363)
Pencarrow, Bodmin (tel: 01208 841369)
Trerice, Newquay (tel: 01637 875404)

► À la Ronde

À la Ronde, near Exmouth in Devon, was the brainchild of two cousins, Jane and Mary Parminter. They built it, in about 1796, in imitation of a church in Ravenna which they had admired on a grand tour of Europe. Though its exterior is extraordinary – it has 16 sides, diamond shaped windows, and a conical roof – its interior is more bizarre still. The cousins decorated the rooms with feathers, shells, dried flowers, marbled paint, cut paper, sand, even seaweed and straw. These fragile decorations have recently been restored to their original condition. (Tel: 01395 265514.)

► Dartmoor longhouses

A defining feature of the longhouse is that humans and livestock lived under a single roof. This arrangement, common on the continent, is very rare in England, and only occurs where it was vital to keep livestock warm and near at hand in harsh winter conditions. Around a hundred longhouses remain on Dartmoor: low, rectangular buildings, built between 1150 and 1700 from huge blocks of granite, often partly recessed into the hillside to maximise shelter.

ISLES OF SCILLY

St Martin's

St Mary's

Hugh Town

5 Miles

5 Kilometres

Ilfracombe
Lynton
Barnstaple
Bideford

DEVON

Holsworthy

Okehampton

Launceston

Tavistock

Ashburton

Wadebridge
Bodmin
Liskeard

CORNWALL

Newquay

Plymouth

Totnes

St Austell
Looe

Truro

Salcombe

Redruth

Falmouth

Penzance
Helston

Colin Earl Cartography

202 WOOLACOMBE BAY HOTEL

🌊🌊🌊🌊🌊 HIGHLY COMMENDED

Woolacombe, Devon EX34 7BN Tel (01271) 870388 Fax (01271) 870613

Set in six acres of quiet gardens gently leading to three miles of EC Blue Flag golden sands. Built in the halcyon days of the mid-1800s, the hotel has a relaxed style of comfort and good living. Guests can enjoy unlimited use of superb sporting facilities, or just relax with a good book in spacious lounges overlooking the Atlantic. The 'Hothouse' offers fitness, massage and beauty treatments. Superb cooking of traditional and French dishes. Shooting, fishing, horse-riding and boating available.

Bed & Breakfast per night: single occupancy from £52.50–£78.75; double room from £105.00–£157.50
Dinner, Bed & Breakfast per person, per night: £73.50–£99.75
Lunch available: 1230–1330 (Sunday only)

Evening meal 1930 (last orders 2100)
Bedrooms: 27 double, 11 twin, 5 triple, 22 family rooms
Bathrooms: 65 en-suite
Parking for 150   Open: February–December
Cards accepted: Mastercard, Visa, Diners, Amex, Switch/Delta

203 WATERSMEET HOTEL

🌊🌊🌊🌊 HIGHLY COMMENDED

Mortehoe, Woolacombe, Devon EX34 7EB Tel (01271) 870333 Fax (01271) 870890 E-mail watersmeethotel@compuserve.com

Set on the National Trust Atlantic coastline with panoramic views of Hartland Point and Lundy Island, the three acres of garden enclose a lawn tennis court, an open air swimming pool and steps to the beach below. A superb new indoor pool and spa is popular with everybody. The resident owners ensure the Watersmeet offers the comfort and peace of a country house, and all the main bedrooms, lounges and the octagonal restaurant overlook the sea. The Watersmeet offers a wine list to complement its national award-winning cuisine and service. www.watersmeethotel.co.uk

Dinner, Bed & Breakfast per person, per night: £70.00–£103.00
Lunch available: 1200–1400
Evening meal 1900 (last orders 2030)

Bedrooms: 3 single, 10 double, 9 twin, 2 triple
Bathrooms: 22 en-suite
Parking for 50   Open: February–November
Cards accepted: Mastercard, Visa, Diners, Amex, Switch/Delta

204 BESSEMER THATCH HOTEL AND RESTAURANT

🌊🌊🌊 HIGHLY COMMENDED

Berrynarbor, Devon EX34 9SE Tel (01271) 882296 Fax (01271) 882296

Situated in one of Devon's prettiest villages and only two miles from the Exmoor border, Bessemer Thatch is the perfect retreat from life's stresses and strains. Four-poster bedrooms with charming decor and furnishings complement this lovely old 13th-century building that offers peace and quiet, with more than a little comfort. In the dining room with its cosy inglenook fireplace enjoy the very best of traditional English menus which are always carefully prepared and presented. Truly somewhere special.

Bed & Breakfast per night: double room from £50.00–£76.00
Dinner, Bed & Breakfast per person, per night: £40.00–£53.00
Evening meal 1830 (last orders 2130)

Bedrooms: 5 double, 1 twin
Bathrooms: 6 en-suite
Cards accepted: Mastercard, Visa, Switch/Delta

205 SEAWOOD HOTEL

 **HIGHLY COMMENDED**

North Walk Drive, Lynton, Devon EX35 6HJ Tel (01598) 752272

Seawood is situated at one of the loveliest spots on the North Devon coast, right in the heart of Lorna Doone country. Nestling on wooded cliffs 400ft above the sea, the hotel has some magnificent views. It looks right out across Lynmouth Bay and the Grand Headland of Countisbury where Exmoor meets the sea. On a clear night you can easily see the twinkling lights of Wales.

Bed & Breakfast per night: single room from
£29.00–£31.00; double room from £58.00–£62.00
Dinner, Bed & Breakfast per person, per night:
£42.00–£44.00
Evening meal 1900 (last orders 1930)

Bedrooms: 1 single, 9 double, 2 twin
Bathrooms: 12 en-suite, 2 public
Parking for 10
Open: April–October

206 RISING SUN HOTEL

 **HIGHLY COMMENDED**

Harbourside, Lynmouth, Devon EX35 6EQ Tel (01598) 753223 Fax (01598) 753480 E-mail RISINGSUNLYNMOUTH@EASYNET.CO.UK

An award-winning 14th-century thatched smugglers' inn overlooking a tiny picturesque harbour and Lynmouth Bay with its stunning backdrop of the highest hogback cliffs in England. The Rising Sun Hotel is steeped in history, with oak panelling, crooked ceilings and creaky, uneven floorboards. Lynmouth Bay lobster, local game and salmon served in the romantic candle-lit, oak-panelled dining room, all add to the atmosphere of quintessential British innkeeping at its best. www.risingsunlynmouth.co.uk

Bed & Breakfast per night: single room from
£59.00–£65.00; double room from £98.00–£130.00
Dinner, Bed & Breakfast per person, per night:
£75.00–£95.00 (min 2 nights, 2 sharing)
Lunch available: 1200–1345

Evening meal 1900 (last orders 2100)
Bedrooms: 2 single, 13 double, 1 twin
Bathrooms: 16 en-suite
Cards accepted: Mastercard, Visa, Diners, Amex,
Switch/Delta

207 SIMONSBATH HOUSE HOTEL

 **HIGHLY COMMENDED**

Simonsbath, Minehead, Somerset TA24 7SH Tel (01643) 831259 Fax (01643) 831557

The first house to be built within the Royal Forest of Exmoor in 1654, Simonsbath House is now a small and friendly family-run country house hotel situated in an ideal position for exploring the Exmoor National Park and the north Devon coastline, on foot or by car. Receive peace and quiet, unstinting comfort, generous and deliciously interesting home-cooked food, rooms with log fires and panelling and some four-poster beds.

Bed & Breakfast per night: single occupancy from
£56.00–£66.00; double room £96.00
Dinner, Bed & Breakfast per person, per night:
£68.00–£76.00
Evening meal 1900 (last orders 2030)

Bedrooms: 4 double, 3 twin
Bathrooms: 7 en-suite
Parking for 30 Open: February–November
Cards accepted: Mastercard, Visa, Diners, Amex,
Switch/Delta

208 GREENHILLS FARM

 HIGHLY COMMENDED

Yeo Mill, West Anstey, South Molton, Devon EX36 3NU Tel (01398) 341300

A warm, friendly atmosphere awaits you at Greenhills. The charming old farmhouse (on a working farm) is on the southern foothills of Exmoor. We offer exceptional, high-standard accommodation and delicious food using home-grown and first class local produce. Care has been taken to preserve the olde worlde charm. Warm and comfortable private suite of rooms. Separate lounge and dining room, both with beams, inglenooks and log fires. Located on the Two Moors Way, this is a country lover's paradise.

Bed & Breakfast per night: single occupancy from £20.00–£24.00; double room from £36.00–£48.00
Dinner, Bed & Breakfast per person, per night: £28.00–£34.00
Evening meal 1830

Bedrooms: 1 double, 1 twin
Bathrooms: 1 en-suite, 2 private, 1 public
Parking for 2
Open: May–October

209 KERSCOTT FARM

HIGHLY COMMENDED

Ash Mill, South Molton, Devon EX36 4QG Tel (01769) 550262

Be a welcome guest at a peaceful rural retreat for non-smoking grown ups. A working farm, mentioned in the Domesday Book, with traditional English sheep and cattle. A solitary, elevated position overlooking Exmoor National Park and the Devon countryside ensures superb views from all windows. Beautiful olde worlde antique interior and furnishings – a rare find. Hearty, flavoursome food for breakfast or dinner. An invited contributor to 'Guide to Good Food in the West Country'.

Bed & Breakfast per night: double room from £38.00–£40.00
Dinner, Bed & Breakfast per person, per night: £27.00–£30.00
Evening meal 1830 (last bookings 1400)

Bedrooms: 2 double, 1 twin
Bathrooms: 3 en-suite
Parking for 8
Open: February–November

210 WHITECHAPEL MANOR

HIGHLY COMMENDED

South Molton, Devon EX36 3EG Tel (01769) 573377 Fax (01769) 573797

Whitechapel Manor is a Grade I Listed Elizabethan manor house set within fifteen acres of terraced gardens, woodlands and pastures. It is the ideal base for exploring Exmoor with its ancient woodlands, dramatic coastline, hidden valleys, high moors and thatched villages. The National Trust has many attractions nearby and The Royal Horticultural Society's gardens at Rosemoor are also close by. The restaurant is recognised as one of the West Country's best and has won many accolades over the years.

Bed & Breakfast per night: single room from £70.00–£85.00; double room from £110.00–£170.00
Dinner, Bed & Breakfast per person, per night: £75.00–£110.00
Lunch available: 1200–1345

Evening meal 1900 (last orders 2045)
Bedrooms: 1 single, 4 double, 5 twin, 1 family room
Bathrooms: 11 en-suite
Parking for 40
Cards accepted: Mastercard, Visa, Diners, Switch/Delta

211 **MARSH HALL COUNTRY HOUSE HOTEL**   ⬇⬇⬇ HIGHLY COMMENDED

Marsh Hall, South Molton, Devon EX36 3HQ Tel (01769) 572666 Fax (01769) 574230

Marsh Hall is a lovely Victorian country house with stained-glass windows, chandeliers and log fires in winter, set in three acres of gardens and woodland. With its spacious lounges, gallery and bedrooms, it is the ideal place in which to relax and enjoy the comforts of life. The delightful AA Rosette award-winning restaurant serves a four-course dinner with mouth-watering dishes devised from local fare and fresh produce grown in the hotel's herb, vegetable and fruit gardens.

Bed & Breakfast per night: single room from £50.00–£70.00; double room from £80.00–£100.00
Dinner, Bed & Breakfast per person, per night: from £54.00
Evening meal 1900 (last orders 2000)

Bedrooms: 1 single, 4 double, 2 twin
Bathrooms: 7 en-suite
Parking for 20
Cards accepted: Mastercard, Visa, Switch/Delta

The Tarka Trail

THE WRITER HENRY WILLIAMSON (1895–1977) was born and bred in London, but in 1921 he decided to leave the city, mounted his motorcycle and headed south-west. His eventual destination was the Devonshire village of Georgeham, near Barnstaple, where he rented a small cottage and stayed for many years. Here he was given an orphaned otter cub which he reared and cared for. It gave him the inspiration for his famous book, *Tarka the Otter*, in which he displayed not only his fascination for these shy and beautiful creatures, but also his deep knowledge and love of the wildlife and landscapes of this most beautiful part of Devon.

An area roughly corresponding to that featured in the book is now being promoted as Tarka Country, a region which extends along Devon's north coast from Bideford to Lynton and southwards to the northern fringes of Dartmoor. As part of a major eco-tourism initiative, the Tarka Country Tourism Association has set up a long-distance route – the Tarka Trail – designed to encourage the visitor to explore the countryside without the use of the car. Describing an irregular figure of eight, the trail loops between Exmoor and Dartmoor, with Barnstaple at its centre, covering 180 miles (290km) of varied and often stunning scenery.

It is of course possible to walk the entire length of the Tarka Trail (except the section between Eggesford and Barnstaple which is a train journey), but shorter walks and cycle routes with starting points on or near the trail have also been devised. Some are circular, some involve a return by bus. Full details of all the different options are available from the Tarka Country Tourism Association (tel: 01837 83399).

The Tarka Trail passes many places mentioned in Williamson's famous book. Tarka's fictional birthplace, for example, is on the Torridge, just upstream from Bideford, while remote Cranmere Pool on Dartmoor was visited by Tarka after the death of his mate, Greymuzzle. But don't expect to see any otters on your travels. Due to river pollution and loss of habitat, otters are one of Europe's most endangered mammals. The best place to see them is at the Tamar Otter Sanctuary, near Launceston, Cornwall (about 25 miles - 40km - from Barnstaple) where otters are bred and re-introduced to the wild in a bid to save them from extinction (tel: 01566 785646).

212 THE RED HOUSE

 HIGHLY COMMENDED

Brynsworthy, Roundswell, Barnstaple, Devon EX31 3NP Tel (01271) 345966

A period country house situated in an elevated position with panoramic views. Although being within two miles of the historic market town of Barnstaple, the house is set in the countryside with its own half acre garden. All rooms have colour TV, showers, hairdryers, tea/coffee-making facilities and central heating. Visitors will find that they are well situated for visiting the historic towns, sandy beaches and natural beauty of the moors, and can enjoy a good and varied selection of pub food, all within a short driving distance.

Bed & Breakfast per night: single occupancy from £18.00–£22.00; double room from £34.00–£38.00

Bedrooms: 1 double, 1 twin
Bathrooms: 2 private showers, 1 public bathroom
Parking for 6
Open: February–November

213 SAUNTON SANDS HOTEL

 HIGHLY COMMENDED

Saunton, Braunton, Devon EX33 1LQ Tel (01271) 890212 Fax (01271) 890145

At the Saunton Sands Hotel you will find the most awe-inspiring coastal views and unspoilt golden beaches in England. Relax and enjoy the cream of West Country hospitality, fine wines, mouth-watering cuisine and the very best in leisure and entertainment. An outdoor adventure play area, games room and nursery make families especially welcome. And you'll find the luxury rooms offer everything you expect from one of Devon's finest hotels, and more.

Bed & Breakfast per night: single room from £67.00–£99.00; double room from £132.00–£208.00
Evening meal 1930 (last orders 2100)

Bedrooms: 17 single, 15 double, 28 twin, 32 family rooms
Bathrooms: 92 en-suite, 5 public
Parking for 200
Cards accepted: Mastercard, Visa, Diners, Amex, Switch/Delta

214 YEOLDON COUNTRY HOUSE HOTEL AND RESTAURANT

 HIGHLY COMMENDED

Durrant Lane, Northam, Bideford, Devon EX39 2RL Tel (01237) 474400 Fax (01237) 476618

Set in two acres of gardens overlooking the River Torridge, Yeoldon House offers real hospitality and a refreshingly casual atmosphere in this uniquely unspoilt part of Devon. Individually decorated rooms with an air of elegance and charm – all en-suite with tea/coffee-making facilities. Imaginative à la carte cuisine using fresh local produce and an extensive wine list.Restaurant awarded an AA Rosette in 1997 and 1998.

Bed & Breakfast per night: single occupancy from £45.00–£55.00; double room from £75.00–£90.00
Dinner, Bed & Breakfast per person, per night: £61.50–£65.00
Evening meal 1900 (last orders 2100)

Bedrooms: 7 double, 3 twin
Bathrooms: 10 en-suite
Parking for 22
Cards accepted: Mastercard, Visa, Diners, Amex, Switch/Delta

215 THE NEW INN

HIGHLY COMMENDED

High Street, Clovelly, Bideford, Devon EX39 5TQ Tel (01237) 431303 Fax (01237) 431636

A fascinating 17th-century inn nestling amongst the cobbled streets and flower-strewn cottages of this historic and picturesque sea-faring village. Luxurious bedrooms with lovely views of the village or the sea. Cosy lounges serving Devon cream teas. A restaurant serving traditional regional dishes and a bar with real ale and, from time to time, interesting local personalities. In this traffic-free village, luggage is portered by sledge. A short break paradise.

Bed & Breakfast per night: single room from £32.75–£54.50; double room from £65.50–£79.00
Dinner, Bed & Breakfast per person, per night: £42.00–£51.25 (min 2 nights, two sharing)
Lunch available: 1200–1430 (bar snacks)

Evening meal 1900 (last orders 2100)
Bedrooms: 1 single, 7 double
Bathrooms: 8 en-suite
Cards accepted: Mastercard, Visa, Amex, Switch/Delta

216 THE FALCON HOTEL

HIGHLY COMMENDED

Breakwater Road, Bude, Cornwall EX23 8SD Tel (01288) 352005 Fax (01288) 356359

Overlooking the famous Bude Canal, with beautiful walled gardens and yet only a short stroll from the beaches and shops, the Falcon has one of the finest settings in North Cornwall. Established in 1798, it still retains an old-world charm and atmosphere. The bedrooms are furnished to a very high standard, and have televisions with Teletext and Sky. Excellent local reputation for the quality of the food, both in the bar and candle-lit restaurant.

Bed & Breakfast per night: single room from £36.00–£38.00; double room from £72.00–£76.00
Dinner, Bed & Breakfast per person, per night: £49.50–£51.50
Lunch available: 1200–1400

Evening meal 1900 (last orders 2100)
Bedrooms: 6 single, 14 double, 6 twin
Bathrooms: 26 en-suite   Parking for 40
Cards accepted: Mastercard, Visa, Diners, Amex, Switch/Delta

217 THE CLIFF HOTEL

HIGHLY COMMENDED

Crooklets Beach, Bude, Cornwall EX23 8NG Tel (01288) 353110 Fax (01288) 353110

The Cliff has a wonderful location, being 200 yards from Crooklets Beach and next to the National Trust cliff walk – "an area of outstanding natural beauty". Our facilities are first class, with indoor swimming pool, gym, all-weather bowling green and tennis court – all set within five acres of lawns and wild-flower meadow. We feel our greatest attribute, though, is the home-cooked fresh food and informal ambience.

Bed & Breakfast per night: single room from £28.00–£38.00; double room from £50.00–£66.00
Dinner, Bed & Breakfast per person, per night: £35.00–£49.00
Lunch available: 1230–1430

Evening meal 1830 (last orders 2030)
Bedrooms: 2 single, 3 double, 1 twin, 9 triple
Bathrooms: 15 en-suite
Parking for 15
Open: April–September

At-a-glance symbols are explained on the flap inside the back cover

218 COURT BARN COUNTRY HOUSE HOTEL

 HIGHLY COMMENDED

Clawton, Holsworthy, Devon EX22 6PS Tel (01409) 271219 Fax (01409) 271309

Pure Devon air, magical skies and countryside, combined with crackling log fires, antiques and fresh flowers, create a warm and relaxing atmosphere for a romantic break. Set in park-like grounds, Court Barn is one of the South West's great small touring hotels. Close to the Atlantic heritage coast, Blue Flag beaches, nature walks, cycle trails, National Trust houses and gardens, and midway between the moors. Our award-winning restaurant, which features an extensive wine list, teas and hospitality make Court Barn a place to remember. Romantic breaks.

Bed & Breakfast per night: single room from
£40.00–£50.00; double room from £76.00–£90.00
Dinner, Bed & Breakfast per person, per night:
£56.00–£66.00 (min 2 nights)
Lunch available: 1200–1400

Evening meal 1900 (last orders 2130)
Bedrooms: 1 single, 3 double, 2 twin, 2 triple
Bathrooms: 8 en-suite, 1 public   Parking for 17
Cards accepted: Mastercard, Visa, Diners, Amex,
Switch/Delta

219 BLAGDON MANOR COUNTRY HOTEL

DE LUXE

Ashwater, Devon EX21 5DF Tel (01409) 211224 Fax (01409) 211634

Welcome to Blagdon Manor. A truly wonderful 17th-century manor nestling in twenty acres with superb views of the rolling countryside. Beautifully appointed en-suite guest rooms. Log fires during the cooler months, and a profusion of fresh flowers throughout the spring and summer, provide a relaxing and welcoming atmosphere. Guests dine together in a country houseparty atmosphere and enjoy the best of English cuisine, the ingredients of which will be the finest available. Smoking restricted.

Bed & Breakfast per night: single occupancy from
£60.00–£70.00; double room from £95.00–£110.00
Evening meal 2000

Bedrooms: 5 double, 2 twin
Bathrooms: 7 en-suite
Parking for 14
Cards accepted: Mastercard, Visa, Amex, Switch/Delta

220 THE OLD VICARAGE

 HIGHLY COMMENDED

Treneglos, Launceston, Cornwall PL15 8UQ Tel (01566) 781351 Fax (01566) 781351 E-mail maggie@fancourt.freeserve.co.uk

An elegant Grade II Listed Georgian vicarage in an idyllic, peaceful rural setting near the spectacular north Cornwall coast. Ideally located as a touring base. Renowned for our hospitality and excellent food, which together with personal service and the highest standards throughout, assure your absolute comfort. A restful conservatory overlooks the garden. The en-suite bedrooms are individually furnished, together with fresh flowers and personal touches. Superb food, imaginative cuisine using produce from our own organic kitchen gardens. Non-smoking.

Bed & Breakfast per night: single occupancy from
£23.00–£25.00; double room from £46.00–£48.00
Dinner, Bed & Breakfast per person, per night:
£38.00–£39.00
Evening meal 1900

Bedrooms: 2 double
Bathrooms: 2 en-suite
Parking for 10
Open: March–November

221 RIVENDELL COURT

≋ ≋ HIGHLY COMMENDED

Boscastle, Cornwall PL35 0BN Tel (01840) 250130

Situated in an elevated position in an area of outstanding natural beauty, Rivendell Court is a spacious, tastefully-converted stone barn retaining many original features and commanding magnificent views of both coastline and countryside. It is here that Maurice and Christine Lovell invite you to share their home, where in peaceful, comfortable surroundings you may relax, enjoy their hospitality and, not least, sample delicious home-cooked food.

Bed & Breakfast per night: double room £45.00
Dinner, Bed & Breakfast per person, per night: £36.00
(min 2 nights)
Evening meal 1930

Bedrooms: 1 double, 1 twin
Bathrooms: 2 en-suite
Parking for 6
Open: March–October

The South-West Coast Path

'POOLE 500 MILES' reads the signpost pointing west along the Somerset coast at Minehead. In this daunting manner begins the South-West Coast Path, a walk around England's 'toe' taking in some of the most magnificent coastal scenery in the land. The walk starts dramatically as it enters the Exmoor National Park, hugging steep, wooded slopes that drop precipitously down to the sea, with stupendous views of the Welsh coast. Further on, the section of Devon coastline from Westward Ho! (the only British placename to include an exclamation mark) to the Cornish border is equally lovely as it passes the huddled village of Clovelly and the heights of Hartland Point with fine views of Lundy Island.

The Cornish Coast, both north and south, displays a stunning array of rocky promontories and soaring cliffs, interspersed with superb sandy beaches and fishing villages nestling in tiny coves. In general, the south coast, here and further on, is harder to negotiate than the north because of the many estuaries cutting into the lower-lying terrain, often requiring long detours inland.

The path re-enters Devon and, almost immediately, Plymouth, the largest city on its route. After rounding the wild promontories of Bolt Head and Prawle Point, it meanders through the gentler landscape of the 'Devon Riviera' and the seaside resorts of Paignton, Torquay, Teignmouth, and Dawlish. In Dorset, chalk cliffs run from Lyme Regis to Lulworth, interrupted by the long finger of shingle, Chesil Bank, pointing out to sea. The walk ends on a scenic high point as it negotiates the limestone heights of the Isle of Purbeck, an island in name only, for it remains firmly attached to the mainland.

As well as offering stunning scenery, the walk is rich in historical interest, from prehistoric hillforts in Dorset to Palmerston forts in Plymouth, or the abandoned village of Tyneham (Dorset) taken over by the army in 1943. In Cornwall, defunct engine houses and empty pilchard 'palaces' are relics of a rich industrial past.

The naturalist, as well as the historian, will find much of interest. The protruding coastline provides a landfall for migrating birds, while sub-tropical species of plants flourish in the mild climes of the South-West. The Lizard, in particular, supports a unique flora, while army ranges at Lulworth, untouched by modern farming practices, have preserved a rare botanical habitat.

There are several guides to the South-West Coast Path available, some suggesting shorter, circular walks and offering advice on accommodation, local attractions and other practical information.

222 POLKERR GUEST HOUSE

HIGHLY COMMENDED

Molesworth Street, Tintagel, Cornwall PL34 0BY Tel (01840) 770382 or (01840) 770132

Somewhere special was what we envisaged when we planned the decor of our bedrooms, dining room and the recently constructed large and restful sun lounge that overlooks the garden: guests visiting Polkerr Guest House enjoy accommodation of the highest standard. Situated within a few minutes' walk of Tintagel village, the historic castle and cliffs that offer superb views of the coast, we are also ideally located for exploring the beauty of the countryside.

Bed & Breakfast per night: double room from
£38.00–£50.00
Dinner, Bed & Breakfast per person, per night:
£29.00–£70.00
Evening meal 1830 (last bookings 1200)

Bedrooms: 1 single, 3 double, 1 twin, 1 triple, 1 family
room
Bathrooms: 6 en-suite, 1 private
Parking for 9

223 THE DOWER HOUSE

HIGHLY COMMENDED

Fentonluna Lane, Padstow, Cornwall PL28 8BA Tel (01841) 532317 Fax (01841) 532667

As you step on to our terrace and smile at this beautiful old house, you'll glance to your right over the rooftops of old Padstow, and marvel at the magnificent view of the Camel Estuary and distant hills of Bodmin Moor. Paul and Patricia will greet you and introduce you to their house. You will be delighted with the individually-decorated rooms and the care with which your breakfast is freshly prepared and presented in their elegant dining room.

Bed & Breakfast per night: single room from
£43.20–£51.20; double room from £54.00–£80.00
Lunch available: 1200–1430
Evening meal 1900 (last bookings 1630)

Bedrooms: 1 single, 3 double, 2 twin
Bathrooms: 6 en-suite
Parking for 8
Open: February–November
Cards accepted: Mastercard, Visa, Switch/Delta

224 DEGEMBRIS FARMHOUSE

HIGHLY COMMENDED

St Newlyn East, Newquay, Cornwall TR8 5HY Tel (01872) 510555 Fax (01872) 510230

If you are searching for a tranquil, undisturbed holiday in a picturesque corner of Cornwall, make your way to Degembris where a warm welcome awaits you. Overlooking a beautiful wooded valley, our farmhouse offers you comfortable accommodation, seasonal log fires and delicious home cooking. Our own country trail allows you to explore the natural surroundings. We will provide you with comfort and a taste of country life.

Bed & Breakfast per night: single room max £20.00;
double room from £40.00–£44.00
Dinner, Bed & Breakfast per person, per night:
£32.00–£34.00
Evening meal 1830

Bedrooms: 1 single, 1 double, 1 twin, 1 triple, 1 family
room
Bathrooms: 3 en-suite, 1 public
Parking for 8
Cards accepted: Mastercard, Visa, Switch/Delta

225 AVIARY COURT HOTEL

〰〰〰〰 HIGHLY COMMENDED

Marys Well, Illogan, Redruth, Cornwall TR16 4QZ Tel (01209) 842256 Fax (01209) 843744 E-mail aviarycourt@connexions.uk

A charming three-hundred-year-old Cornish country house set in its own grounds on the edge of Illogan Woods, ideal for touring the South West peninsular and its many local attractions. Six well-equipped individual bedrooms with tea/coffee-making facilities, biscuits, mineral water, fresh fruit, direct dial telephone, remote control television and a view of the gardens. The resident family proprietors ensure personal service, offering well-cooked varied food that uses as much Cornish produce as possible.

Bed & Breakfast per night: single occupancy from £40.00–£44.00; double room from £58.00–£62.00
Dinner, Bed & Breakfast per person, per night: £55.00–£60.00
Lunch available: 1230–1330 (Sunday only)

Evening meal 1900 (last orders 2030)
Bedrooms: 4 double, 1 twin, 1 triple
Bathrooms: 6 en-suite
Parking for 25
Cards accepted: Mastercard, Visa, Switch/Delta

The Leach Pottery

A LARGE ARTISTS' COLONY had been established in St Ives for several decades when in 1920 Bernard Leach returned to England from Japan and set up a pottery here with his lifelong Japanese friend, Shoji Hamada. Leach was born in Hong Kong, of English parents, in 1887 and lived in the Far East as a child. He returned to Japan in 1909 to study pottery, one of the first Westerners to learn the techniques of Oriental pottery. Leach and Hamada chose a site three-quarters of a mile up the hill from the town centre, by the Stennack stream. They wanted to produce 'genuine handicrafts of quality rather than machine craft in quantity', the aim being to combine the traditions of craftsmanship that were still alive in the East with pre-Industrial Revolution English handcrafted pottery. Leach was ideally suited to this, a man able to bridge the spirit of the West and the East, and he was quickly established as the leader of the studio pottery movement. He proved too to be an inspirational teacher, passing on not only practical skills but his philosophy of what it meant to be an artist potter, and always attracted visitors and students from all over the world, the first being Michael Cardew, who later built Wenfordbridge pottery, near Bodmin. In 1923 Hamada went back to Japan, but remained in close touch with Leach. Bernard's son David joined the pottery in 1930, aged 19, and worked as his father's right-hand man for 25 years before starting up on his own in Bovey Tracey, Devon. David's brother, Michael, also worked in St Ives between 1950 and 1955, when he moved to Yelland, North Devon. His son John maintains the family tradition at Mulchelney Pottery in Somerset.

In 1956 Bernard married an American potter, Janet Darnell, and she took over the management of the pottery, showroom and students, while continuing to pot in her own right. Bernard was therefore freed up for more writing and travel, only giving up potting when his sight began to fail in the mid-1970s. After his death in 1979, Janet Leach kept the pottery going, a mecca for collectors and admirers of the art. There is a big collection of Leach and Hamada pots, and work for sale by Trevor Corser and Joanna Wason, who work there. (tel: 01736 796398.)

Bernard Leach/Crafts Council

226 CARBIS BAY HOTEL

HIGHLY COMMENDED

Carbis Bay, St Ives, Cornwall TR26 2NP Tel (01736) 795311 Fax (01736) 797677

Built in 1894 by the famous Cornish architect Sylvanus Trevail, this award-winning hotel has one of the most enchanting and romantic locations in the country – situated on the perfect golden sands of Carbis Bay beach itself. The idyllic surroundings offer peace and tranquillity, making it a natural haven for visitors wishing to escape the stresses and strains of everyday life. Set in its own grounds, the hotel commands breathtaking views across the beautiful landlocked bay of St Ives to Godrevy lighthouse and beyond.

Bed & Breakfast per night: single room from £35.00–£60.00; double room from £60.00–£140.00
Dinner, Bed & Breakfast per person, per night: £45.00–£89.00
Evening meal 1800 (last orders 2030)

Bedrooms: 3 single, 13 double, 6 twin, 4 triple, 7 family rooms
Bathrooms: 33 en-suite
Parking for 60   Open: February–December
Cards accepted: Mastercard, Visa, Diners, Amex, Switch/Delta

227 TREGILDRY HOTEL

HIGHLY COMMENDED

Gillan, Manaccan, Helston, Cornwall TR12 6HG Tel (01326) 231378 Fax (01326) 231561

An elegant small hotel with stunning sea views. Tucked away in an undiscovered corner of the Lizard Peninsula, this is for those seeking relaxed and stylish comfort in "away from it all" surroundings. Large, light lounges with panoramic sea views have comfy sofas, fresh flowers and the latest books and magazines. The stylish restaurant has won awards for cuisine and the pretty sea-view bedrooms are attractively decorated with colourful fabrics. Near coastal path walks and an ideal peaceful base for exploring Cornwall.

Dinner, Bed & Breakfast per person, per night: £60.00–£65.00
Evening meal 1900 (last orders 2030)

Bedrooms: 7 double, 3 twin
Bathrooms: 10 en-suite
Parking for 15
Open: March–October
Cards accepted: Mastercard, Visa, Switch/Delta

228 POLURRIAN HOTEL, APARTMENTS AND LEISURE CLUB

HIGHLY COMMENDED

Polurrian Cove, Mullion, Helston, Cornwall TR12 7EN Tel (01326) 240421 or (01326) 240929 Fax (01326) 240083

Polurrian is a family-run hotel in a magnificent cliff-top setting with 12 acres of gardens leading down to a secluded sandy cove. The National Trust coastline surrounding the hotel offers unrivalled scenic walks and there are many interesting and historic places to visit, all within easy distance. At Polurrian, our aim is to offer good value, quality and service in an atmosphere of comfort and friendliness.

Bed & Breakfast per night: single occupancy from £40.00–£89.00
Dinner, Bed & Breakfast per person, per night: £50.00–£99.00
Lunch available: 1200–1430

Evening meal 1900 (last orders 2100)
Bedrooms: 18 double, 17 twin, 4 triple
Bathrooms: 39 en-suite
Parking for 60
Cards accepted: Mastercard, Visa, Diners, Amex

229 HOUSEL BAY HOTEL

🌊🌊🌊 HIGHLY COMMENDED

Housel Cove, The Lizard, Helston, Cornwall TR12 7PG Tel (01326) 290417 or (01326) 290917 Fax (01326) 290359

An elegant Victorian hotel at Britain's most southerly coast. The views across the ocean are spectacular and a secluded and sandy beach nestles below the hotel. The Cornish coastal path, which runs through the hotel gardens, leads east towards Cadgwith and Coverack and west towards Kynance Cove. Fully licensed with a stylish restaurant and a bar with panoramic views. All bedrooms are en-suite with satellite television and there is a passenger lift.

Bed & Breakfast per night: single room from
£30.00–£68.00; double room from £60.00–£98.00
Dinner, Bed & Breakfast per person, per night:
£49.50–£70.00
Lunch available: 1200–1415 (in Ocean View bar)

Evening meal 1900 (last orders 2130)
Bedrooms: 4 single, 10 double, 5 twin, 1 family room
Bathrooms: 20 en-suite
Parking for 34
Cards accepted: Mastercard, Visa, Amex, Switch/Delta

230 THE BAY HOTEL

🌊🌊🌊 HIGHLY COMMENDED

Coverack, Helston, Cornwall TR12 6TF Tel (01326) 280464 Fax (01326) 280464

This very comfortable family-run hotel, which is exclusively for adults, combines good food and wines, fresh air, exhilarating walks and good company to provide a tonic for all. We take great pleasure in preparing fine food for you, from local lobster and Helford oysters to traditional dishes such as roast lamb in the hay and grilled local fish. Our wine list boasts over eighty wines from which to choose. There is nowhere quite like it!

Bed & Breakfast per night: single room from
£35.00–£46.50; double room from £70.00–£93.00
Dinner, Bed & Breakfast per person, per night:
£45.00–£56.50
Lunch available: 1200–1400

Evening meal 1830 (last orders 2030)
Bedrooms: 1 single, 7 double, 6 twin
Bathrooms: 13 en-suite, 1 private
Parking for 14
Cards accepted: Mastercard, Visa, Switch/Delta

231 GREEN LAWNS HOTEL

🌊🌊🌊 HIGHLY COMMENDED

Western Terrace, Falmouth, Cornwall TR11 4QJ Tel (01326) 312734 or (01326) 312007 Fax (01326) 211427 E-mail green.lawns@dial.pipex.com

Where can you relax in an elegant, centrally positioned, chateau-style hotel with views across a beautiful bay? The Green Lawns Hotel and the famous Garras restaurant! If you are looking for a holiday where high standards and personal attention are paramount, you will enjoy an excellent choice of imaginative cuisine from a table d' hôte or à la carte menu. All our guests enjoy free membership of the Garras Leisure Club with its magnificent indoor swimming pool. 'Britain in Bloom' winners 1995, 1996 and 1997.

Bed & Breakfast per night: single room from
£50.00–£90.00; double room from £90.00–£130.00
Dinner, Bed & Breakfast per person, per night:
£55.00–£110.00 (min 2 nights)
Lunch available: 1200–1345

Evening meal 1845 (last orders 2145)
Bedrooms: 6 single, 16 double, 9 twin, 2 triple, 6 family rooms
Bathrooms: 39 en-suite   Parking for 60
Cards accepted: Mastercard, Visa, Diners, Amex, Switch/Delta

At-a-glance symbols are explained on the flap inside the back cover

232 THE HUNDRED HOUSE HOTEL

〰〰〰 HIGHLY COMMENDED

Ruan Highlanes, near Truro, Cornwall TR2 5JR Tel (01872) 501336 Fax (01872) 501151

Delightful 19th-century Cornish country house set in three acres. Near St Mawes on the Fal estuary and surrounded by superb countryside and unspoilt sandy coves. It is now a charming small hotel, beautifully decorated and furnished like an elegant English home. Delicious candle-lit dinners, Cornish cream teas, log fires and croquet on the lawn make a relaxing short break or a longer stay a memorable delight. Ideal for exploring Cornwall, its sub-tropical gardens or walking the coastal path. AA Rosette for food.

Bed & Breakfast per night: single room from £40.00–£44.00; double room from £80.00–£88.00
Dinner, Bed & Breakfast per person, per night: £52.00–£65.00
Evening meal 1930 (last orders 2000)

Bedrooms: 2 single, 4 double, 4 twin, 1 triple, 1 family room
Bathrooms: 10 en-suite
Parking for 15
Open: March–October
Cards accepted: Mastercard, Visa, Amex, Switch/Delta

233 LUGGER HOTEL AND RESTAURANT

〰〰〰〰 HIGHLY COMMENDED

Portloe, Truro, Cornwall TR2 5RD Tel (01872) 501322 Fax (01872) 501691

Dating from the 17th century and originally an inn frequented by smugglers, the Lugger is situated at the very water's edge of a picturesque cove on the beautiful and unspoilt Cornish Roseland Peninsula. Internationally renowned for its first-class accommodation, superb food and wide selection of wines, the hotel has been in the ownership of the welcoming Powell family for three generations. It is the perfect place for lovers of nature and those in search of peace and seclusion.

Bed & Breakfast per night: single room from £55.00–£60.00; double room from £110.00–£120.00
Dinner, Bed & Breakfast per person, per night: £63.00–£80.00
Lunch available: 1200–1400

Evening meal 1900 (last orders 2130)
Bedrooms: 3 single, 9 double, 7 twin
Bathrooms: 19 en-suite
Parking for 25   Open: March–October
Cards accepted: Mastercard, Visa, Diners, Amex, Switch/Delta

234 BOKIDDICK FARM

〰〰 HIGHLY COMMENDED

Lanivet, Bodmin, Cornwall PL30 5HP Tel (01208) 831481 Fax (01208) 831481

Lovely Georgian farmhouse, with oak beams and wood panelling, nestling in beautiful Cornish countryside. Magnificent views and a peaceful location. The central position of our 180-acre dairy farm makes it an ideal base for touring all of Cornwall. Close to National Trust Lanhydrock House and on the Saint's Way walk. Lovely en-suite bedrooms, delicious breakfasts cooked on the Aga and a relaxed, friendly atmosphere. The warmest of welcomes awaits you.

Bed & Breakfast per night: single occupancy from £25.00; double room from £40.00–£42.00

Bedrooms: 1 double, 1 triple
Bathrooms: 2 en-suite
Parking for 4

Entries are cross referenced by number to the maps on pages 110–111

235 BOSCUNDLE MANOR

HIGHLY COMMENDED

Tregrehan, St Austell, Cornwall PL25 3RL Tel (01726) 813557 Fax (01726) 814997

A lovely house in over twelve acres of secluded grounds with a practice golf area. The rooms are very attractively furnished with antiques, pictures and family possessions. The bedrooms are extremely comfortable and most have spa baths and power showers. There is an outstanding wine list and beautifully prepared fresh food is served. Andrew and Mary Flint have been here for over twenty years and their personal involvement and enthusiasm create a relaxed and happy atmosphere.

Bed & Breakfast per night: single room from
£65.00–£75.00; double room from £110.00–£130.00
Dinner, Bed & Breakfast per person, per night:
£75.00–£90.00
Evening meal 1930 (last orders 2030)

Bedrooms: 2 single, 4 double, 5 twin, 1 family room
Bathrooms: 12 en-suite
Parking for 15
Open: April–October
Cards accepted: Mastercard, Visa, Amex, Switch/Delta

236 CARLYON BAY HOTEL

HIGHLY COMMENDED

Sea Road, Carlyon Bay, St Austell, Cornwall PL25 3RD Tel (01726) 812304 Fax (01726) 814938

Set in 250 acres of exquisite grounds, including its own championship golf course, the Carlyon Bay Hotel is blessed with a setting that is unique. Renowned for its spectacular coastal views and outstanding hospitality, every comfort and luxury is catered for. From the magnificent indoor and outdoor heated swimming pools to the award-winning Bay View Restaurant. A relaxing, peaceful retreat or delightful family holiday, the Carlyon Bay Hotel combines the finest facilities with the warmest of West Country welcomes.

Bed & Breakfast per night: single room from
£72.00–£87.00; double room from £130.00–£220.00
Evening meal 1900 (last orders 2100)

Bedrooms: 13 single, 16 double, 41 twin, 2 triple
Bathrooms: 72 en-suite
Parking for 74
Cards accepted: Mastercard, Visa, Diners, Amex,
Switch/Delta

237 MARINA HOTEL

HIGHLY COMMENDED

Esplanade, Fowey, Cornwall PL23 1HY Tel (01726) 833315 Fax (01726) 832779 E-mail marina.hotel@dial.pipex.com

This Georgian hotel, originally built as the summer residence of the Bishop of Truro, is situated on the waterside with its own moorings. The hotel faces south and most rooms (four have balconies) overlook the estuary. The walled garden provides an ideal spot for observing the waterside traffic. The award-winning restaurant overlooking the water provides a feast of local fish, shellfish and meat. Early and late season offers of two nights for the price of one. www.cornwall-online.co.uk/marina_hotel/

Bed & Breakfast per night: single occupancy from
£45.00–£57.00; double room from £60.00–£98.00
Dinner, Bed & Breakfast per person, per night:
£54.00–£67.00
Lunch available: 1200–1700

Evening meal 1900 (last orders 2030)
Bedrooms: 7 double, 4 twin
Bathrooms: 11 en-suite
Open: March–December
Cards accepted: Mastercard, Visa, Amex, Switch/Delta

At-a-glance symbols are explained on the flap inside the back cover

238 TALLAND BAY HOTEL

~~~ ~~~ ~~~ ~~~ HIGHLY COMMENDED

Talland Bay, Looe, Cornwall PL13 2JB Tel (01503) 272667 Fax (01503) 272940

A delightful old Cornish manor house set in two acres of gardens overlooking the sea. All bedrooms are furnished to a high standard and many have sea views. Dinners feature fresh regional produce – local seafood, Cornish lamb, West Country cheeses. AA Rosette. Talland Bay is a magically peaceful spot from which to explore this part of Cornwall. Breathtaking cliff paths lead to Looe and Polperro, and there are fascinating sub-tropical gardens and National Trust properties within easy reach.

Bed & Breakfast per night: single room from £49.00–£79.00; double room from £98.00–£158.00
Dinner, Bed & Breakfast per person, per night: £67.00–£95.00
Lunch available: 1230–1400 (bar lunches)

Evening meal 1900 (last orders 2100)
Bedrooms: 3 single, 5 double, 9 twin, 2 family rooms
Bathrooms: 19 en-suite
Parking for 20 Open: March–December
Cards accepted: Mastercard, Visa, Diners, Amex, Switch/Delta

239 TRELASKE HOTEL AND RESTAURANT

~~~ ~~~ ~~~ ~~~ HIGHLY COMMENDED

Polperro Road, Looe, Cornwall PL13 2JS Tel (01503) 262159 Fax (01503) 265360

Trelaske is situated just off, but not visible from, the main Looe to Polperro Road, making it a perfect place for peace and tranquillity. The hotel is privately owned by Sylvia and Roger Rawlings, who are both Cornish and local to the area. Trelaske has an enviable reputation for fine food and luxurious accommodation. Each of the seven bedrooms has been individually furnished to the highest possible standard. Executive rooms with jacuzzi. Set in four acres of beautiful mature gardens, making a perfect retreat to return to after visiting Poldark country.

Bed & Breakfast per night: single occupancy from £45.00; double room from £70.00
Dinner, Bed & Breakfast per person, per night: from £55.00
Evening meal 1900 (last orders 2130)

Bedrooms: 3 double, 2 twin, 1 triple, 1 family room
Bathrooms: 7 en-suite
Parking for 50
Cards accepted: Mastercard, Visa, Amex, Switch/Delta

240 THE OLD RECTORY COUNTRY HOUSE HOTEL

~~~ ~~~ ~~~ HIGHLY COMMENDED

St Keyne, Liskeard, Cornwall PL14 4RL Tel (01579) 342617 Fax (01579) 342293

If you were to quote the Bible, "the peace that passeth all understanding", it would be applicable to The Old Rectory. The view from the grounds and windows merely enhances the image. Built in the 1800s, this is a family run hotel with en-suite bedrooms which are tastefully decorated (two rooms with four-poster beds). A sumptuous breakfast, an à la carte dinner with fine English cooking, and the adventure of continental cuisine complete the picture. AA 2 Rosettes.

Bed & Breakfast per night: single room from £35.00–£40.00; double room from £58.00–£70.00
Dinner, Bed & Breakfast per person, per night: £49.00
Evening meal 1900 (last orders 2100)

Bedrooms: 1 single, 5 double, 2 twin
Bathrooms: 7 en-suite, 1 private
Parking for 30
Cards accepted: Mastercard

241 COOMBE FARM

HIGHLY COMMENDED

Widegates, near Looe, Cornwall PL13 1QN Tel (01503) 240223 Fax (01503) 240895

Relax in a wonderful tranquil setting of lawns, meadows, woods and streams, with superb views down a wooded valley to the sea. Enjoy warm friendly hospitality in a house lovingly furnished with antiques and interesting objects. There are open log fires, a beautiful outdoor pool, a stone barn for snooker and table tennis, and a candlelit dining room in which we serve a delicious four-course dinner every evening. Nearby glorious walks and beaches, and splendid National Trust properties.

Bed & Breakfast per night: single occupancy from £28.00–£36.00; double room from £56.00–£72.00; Dinner, Bed & Breakfast per person, per night: £44.00–£52.00
Evening meal 1900

Bedrooms: 3 double, 3 twin, 2 triple, 2 family rooms
Bathrooms: 10 en-suite, 1 public
Parking for 12 Open: March–October
Cards accepted: Mastercard, Visa, Diners, Amex, Switch/Delta

Cornish customs

HISTORICALLY, CORNWALL WAS a wild and remote county, with a culture and language of its own. Little affected by the Romans, it established closer ties to its Celtic neighbours than to the rest of England, and many of its customs have origins in its dim Celtic past. Though occasionally tenuously linked to an obscure Cornish saint (of which there is no shortage), Cornish customs tend to have a distinctly pagan flavour and involve much incantatory music, drumming and dancing.

One such Cornish event, the famous Helston Floral Dance (on or around 8 May) probably began as a pagan celebration of Spring's arrival, but the festivities also mark the feast of the Apparition of St Michael, patron saint of Helston. Its popular name is a misnomer born of the customary decoration of the town with greenery; the actual name – Furry Dance – is from feriae, Latin for festival. In the main dance, gentlemen in morning-coats and ladies in bonnets cavort in a crocodile through the town, diving into gardens, yards and shops as they go.

May Day is celebrated in Padstow with even greater energy. Its high-point is the appearance of the hobby horse (or 'Obby 'Oss) – or rather horses, for there are two of them: the Temperance Oss and the Old Oss. Both are extraordinary: black and circular, with a small decorated head protruding from the side, and the wearer's head, in the centre, obscured by a grotesque mask. The Old Oss has all the fun: accompanied by his 'teaser' and a band of followers all singing a special song, he leaps through the streets in pursuit of pretty girls who, if caught in his voluminous skirts, are deemed extremely lucky. The custom's origins are shrouded in obscurity, but are said by some to represent the luring away of a dragon by St Petrioc in the 6th century.

Some lesser-known Cornish customs have been initiated in memory of particular individuals. The one-time mayor of St Ives, John Knill, made sure he would be remembered by posterity by leaving a sum of £100 in his will for the initiation of a five-yearly custom. Though wholly artificially devised, the ceremony incorporates all the typical elements of a true Cornish tradition: much processing, singing and dancing at the top of steep Warvas Hill, just outside St Ives, where Knill's Steeple stands. Though the purpose of the custom was to preserve his memory after his death, Knill made certain all was to his liking by having the rigmarole enacted in 1801, ten years before he actually died!

The famous Helston Floral Dance

At-a-glance symbols are explained on the flap inside the back cover

242 LYDFORD HOUSE HOTEL

 HIGHLY COMMENDED

Lydford, Okehampton, Devon EX20 4AU Tel (01822) 820347 Fax (01822) 820442 E-mail lydfordhousehotel@compuserve.com

A country house hotel of considerable charm in a beautiful garden setting just on the edge of Dartmoor. There are delightful bedrooms with every facility, comfortable lounges and a well-stocked bar. The restaurant offers the finest traditional English fare and an interesting wine list. Service is by friendly, efficient staff and the resident proprietors are always on hand to ensure that guests receive personal attention. Riding stables in the grounds provide superb hacking over Dartmoor. www.westcountry-hotels.co.uk/lydford

Bed & Breakfast per night: single room from £37.00–£43.00; double room £74.00
Evening meal 1900 (last orders 2030)

Bedrooms: 2 single, 3 double, 3 twin, 1 triple, 3 family rooms
Bathrooms: 11 en-suite, 1 private
Parking for 30
Cards accepted: Mastercard, Visa, Switch/Delta

243 TOR COTTAGE

 DE LUXE

Chillaton, Lifton, Devon PL16 OJE Tel (01822) 860248 Fax (01822) 860126 E-mail info@torcottage.demon.co.uk

National winner of the English Tourist Board and the West Country Tourist Board's 'England for Excellence' Gold Award for Bed & Breakfast of the Year 1998. Tor Cottage has a warm and relaxed atmosphere and nestles in its own private valley. Streamside setting, lovely gardens and eighteen acres of hillside full of wildlife. Enjoy the ambience of this special place and its many luxuries. Peace, tranquillity and complete privacy in beautiful bed-sitting rooms, each with a log fire and private garden/terrace. Renowned vegetarian cuisine and traditional meals. Heated pool (summer), indoor jacuzzi (winter). www.torcottage.demon.co.uk

Bed & Breakfast per night: single occupancy £68.00; double room £76.00
Dinner, Bed & Breakfast per person, per night: £45.50–£63.00
Evening meal 1930 (last orders 2130)

Bedrooms: 3 double, 1 twin
Bathrooms: 4 en-suite
Parking for 8
Cards accepted: Mastercard, Visa, Switch/Delta

244 STORE COTTAGE

HIGHLY COMMENDED

19 The Village, Buckland Monachorum, Yelverton, Devon PL20 7NA Tel (01822) 853117 Fax (01822) 853117

Store Cottage is a listed building in the centre of Buckland Monachorum, not far from the church and village pub. There are two rooms with en-suite bathrooms. The guests' lounge has a wood burning stove and plenty of good local maps and books. We provide a choice of breakfasts using local Devon produce wherever possible. The village is to the west of Dartmoor and several gardens and National Trust houses are nearby. Dogs welcome.

Bed & Breakfast per night: double room £40.00

Bedrooms: 1 double, 1 twin
Bathrooms: 2 en-suite
Parking for 3

245 PRINCE HALL HOTEL

HIGHLY COMMENDED

nr Two Bridges, Dartmoor, Devon PL20 6SA Tel (01822) 890403 Fax (01822) 890676

A warm welcome awaits you at Prince Hall, set in the very heart of Dartmoor's breathtaking scenery. Peacefulness prevails in this relaxed and friendly country house. We offer eight spacious, individually decorated en-suite bedrooms, a cosy bar and elegant sitting room. Our AA 2 Rosette award-winning restaurant is overseen by the owner/chef using the very best local produce, and this is complemented by an extensive international wine list. The ideal location for walking, fishing, riding or just relaxing. Well behaved dogs welcome free of charge.

Bed & Breakfast per night: single room £35.00; double room from £75.00–£85.00
Dinner, Bed & Breakfast per person, per night: £59.50–£64.50
Evening meal 1900 (last orders 2030)

Bedrooms: 1 single, 3 double, 3 twin, 1 triple
Bathrooms: 8 en-suite
Parking for 16
Open: February–December
Cards accepted: Mastercard, Diners, Amex, Switch/Delta

246 BORINGDON HALL HOTEL

HIGHLY COMMENDED

Colebrook, Plympton, Plymouth, Devon PL7 4DP Tel (01752) 344455 Fax (01752) 346578

Boringdon Hall Hotel is a Grade I Listed Elizabethan manor house where Queen Elizabeth may have stayed. Situated on the edge of Dartmoor – a place of tranquil calm in a world of hustle and bustle. The Hall and historic outbuildings have been tastefully restored to their former glory. The forty luxury bedrooms stand around a courtyard, along with the leisure facilities which include a swimming pool, sauna, nine-hole pitch and putt, and a tennis court. Our Gallery restaurant now has an AA Rosette.
www.g-p.uk/hotels/boringdon

Bed & Breakfast per night: single room from £75.00–£120.00; double room from £95.00–£130.00
Dinner, Bed & Breakfast per person, per night: £50.50–£60.50 (min 2 nights)
Lunch available: 1200–1400

Evening meal 1900 (last orders 2130)
Bedrooms: 1 single, 20 double, 15 twin, 4 triple
Bathrooms: 40 en-suite
Parking for 250
Cards accepted: Mastercard, Visa, Amex, Switch/Delta

247 BOWLING GREEN HOTEL

HIGHLY COMMENDED

9-10 Osborne Place, Lockyer Street, Plymouth, Devon PL1 2PU Tel (01752) 209090 Fax (01752) 209092

Situated in the historic naval city of Plymouth opposite the world famous 'Drake's Bowling Green', this elegant Georgian hotel has superbly appointed bedrooms offering all the modern facilities the traveller requires. With a full breakfast menu and friendly and efficient family staff, you can be sure of a memorable visit to Plymouth. The Bowling Green Hotel is centrally situated for the Barbican, Theatre Royal, leisure/conference centre and ferry port, with Dartmoor only a few miles away.

Bed & Breakfast per night: single room from £36.00–£37.00; double room from £46.00–£50.00

Bedrooms: 1 single, 9 double, 1 twin, 1 triple
Bathrooms: 12 en-suite
Parking for 4
Cards accepted: Mastercard, Diners, Amex, Switch/Delta

248 HALFWAY HOUSE INN

HIGHLY COMMENDED

Fore Street, Kingsand, Torpoint, Cornwall PL10 1NA   Tel (01752) 822279 Fax (01752) 823146 E-mail david.riggs@virgin.net

Situated on the Cornwall coastal path, just thirty yards from the beach. At the heart of the historical colour-washed villages of Kingsand and Cawsand, adjacent to Mount Edgcumbe Park and a ferry ride away from the great naval city of Plymouth. The intimate restaurant specialises in locally-caught seafood, complemented by a selection of fine wines and real ales. A haven of peace and tranquillity, your stay here will be a truly unforgettable experience.   www.connexions.co.uk/halfway/index.htm

Bed & Breakfast per night: single room from £25.00–£30.00; double room from £50.00–£60.00 Dinner, Bed & Breakfast per person, per night: £35.00–£45.00 Lunch available: 1200–1430

Evening meal 1900 (last orders 2130) Bedrooms: 1 single, 3 double, 1 family room Bathrooms: 5 en-suite Cards accepted: Mastercard, Visa, Diners, Amex, Switch/Delta

249 TIDES REACH HOTEL

HIGHLY COMMENDED

South Sands, Salcombe, Devon TQ8 8LJ Tel (01548) 843466 Fax (01548) 843954

Located in a tree-fringed sandy cove where country meets the sea, with a glorious view across the Salcombe Estuary, you can relax in style in this beautifully furnished and decorated hotel. Pamper yourself in the superb leisure complex, extensively-equipped and with a sunny tropical atmosphere. Award-winning creative cuisine (AA 2 Rosettes) served with courtesy and care in our garden-room restaurant.

Dinner, Bed & Breakfast per person, per night: £72.00–£116.00 (2 sharing) Evening meal 1900 (last orders 2100)

Bedrooms: 18 double, 17 twin, 3 family rooms Bathrooms: 38 en-suite, 2 public Parking for 100   Open: February–December Cards accepted: Mastercard, Visa, Diners, Amex, Switch/Delta

250 LANTERN LODGE HOTEL

HIGHLY COMMENDED

Hope Cove, Kingsbridge, Devon TQ7 3HE Tel (01548) 561280 Fax (01548) 561736

Situated overlooking the unspoilt fishing village of Hope Cove, Lantern Lodge Hotel is renowned for comfort, superb food, peace, quiet and excellent service. Four-poster bedrooms available, all with a sea view. All rooms have en-suite facilities, tea/coffee-making and colour television. Indoor heated swimming pool, sauna and solarium. No children under twelve years. No pets.

Bed & Breakfast per night: single occupancy from £40.00–£50.00; double room from £70.00–£90.00 Dinner, Bed & Breakfast per person, per night: £47.00–£67.00 Evening meal 1900 (last orders 2030)

Bedrooms: 10 double, 3 twin, 1 triple Bathrooms: 14 en-suite Parking for 20 Open: March–November Cards accepted: Mastercard, Visa, Switch/Delta

251 THURLESTONE HOTEL

HIGHLY COMMENDED

Thurlestone, Kingsbridge, Devon TQ7 3NN Tel (01548) 560382 Fax (01548) 561069 E-mail enquiries@thurlestone.co.uk

An intimate atmosphere, characteristic of grand establishments, distinguishes us from others due to our location on the Devon coast, in an area of outstanding natural beauty. Sixty four en-suite bedrooms (includes four suites), well furnished with every facility, including video in some rooms. A restaurant with a reputation for fine rosette food, superb wine and long-serving staff. Leisure activities include indoor swimming pool, spa bath, sauna, solarium, 9-hole championship golf course and tennis, squash and badminton courts as well as opportunities for walks and fishing. Please telephone for brochure. www.thurlestone.co.uk

Bed & Breakfast per night: single room from £60.00–£105.00; double room from £120.00–£210.00 Dinner, Bed & Breakfast per person, per night: £47.00–£118.00
Lunch available: 1230–1400

Evening meal 1930 (last orders 2100)
Bedrooms: 5 single, 18 double, 26 twin, 13 triple, 3 family rooms
Bathrooms: 64 en-suite   Parking for 119
Cards accepted: Mastercard, Visa, Amex, Switch/Delta

252 HELLIERS FARM

HIGHLY COMMENDED

Ashford, Aveton Gifford, Kingsbridge, Devon TQ7 4ND   Tel (01548) 550689 Fax (01548) 550689

Helliers Farm is a small sheep farm set on a hill overlooking a lovely valley in the South Hams. An ideal centre for touring the coasts, moors, golf courses (Bigbury, Thurlestone and Dartmouth), National Trust houses and walks, and the city of Plymouth. Tastefully appointed en-suite bedrooms and a comfortable lounge and dining room where excellent farmhouse breakfasts are served. No smoking.

Bed & Breakfast per night: single room from £20.00–£22.00; double room from £40.00–£56.00

Bedrooms: 1 single, 1 double, 1 twin, 1 family room
Bathrooms: 2 en-suite, 1 private, 1 public
Parking for 6

253 WHITE HOUSE HOTEL

HIGHLY COMMENDED

Chillington, Kingsbridge, Devon TQ7 2JX Tel (01548) 580580 Fax (01548) 581124

The White House is a lovely Grade II Listed building of great aesthetic and architectural appeal. Set in an acre of lawned and terraced gardens in one of the most beautiful corners of coastal England, the house has a special atmosphere reminiscent of a quieter and less hurried age. An elegant restaurant and cosy bar, comfortable lounges with log fires, interesting wines and home cooking are all here for your delight.

Bed & Breakfast per night: single occupancy from £35.00–£45.00; double room from £60.00–£120.00 Dinner, Bed & Breakfast per person, per night: £45.00–£75.00
Evening meal 1900 (last orders 2030)

Bedrooms: 3 double, 5 double/twin
Bathrooms: 7 en-suite, 1 private
Parking for 12
Open: March–December
Cards accepted: Mastercard, Visa, Switch/Delta

254 WOODSIDE COTTAGE

HIGHLY COMMENDED

Blackawton, Totnes, Devon TQ9 7BL Tel (01803) 712375 Fax (01803) 712605 E-mail b&b@woodside-cottage.demon.co.uk

A fine old 18th-century Devon house, formerly a gamekeeper's cottage, built of local stone and set in the side of a beautiful valley with a small stream. A full English breakfast is served in the dining room, which has a beamed ceiling, natural stone fireplaces and is furnished with antiques.
A conservatory lounge is available for coffee, with panoramic views over the valleys. Ample car parking. Bike and boat hire. The ancient village of Blackawton, with two nice country inns serving evening meals, is just a short walk away. An 18-hole golf course, with indoor swimming pool, is close by. Sorry, no family rooms, smoking or pets.

Bed & Breakfast per night: double room from
£36.00–£44.00

Bedrooms: 3 double
Bathrooms: 3 en-suite
Parking for 6
Open: February–November

---

255 KNOWLE FARM

HIGHLY COMMENDED

Rattery, nr Totnes, Devon TQ10 9JY Tel (01364) 73914 Fax (01364) 73914

Four-poster, pretty linen, beams, wood-panelled dining room and Aga-cooked breakfasts in our 17th-century Devon longhouse. Set in 44 acres of beautiful farmland, Knowle Farm is close to Totnes and Dartmoor, and within easy reach of the wonderful coastline and sandy beaches. Pet farm animals abound. There is a heated pool from May to September, tennis, an indoor purpose-built toddlers' soft play area and table tennis. We have a kingsize four-poster room and a twin room, both en-suite, as well as a children's twin room adjacent (adaptable for adults) which shares the en-suite facilities.

Bed & Breakfast per night: single occupancy from
£35.00–£40.00; double room from £47.00–£55.00

Bedrooms: 1 double, 2 twin
Bathrooms: 2 en-suite
Parking for 9

---

256 THE OLD FORGE AT TOTNES

HIGHLY COMMENDED

Seymour Place, Totnes, Devon TQ9 5AY Tel (01803) 862174 Fax (01803) 865385

This beautiful 600-year-old building is a haven of comfort and relaxation, not far from the town centre. Rooms are delightfully co-ordinated, offering hairdryer, radio alarm, telephone, central heating, colour TV, beverage tray, continental bedding and direct dial telephone. We also have ground floor rooms and a family cottage suite. Leisure lounge with whirlpool spa. Enjoy breakfast in the Tudor-style dining room which offers a wide choice of menu. Specialities: golf breaks (near 15 courses), adventure sport breaks, dance holidays, 'hands on' blacksmithing. No smoking indoors. Extensive afternoon tea menu served in the walled tea garden or conservatory.

Bed & Breakfast per night: single room from
£40.00–£46.00; double room from £52.00–£72.00

Bedrooms: 1 single, 2 double, 2 twin, 5 family rooms
Bathrooms: 9 en-suite, 1 private, 1 public
Parking for 10
Cards accepted: Mastercard, Visa, Switch/Delta

257 EDGEMOOR HOTEL

HIGHLY COMMENDED

Haytor Road, Bovey Tracey, Devon TQ13 9LE Tel (01626) 832466 Fax (01626) 834760 E-mail edgemoor@btinternet.com

'Loaded with charm', this wisteria-clad country house hotel is personally run by resident proprietors Rod and Pat Day. With its beautiful gardens and lovely en-suite bedrooms (including some four-posters) the Edgemoor provides the ideal setting in which to unwind from the cares of modern life. Good food (AA 2 Rosettes), fine wines and beautiful countryside combine to help make your stay memorable and enjoyable. www.edgemoor.co.uk

Bed & Breakfast per night: single room from
£48.50–£55.00; double room from £77.50–£100.00
Dinner, Bed & Breakfast per person, per night:
£52.50–£65.00 (min 2 nights)
Lunch available: 1200–1345

Evening meal 1900 (last orders 2100)
Bedrooms: 3 single, 9 double, 3 twin, 1 triple, 1 family room
Bathrooms: 17 en-suite   Parking for 50
Cards accepted: Mastercard, Visa, Diners, Amex,
Switch/Delta

258 GREAT SLONCOMBE FARM

HIGHLY COMMENDED

Moretonhampstead, Newton Abbot, Devon TQ13 8QF Tel (01647) 440595 Fax (01647) 440595

Share the magic of Dartmoor all year round while staying in our lovely rambling 13th-century farmhouse, which is full of interesting historical features. A working dairy farm set amongst peaceful meadows and woodland abundant in wild flowers and animals. A welcoming and informal place to relax and explore the countryside. Comfortable en-suite rooms, one with a four-poster bed, central heating, TVs and tea/coffee-making facilities. Delicious Devonshire suppers and breakfasts with new-baked bread.

Bed & Breakfast per night: single occupancy from
£21.00–£22.00; double room from £42.00–£44.00
Dinner, Bed & Breakfast per person, per night:
£32.00–£48.00
Evening meal 1830 (last bookings 1000)

Bedrooms: 2 double, 1 twin
Bathrooms: 3 en-suite
Parking for 3

259 WOOSTON FARM

HIGHLY COMMENDED

Moretonhampstead, Newton Abbot, Devon TQ13 8QA Tel (01647) 440367 or (0498) 670590 Fax (01647) 440367

Wooston Farm is situated above the Teign Valley in the Dartmoor National Park, with views over open moorland. The farmhouse is surrounded by a delightful garden. There are plenty of walks to take on the moor and in the wooded Teign Valley. Good home cooking and cosy log fires await you at Wooston with two double (one four-poster) and one twin room. Mountain bikes available. Open all year except Christmas.

Bed & Breakfast per night: double room from
£40.00–£44.00
Evening meal 1800 (last orders 1830)

Bedrooms: 2 double, 1 twin
Bathrooms: 2 en-suite, 2 private
Parking for 3

260 LOWER NICHOLS NYMET FARM

 HIGHLY COMMENDED

Lower Nichols Nymet, North Tawton, Devon EX20 2BW Tel (01363) 82510 Fax (01363) 82510

We offer a haven of comfort and rest on our farm that is set in rolling countryside in the centre of Devon. On holiday, food becomes important – we serve hearty and healthy breakfasts and candle-lit dinners using local produce. Our elegantly furnished en-suite bedrooms have glorious views. There are many National Trust properties and other attractions to visit. This is a perfect base for exploring the beauties of the West Country. A no smoking establishment. Brochure available.

Bed & Breakfast per night: double room from
£36.00–£39.00
Dinner, Bed & Breakfast per person, per night:
£28.00–£29.50
Evening meal 1830

Bedrooms: 1 double, 1 family room
Bathrooms: 2 en-suite
Parking for 4
Open: March–October

Clapperbridges

NEAR ASHWAY IN EXMOOR, the river Barle flows wide and shallow over its brown stony bed. On either side, the road ends abruptly in a somewhat intimidating ford, but walkers may remain dry-shod, crossing the Barle via a magnificent walkway of vast stone slabs, known as Tarr Steps.

Tarr Steps is a type of ancient bridge known as a clapperbridge, and at 177ft (54m) in length is the largest and most elaborate of its type in England. The term 'clapperbridge' is used for any bridge constructed from large, flat slabs of stone forming a level pathway over a river or stream; the word probably developed from the Anglo Saxon *cleaca* meaning 'stepping stones'. Indeed a number of clapperbridges may well have begun as simple stepping-stones, which later formed the piers upon which linking slabs of stone were balanced. While some clapperbridges consist simply of a single slab thrown across the stream, multi-span bridges have typically between two and five spans (Tarr Steps with its magnificent 17 spans, is actually something of an anomaly).

No-one knows exactly when Tarr Steps was built, and, although for many years considered a pre-historic monument, it is now thought to be of much more recent construction. Most clapperbridges were built in the 14th century on packhorse routes, but a few appeared as late as the 18th and 19th centuries. They were simple and functional, and when routes changed or more superior structures superseded them, they were very often allowed to disappear. Today, only about 40 remain in England.

ERJ Davey

Clapperbridges are found in parts of the country where the local rock yields large slabs of strong stone. There are consequently two main concentrations: one in north and west Yorkshire, the other in Devon and Cornwall. The greatest number are in Dartmoor, which boasts a wide range of variations. Postbridge, a lonely village in the heart of the moor, has one of the finest of its type (shown above). It consists of three vast slabs of granite, some 17ft (5m) by 7ft (2m) in size, supported by four piers of granite blocks. Also on Dartmoor are Teignhead's bridge, built in 1790, and one over the Cowsic River at Two Bridges, built in 1837. At Wallabrook is a single-span clapperbridge, while the bridge at Yar Tor Down, Hexworthy, has three spans. Runnage bridge, near Postbridge, is a late example fitted with parapets.

261 SAVERY'S AT KARSLAKE HOUSE

HIGHLY COMMENDED

Halse Lane, Winsford, Minehead, Somerset TA24 7JE Tel (01643) 851242 Fax (01643) 851242

The spacious restaurant in this 15th-century malthouse has quickly gained recognition in the major food guides. The pretty village of Winsford is a peaceful centre from which to tour Devon and Somerset, and its reputation for riding, shooting and fishing is legendary. With seven bedrooms and a relaxed atmosphere, Karslake House is perfect for private house parties.

Bed & Breakfast per night: double room from £50.00–£80.00
Dinner, Bed & Breakfast per person, per night:
£51.00–£65.00 (min 2 nights on summer weekends and Bank Holidays)
Lunch available: by arrangement

Evening meal 1900 (last orders 2115)
Bedrooms: 6 double, 1 twin
Bathrooms: 4 en-suite, 2 private, 2 private showers, 1 public
Parking for 15
Cards accepted: Mastercard, Visa, Switch/Delta

262 RALEIGH MANOR COUNTRY HOUSE HOTEL

HIGHLY COMMENDED

Wheddon Cross, Dunster, Somerset TA24 7BB Tel (01643) 841484

Raleigh Manor is a fine Victorian country house, totally secluded with beautiful far-reaching views set amidst the Exmoor National Park. Offering tea and home-made cakes on arrival, delicious freshly-prepared home-cooked dinners, fine wines and log fires, a relaxing atmosphere has been created and a warm welcome awaits. Ideally situated for exploring the moorland, wooded valleys and coastline of Exmoor. Close to Dunster, Dunkery Beacon and many National Trust properties. A no smoking house.

Bed & Breakfast per night: single room from £27.00–£31.00; double room from £54.00–£62.00
Dinner, Bed & Breakfast per person, per night:
£43.50–£47.50
Evening meal 1930 (last orders 2030)

Bedrooms: 1 single, 3 double, 2 twin
Bathrooms: 6 en-suite
Parking for 10
Open: March–November
Cards accepted: Mastercard, Visa, Switch/Delta

263 PORLOCK VALE HOUSE

HIGHLY COMMENDED

Porlock Weir, Somerset TA24 8NY Tel (01643) 862338 Fax (01643) 863338 E-mail info@porlockvale.co.uk

Formerly a hunting lodge, now a magnificent Edwardian country house hotel in a wonderful situation. Set in twenty five acres of grounds which sweep down to the sea, Porlock Vale House nestles at the foot of the ancient wooded fringe where Exmoor meets the coast. A friendly, unpretentious hotel where you can enjoy good food and fine wines served in a relaxed, informal atmosphere, with beautiful, uninterrupted views across Porlock Bay. Whether you enjoy the great outdoors, or sitting by a log fire, Porlock Vale is the perfect place for a short break at any time of the year.

Bed & Breakfast per night: single occupancy from £45.00–£65.00; double room from £70.00–£90.00
Dinner, Bed & Breakfast per person, per night:
£56.00–£72.00 (2 sharing)
Lunch available: 1200–1400

Bedrooms: 10 double, 5 twin
Bathrooms: 15 en-suite, 2 public
Parking for 20
Cards accepted: Mastercard, Visa, Amex, Switch/Delta

At-a-glance symbols are explained on the flap inside the back cover

264 CHANNEL HOUSE HOTEL

 HIGHLY COMMENDED

Church Path, Off Northfield Road, Minehead, Somerset TA24 5QG Tel (01643) 703229 Fax (01643) 708925 E-mail channel.house@virgin.net

An elegant Edwardian country house perfectly located for exploring the beauty of Exmoor and situated on the lower slopes of Minehead's picturesque North Hill where it nestles in two acres of award-winning gardens. The high standards of cuisine and accommodation will best suit those seeking superior quality and comfort. If you would like to experience smiling service in the tranquil elegance of this lovely hotel, we will be delighted to send you our brochure and sample menu.

Bed & Breakfast per night: single occupancy £70.00; double room £110.00
Dinner, Bed & Breakfast per person, per night: £51.00–£65.00 (2 sharing)
Evening meal 1900 (last orders 2030)

Bedrooms: 2 double, 5 twin, 1 triple
Bathrooms: 8 en-suite   Parking for 10
Open: March–November and Christmas
Cards accepted: Mastercard, Visa, Diners, Amex, Switch/Delta

265 DOLLONS HOUSE

 HIGHLY COMMENDED

10 Church Street, Dunster, Somerset TA24 6SH Tel (01643) 821880 Fax (01643) 822016

A 16th-century listed building, Dollons is a delightul house in the centre of the village with castle views and a small walled garden. Years ago Dollons was the village pharmacy and also supplied marmalade to the Houses of Parliament. The shop now sells good local crafts. All the rooms are en-suite, well furnished and decorated with their own theme. There is a well-appointed guests' sitting room with access to the verandah and garden. Totally non-smoking.

Bed & Breakfast per night: single occupancy from £35.00–£40.00; double room from £50.00–£55.00

Bedrooms: 2 double, 1 twin
Bathrooms: 3 en-suite
Cards accepted: Mastercard, Visa

266 COMBE HOUSE HOTEL

 HIGHLY COMMENDED

Holford, Bridgwater, Somerset TA5 1RZ Tel (01278) 741382 Fax (01278) 741322 E-mail enquiries@combehouse.co.uk

In the heart of the Quantock Hills (renowned as an area of outstanding natural beauty) lies this 17th-century house of great character. Once a tannery, this cottage-style hotel offers absolute peace and quiet in beautiful surroundings. Inside the beamed building, with its charming collection of pictures, pottery and period furniture, the visitor will find the relaxed atmosphere and friendly service ideal to enjoy Combe House, its AA Rosette restaurant, the Quantocks and the many attractions in the area.

Bed & Breakfast per night: single room from £28.00–£38.00; double room from £56.00–£87.00
Dinner, Bed & Breakfast per person, per night: £46.75–£62.25
Evening meal 1930 (last orders 2030)

Bedrooms: 4 single, 5 double, 7 twin
Bathrooms: 16 en-suite, 1 public
Parking for 20
Cards accepted: Mastercard, Visa, Amex, Switch/Delta

267 BLACKMORE FARM

HIGHLY COMMENDED

Cannington, Bridgwater, Somerset TA5 2NE Tel (01278) 653442 Fax (01278) 653427 E-mail dyerfarm@aol.com

A rare Grade I Listed 14th-century manor house retaining many period features including oak beams, stone archways, log fires and its own private chapel. A traditional farmhouse breakfast is served in the Great Hall. All the bedrooms are en-suite, one with a four-poster bed. You can be assured of a warm welcome to this family home situated in a quiet, rural location, with views of the Quantock Hills. An ideal base for touring Bath, Somerset and Exmoor. Facilities for disabled guests. CATEGORY 2

Bed & Breakfast per night: single occupancy from £25.00–£35.00; double room from £40.00–£50.00

Bedrooms: 3 double, 1 triple
Bathrooms: 4 en-suite
Parking for 6
Cards accepted: Mastercard, Visa, Amex

West Country Cheeses

THE WEST COUNTRY is ideal cattle-rearing country: its climate is mild and damp, its grass lush, and much of its landscape too hilly and higgledy-piggledy to make good arable farmland. At one time almost every small region had its own variety of cheese, and though many have disappeared, the region has preserved some of its most popular old varieties and has developed many new ones, too.

Somerset is the home of the acknowledged 'king of cheeses', the great and versatile Cheddar. Sixty percent of all cheese produced in creameries throughout England and Wales is Cheddar. First recorded in the early 16th century, it got its name because visitors to the famous Cheddar Gorge bought the flavoursome hard cheese there. Today visitors to the Cheddar Rural Village (tel: 01934 742810) may watch cheesemaking displays, while not far away, Chewton Cheese Dairy, near Wells (open to the public, tel: 01761 241666) continues to make Cheddar to traditional methods.

Cheddar's nearest rival, also a full-flavoured hard cheese, is double Gloucester, originally made from the rich milk of the Gloucester black cattle. A 'single' variety, known as the 'haymaking cheese' was made from early-season milk, and was matured quickly, resulting in a light colour. The larger 'double' Gloucesters were allowed to mature longer and were consequently darker. Both are made at Old Ley Court near Birdwood, Gloucestershire (tel: 01452 421188), where cheese-making demonstrations can be seen on certain days.

At one time, Dorset blue vinney, a hard blue-veined cheese, was made on numerous farms throughout Dorset. Though it went out of production in the 1980s, it is again produced near Sherborne (not open to the public, but the cheese is readily available in local shops). Cornish yarg, by contrast, is a recent innovation, a crumbly white cheese with a black covering of nettle leaves, first produced in the 1980s by the Gray family – yarg is Gray backwards – at Lynher Valley Dairy near Liskeard (open in summer: tel: 01579 362244).

Another new development is the creation in the West Country of French-type soft cheeses, with Somerset brie and Somerset camembert now widely available. The range of West Country cheeses is wide, and although little can beat a slice of tasty traditional farmhouse Cheddar, look out for some more unusual varieties: brendon blue, vulscombe, cloisters, tala, wedmore, little rydings, hazlewood, Devon oke, blackdown, capricorn and the irresistible stinking bishop.

Chewton Cheese Dairy

268 WEMBDON FARM

Hollow Lane, Wembdon, Bridgwater, Somerset TA5 2BD Tel (01278) 453097 or (0402) 272755 Fax (01278) 445856 E-mail mary.rowe@btinternet.com

Enjoy a refreshing change and a memorable stay at our homely Georgian farmhouse. Our working farm is situated near the Quantock Hills, an area of outstanding natural beauty. Conveniently central for all that Somerset has to offer. Elegant and romantic bedrooms – 2 double en-suite, 1 twin with private bathroom. Guests have their own lounge and dining room. Relax in our pretty garden. Off-road parking. Quietly tucked away, yet easy to find – a place for all seasons.

Bed & Breakfast per night: single occupancy from £22.00–£25.00; double room from £40.00–£44.00

Bedrooms: 2 double, 1 twin
Bathrooms: 2 en-suite, 1 private
Parking for 4
Open: February–November

269 WALNUT TREE HOTEL

 HIGHLY COMMENDED

North Petherton, Bridgwater, Somerset TA6 6QA Tel (01278) 662255 Fax (01278) 663946 E-mail sales.walnuttree@btinternet.com

It is rare to find a delightful hotel with such easy access to the M5 as the Walnut Tree. This former 18th-century coaching inn has been tastefully designed with the accent on comfort. All bedrooms are individually designed with every facility for today's travellers. Good food is served in the pleasing surroundings of the Sedgemoor Restaurant, whilst with its four meeting rooms, cosy bar and friendly staff, the Walnut Tree is a popular venue for honeymooners, travellers and those seeking a relaxing break.

Bed & Breakfast per night: single room from £40.00–£58.00; double room from £56.00–£76.00
Dinner, Bed & Breakfast per person, per night: £50.00
Lunch available: 1200–1400
Evening meal 1900 (last orders 2200)

Bedrooms: 2 single, 22 double, 8 twin
Bathrooms: 32 en-suite
Parking for 74
Cards accepted: Mastercard, Visa, Diners, Amex, Switch/Delta

270 ALLERFORD FARM

⬛⬛⬛ DE LUXE

Norton Fitzwarren, Taunton, Somerset TA4 1AL Tel (01823) 461210 Fax (01823) 461210

Set in two hundred acres and central to Exmoor and Blackdown and Brendon Hills. Every room has been decorated with the same care, flair and attention to detail, resulting in a house which combines comfort with style. The oak staircase leads to three spacious, entrancing bedrooms which are adorned with carefully chosen fabrics and fine furniture. Breakfast is served in the elegant dining room. Dinner available by arrangement. Allerford Farm has one of the UK's top dairy herds.

Bed & Breakfast per night: single occupancy from £30.00–£40.00; double room from £50.00–£60.00
Dinner, Bed & Breakfast per person, per night: £40.00–£55.00

Bedrooms: 2 double
Bathrooms: 1 en-suite, 2 private
Parking for 6

271 HORNHILL

 HIGHLY COMMENDED

Exeter Hill, Tiverton, Devon EX16 4PL Tel (01884) 253352 Fax (01884) 253352

Overlooking the beautiful Exe valley, Hornhill is the perfect place to stay and relax. In our 200-year-old home we offer peaceful country bedrooms with en-suite and private bathrooms. One has a Victorian four-poster bed, and another, on the ground floor, is suitable for the 'not so able'. The comfortable, sunny sitting room has lots of books and heating for chilly evenings. We are ideally placed for exploring Devon. Large garden and ample parking.

Bed & Breakfast per night: single occupancy from £20.00–£25.00; double room from £40.00–£42.00

Bedrooms: 2 double, 1 twin
Bathrooms: 1 en-suite, 2 private
Parking for 4

272 WEIR MILL FARM

 HIGHLY COMMENDED

Jaycroft, Willand, Cullompton, Devon EX15 2RE Tel (01884) 820803 Fax (01884) 820973

Luxurious rooms, beautiful views and peaceful surroundings make Weir Mill something very special in the beautiful Culm Valley. Only three miles from Junction 27 of the M5, giving easy access to coasts, moors and National Trust properties. There is one en-suite family room, one en-suite double room and one double room with a private bathroom. Heating, TV and tea/coffee-making facilities. Large garden. Ample parking. Dinners by arrangement. Open all year.

Bed & Breakfast per night: single occupancy £20.00; double room £36.00
Dinner, Bed & Breakfast per person, per night: £28.00
Evening meal 1830 (last bookings 0900)

Bedrooms: 2 double, 1 family room
Bathrooms: 2 en-suite, 1 private
Parking for 5

273 UPTON

 HIGHLY COMMENDED

Cullompton, Devon EX15 1RA Tel (01884) 33097 Fax (01884) 33097

Beautiful 17th-century country house, charmingly furnished with a wealth of beams and inglenook fireplaces, in a tranquil parkland setting with superb views. All bedrooms are spacious and tastefully decorated, with en-suite bath or shower room, hot drink facilities, television and hairdryer. Wonderful inns and restaurants within two miles. Ideally placed for exploring Dartmoor, Exmoor, the north and south Devon coasts and many National Trust properties. Corse fishing lake in picturesque setting, with free fishing for guests. All within one and a half miles of M5, junction 28. Free brochure on request.

Bed & Breakfast per night: single occupancy from £22.00–£25.00; double room from £40.00–£50.00

Bedrooms: 2 double, 1 twin
Bathrooms: 3 en-suite
Parking for 6

At-a-glance symbols are explained on the flap inside the back cover

274 THOMAS LUNY HOUSE

 DE LUXE

Teign Street, Teignmouth, Devon TQ14 8EG   Tel (01626) 772976

Thomas Luny House – built by the marine artist Thomas Luny around 1800 – is tucked away in a conservation area. It is now the home of Alison and John Allan and their young family. The house, which is surrounded by a secluded garden, is furnished tastefully with antiques and has four themed en-suite rooms, two with views to the river. Drive under an archway (beware: the entrance is narrow) and enjoy a warm welcome.

Bed & Breakfast per night: single occupancy from £30.00–£35.00; double room from £50.00–£70.00

Bedrooms: 2 double, 2 twin
Bathrooms: 4 en-suite
Parking for 6
Open: February–December

275 BARN HAYES COUNTRY HOTEL

HIGHLY COMMENDED

Brim Hill, Maidencombe, Torquay, Devon TQ1 4TR   Tel (01803) 327980 Fax (01803) 327980

Warm, friendly and comfortable hotel, with a swimming pool, in beautiful gardens which overlook both countryside and sea, set in a lovely walking area of outstanding natural beauty. Your total relaxation is guaranteed in our lovely hotel, with genuine hospitality and excellent home cooking, Delia Smith-style, using fresh local produce. We are ideally placed as a touring base to discover the diverse delights that Devon has to offer, whatever the season. Children and dogs are welcome too. A brochure will be sent with pleasure.

Bed & Breakfast per night: single occupancy from £28.00–£30.00; double room from £56.00–£60.00
Dinner, Bed & Breakfast per person, per night: £42.00–£44.00
Lunch available: 1230–1400

Evening meal 1830 (last orders 1900)
Bedrooms: 4 double, 2 twin, 2 triple, 2 family rooms
Bathrooms: 10 en-suite
Parking for 16   Open: February–December
Cards accepted: Mastercard, Visa

276 SUITE DREAMS HOTEL

HIGHLY COMMENDED

Steep Hill, Maidencombe, Torquay, Devon TQ1 4TS   Tel (01803) 313900 Fax (01803) 313841

Set in the tranquil heart of the West Country with spectacular, panoramic valley and sea views, we are able to guarantee our guests a relaxing stay in peaceful surroundings. The hotel itself is spaciously fitted to the highest standard, whilst all the rooms offer a wide range of facilities including colour television, hospitality tray, fridge and en-suite bathroom. This special combination of style and comfort allows us to ensure that we offer an excellent service.

Bed & Breakfast per night: single occupancy from £29.50–£43.00; double room from £39.00–£66.00

Bedrooms: 9 double, 3 twin
Bathrooms: 12 en-suite
Parking for 12
Cards accepted: Mastercard, Amex

277 BLUE HAZE HOTEL

≋ ≋ ≋ HIGHLY COMMENDED

Seaway Lane, Torquay, Devon TQ2 6PS Tel (01803) 607186 or (01803) 606205 Fax (01803) 607186

A small friendly hotel set in lovely grounds in a quiet country lane leading down to the sea. Spacious quality en-suite bedrooms which are sparkling clean, pleasantly decorated, well appointed and all non-smoking. You are welcome to book bed and breakfast only, or you may wish to enjoy our traditional home cooking which is served straight from the oven and made from fresh local produce wherever possible. Parking is no problem in our large car park. Truly 'Somewhere Special'.

Bed & Breakfast per night: double room from £58.00–£62.00
Dinner, Bed & Breakfast per person, per night: £43.00–£45.00
Evening meal 1900

Bedrooms: 4 double, 2 twin, 2 triple, 1 family room
Bathrooms: 9 en-suite
Parking for 15
Open: April–October
Cards accepted: Mastercard, Visa, Amex

278 OSBORNE HOTEL & LANGTRY'S RESTAURANT

≋ ≋ ≋ HIGHLY COMMENDED

Hesketh Crescent, Meadfoot Beach, Torquay, Devon TQ1 2LL Tel (01803) 213311 Fax (01803) 296788

This 29-bedroomed hotel, centrepiece of an elegant Regency crescent, overlooks the seclusion of Meadfoot Beach. The hotel offers the friendly ambience of a country home complemented by superior standards of comfort, five acres of gardens, indoor/outdoor pools, tennis court, gym, sauna, solarium, snooker room and putting green. Langtry's guide-acclaimed restaurant offers superlative food every evening and is one of the foremost restaurants on the English Riviera. The all-day Brasserie serves an international selection of food and drinks.

Bed & Breakfast per night: single room from £40.00–£70.00; double room from £70.00–£120.00
Dinner, Bed & Breakfast per person, per night: £50.00–£80.00
Evening meal 1900 (last orders 2145)

Bedrooms: 1 single, 26 double, 2 family rooms
Bathrooms: 29 en-suite
Parking for 100
Cards accepted: Mastercard, Visa, Amex, Switch/Delta

279 ROYAL CASTLE HOTEL

≋ ≋ ≋ HIGHLY COMMENDED

11 The Quay, Dartmouth, Devon TQ6 9PS Tel (01803) 833033 Fax (01803) 835445

An unusual 17th-century coaching hostelry in the heart of the historic port of Dartmouth – an unrivalled location ideal for short breaks at any time of year. Twenty five luxuriously appointed en-suite bedrooms are individually decorated and furnished, some with four-poster or brass beds and jacuzzis. The elegant restaurant on the first floor overlooks the estuary and specialises in select regional produce and locally-caught seafood. Two bars serve delicious food, traditional ales and a good choice of wines. We look forward to welcoming you.

Bed & Breakfast per night: single room from £41.95–£58.55; double room from £84.00–£130.00
Dinner, Bed & Breakfast per person, per night: £53.00–£76.00 (min 2 nights)
Lunch available: 1130–1500

Evening meal 1845 (last orders 2200)
Bedrooms: 4 single, 10 double, 8 twin, 3 triple
Bathrooms: 25 en-suite
Parking for 10
Cards accepted: Mastercard, Visa, Amex, Switch/Delta

280 FORD HOUSE

 HIGHLY COMMENDED

44 Victoria Road, Dartmouth, Devon TQ6 9DX Tel (01803) 834047

Situated within walking distance from Dartmouth's historic quay and town centre, Ford House has a friendly, lived-in atmosphere with three attractively decorated and fully equipped en-suite rooms. Breakfast is served until noon around a large mahogany dining table, with smoked haddock, kippers, scrambled egg with smoked salmon, freshly squeezed orange juice, bacon and eggs. Special mid-week dinner, bed & breakfast packages have been arranged with the famous Carved Angel restaurant.

Bed & Breakfast per night: double room from
£45.00–£75.00
Dinner, Bed & Breakfast per person, per night:
£52.50–£70.00
Evening meal 1900 (last orders 2100)

Bedrooms: 3 double, 1 twin
Bathrooms: 3 en-suite, 2 private
Parking for 5
Open: April–October
Cards accepted: Mastercard, Visa, Amex

281 THE CAPTAINS HOUSE

 HIGHLY COMMENDED

18 Clarence Street, Dartmouth, Devon TQ6 9NW Tel (01803) 832133

A charming small Grade II Listed house built c1730 and containing the original staircase and Adam-style fire surroundings. It is conveniently situated in a quiet street just off the River Dart, and a three minute walk from the harbour and historic town centre. Each bedroom is individually furnished and decorated but with every modern facility. Full English breakfast with a choice, served with home-made breads and preserves, can be taken either downstairs or upstairs.

Bed & Breakfast per night: single occupancy £35.00;
double room £55.00

Bedrooms: 3 double, 1 twin
Bathrooms: 4 en-suite
Open: March–October and Christmas

282 CAMPBELLS

 HIGHLY COMMENDED

5 Mount Boone, Dartmouth, Devon TQ6 9PB Tel (01803) 833438 Fax (01803) 833438

Most people immediately warm to the relaxed and friendly atmosphere of our home. We previously owned a small award-winning hotel in Scotland. Both bedrooms have this panoramic view, and yet we're only a few minutes' walk from the centre of Dartmouth. Take tea on the terrace, leave your car in the drive and try one of the many excellent restaurants in Dartmouth. At breakfast, enjoy home-made bread and fruit from our garden.

Bed & Breakfast per night: double room from
£50.00–£60.00
Dinner, Bed & Breakfast per person, per night:
£35.00–£55.00
Evening meal by prior arrangement

Bedrooms: 2 double
Bathrooms: 2 en-suite
Parking for 4

283 HOTEL RIVIERA

DE LUXE

The Esplanade, Sidmouth, Devon EX10 8AY Tel (01395) 515201 Fax (01395) 577775 E-mail enquiries@hotelriviera.co.uk

Splendidly positioned at the centre of Sidmouth's esplanade, overlooking Lyme Bay. With its mild climate and the beach just on the doorstep, the setting echoes the south of France and is the choice for the discerning visitor. Behind the hotel's fine Regency façade lies an alluring blend of old-fashioned service and present-day comforts. Glorious sea views can be enjoyed from the recently redesigned en-suite bedrooms, which are fully appointed and have many thoughtful extras. In the elegant bay-view dining room guests are offered a fine choice of dishes from extensive menus, prepared by French and Swiss-trained chefs, with local seafood being a particular speciality. www.hotelriviera.co.uk

Bed & Breakfast per night: single room from £70.00–£95.00; double room from £120.00–£170.00
Dinner, Bed & Breakfast per person, per night: £70.00–£105.00
Lunch available: 1230–1400

Evening meal 1900 (last orders 2100)
Bedrooms: 7 single, 6 double, 14 twin
Bathrooms: 27 en-suite, 1 public
Parking for 26
Cards accepted: Mastercard, Visa, Diners, Amex

284 SWALLOWS EAVES HOTEL

HIGHLY COMMENDED

Colyford, Colyton, Devon EX13 6QJ Tel (01297) 553184 Fax (01297) 553574

Enjoy the beauty and treasures of Devon and Dorset from this attractive wisteria-clad small hotel. In a village setting with spacious gardens and glorious views towards the heritage coast, between Lyme Regis and Sidmouth. An abundance of walks, gardens and National Trust properties nearby. Only eight delightful en-suite rooms and wonderful home-cooked meals. Ground floor room available, easy parking. No children, no dogs, no smoking rooms. Complimentary use of nearby private swimming club, heated indoor pool (88°F) and outdoor pool, sauna, solarium.

Bed & Breakfast per night: single room from £39.00–£49.00; double room from £58.00–£84.00
Dinner, Bed & Breakfast per person, per night: £50.00–£60.00
Evening meal 1900 (last orders 2000)

Bedrooms: 1 single, 3 double, 4 twin
Bathrooms: 8 en-suite
Parking for 10
Open: February–November
Cards accepted: Visa, Amex, Switch/Delta

285 THE DOWER HOUSE HOTEL

HIGHLY COMMENDED

Rousdon, Lyme Regis, Dorset DT7 3RB Tel (01297) 21047 Fax (01297) 24748

Welcome to a world of tranquil charm! The Dower House, created in true country house hotel tradition, stands in its own lawned, wooded grounds ensuring safe easy parking. Rooms are en-suite and we also have an indoor heated swimming pool and sauna, central heating, colour television, radio, telephone, beverage tray, hairdryers, open fires, fine cuisine plus old fashioned courteous service. Enjoy the many nearby local walks, bracing coastal footpath walks, and golf. Special Winter and Spring breaks.

Bed & Breakfast per night: single room from £40.00–£50.00; double room from £60.00–£80.00
Dinner, Bed & Breakfast per person, per night: £45.00–£58.50
Lunch available: 1200–1400

Evening meal 1900 (last orders 2100)
Bedrooms: 1 single, 3 double, 2 twin, 3 triple
Bathrooms: 9 en-suite, 1 public
Parking for 48 Open: February–November and Christmas
Cards accepted: Mastercard, Amex, Switch/Delta

At-a-glance symbols are explained on the flap inside the back cover

286 THATCH LODGE HOTEL

≋≋≋ HIGHLY COMMENDED

The Street, Charmouth, near Lyme Regis, Dorset DT6 6PQ Tel (01297) 560407 Fax (01297) 560407

'Picture postcard' 14th-century thatched hotel, originally a monks' retreat for nearby Forde Abbey. Four-poster and half-tester bedrooms with many thoughtful extras. Antiques, grapes cascading from a two hundred year-old vine, and beautiful walled gardens make this an ideal retreat. Situated in an area of outstanding natural beauty, just three minutes' walk from the world-famous fossil beach. Discover the coastal location chosen for 'Emma', 'Restoration' and BBC's 'Harbour Lights'. We offer tranquillity, discerning quality and superb chef-inspired, 2 Rosette cuisine. Non-smoking throughout.

Bed & Breakfast per night: double room from
£60.00–£100.00
Dinner, Bed & Breakfast per person, per night:
£54.00–£74.00
Evening meal 1930

Bedrooms: 6 double, 1 twin
Bathrooms: 6 en-suite, 1 private
Parking for 10
Cards accepted: Mastercard, Visa, Switch/Delta

287 HENSLEIGH HOTEL

≋≋≋ HIGHLY COMMENDED

Lower Sea Lane, Charmouth, Bridport, Dorset DT6 6LW Tel (01297) 560830 Fax (01297) 560830

A family-run hotel with a reputation for friendly service, comfort and hospitality complemented by a relaxing atmosphere which has made it a favourite with visitors to Charmouth. Situated just three hundred metres from the beach, in an area of outstanding beauty, with spectacular cliff walks and fossil hunting, we have ample car parking within the grounds.

Bed & Breakfast per night: single room from
£25.00–£27.00; double room from £50.00–£54.00
Evening meal 1830 (last orders 1930)

Bedrooms: 2 single, 4 double, 4 twin, 1 triple
Bathrooms: 11 en-suite
Parking for 15
Open: March–October
Cards accepted: Mastercard, Visa, Amex, Switch/Delta

288 ROUNDHAM HOUSE HOTEL

≋≋≋ HIGHLY COMMENDED

Roundham Gardens, West Bay Road, Bridport, Dorset DT6 4BD Tel (01308) 422753 Fax (01308) 421500

Owned and personally managed by Daphne and Jeremy Thomas, Roundham House is situated in an enviable position within an acre of feature gardens, with westerly views over the Dorset countryside and Lyme Bay. Built of local stone in 1903, the hotel offers every modern amenity for the discerning guest and is renowned for its excellent food, wine and hospitality. The table d'hôte and à la carte menus offer a wide choice, including vegetarian options, and feature local produce and fresh vegetables from the kitchen garden. The hotel is an ideal base for walking, touring or just relaxing in an area of outstanding beauty.

Bed & Breakfast per night: single room from
£30.00–£40.00; double room from £55.00–£75.00
Dinner, Bed & Breakfast per person, per night:
£45.00–£55.00

Evening meal 1900 (last orders 2030)
Bedrooms: 1 single, 3 double, 2 twin, 2 family rooms
Bathrooms: 7 en-suite, 1 private
Parking for 12   Open: March–December
Cards accepted: Mastercard, Visa

289 BRITMEAD HOUSE

 HIGHLY COMMENDED

West Bay Road, Bridport, Dorset DT6 4EG Tel (01308) 422941 Fax (01308) 422516

An elegant and spacious, recently refurbished detached house. Situated between Bridport and West Bay harbour with its beaches, Chesil Beach and the Dorset Coastal Path. An ideal base from which to discover Dorset. The spacious south-west facing dining room and lounge overlook an attractive garden and open countryside beyond. Well-appointed bedrooms, all with many thoughtful extras. Delicious meals, table d'hôte dinner. Quite simply everything, where possible, is tailored to suit your needs.

Bed & Breakfast per night: single occupancy from £26.00–£37.00; double room from £42.00–£60.00
Dinner, Bed & Breakfast per person, per night: £40.00–£51.00
Evening meal 1900 (last bookings 1700)

Bedrooms: 4 double, 3 twin
Bathrooms: 6 en-suite, 2 private
Parking for 8
Cards accepted: Mastercard, Visa, Diners, Amex

290 BAY LODGE

HIGHLY COMMENDED

27 Greenhill, Weymouth, Dorset DT4 7SW Tel (01305) 782419 Fax (01305) 782828 E-mail barbara@baylodge.co.uk

Bay Lodge is set in a tranquil position in its own grounds at the centre of Weymouth Bay and enjoys extensive sea views towards the harbour and surrounding cliffs. The luxurious bedrooms, some of which are on the ground floor, are furnished to accentuate their own unique features with king-size beds, jacuzzi bathrooms and open log fires. We have an elegant dining room where our chef prides himself on serving fresh local produce. The lounges have deep, comfortable armchairs and, together with the dining room, have open log/coal fires. Private car park. Three-day bargain breaks from £99 per person. www.baylodge.co.uk

Bed & Breakfast per night: single room from £29.50–£45.00; double room from £52.00–£62.00
Dinner, Bed & Breakfast per person, per night: £39.50–£47.00
Lunch available: 1200–1345

Evening meal 1830 (last orders 1900)
Bedrooms: 1 single, 5 double, 4 twin, 2 triple
Bathrooms: 12 en-suite   Parking for 18
Cards accepted: Mastercard, Visa, Diners, Amex, Switch/Delta

291 THE OLD RECTORY

HIGHLY COMMENDED

Winterbourne Steepleton, Dorchester, Dorset DT2 9LG Tel (01305) 889468 Fax (01305) 889737 E-mail trees@eurobell.co.uk.

Genuine 1850 Victorian rectory situated in a quiet hamlet, surrounded by breathtaking countryside. Close to historic Dorchester and Weymouth's sandy beaches. We specialise in providing a quiet comfortable night's sleep followed by a copious English, vegetarian or continental breakfast, with fresh organic home produce. The Crystal Dining Room is available for celebration dinners and cordon bleu cuisine (minimum 6 people). Enjoy our superbly appointed lounge, croquet lawn and putting green. Local pub within walking distance. www.homepage.eurobell.co.uk/trees/welcome.html

Bed & Breakfast per night: single occupancy from £27.50–£30.00; double room from £40.00–£80.00

Bedrooms: 4 double/twin
Bathrooms: 3 en-suite, 1 private
Parking for 10

292 YALBURY COTTAGE HOTEL AND RESTAURANT

 HIGHLY COMMENDED

Lower Bockhampton, Dorchester, Dorset DT2 8PZ Tel (01305) 262382 Fax (01305) 266412

Surrounded by green fields and woodland and 200 yards from the River Frome, peaceful Yalbury Cottage is the ideal place to 'relax and unwind'. This friendly, 17th-century, family-run, thatched hotel is in a quiet hamlet at the heart of Thomas Hardy's Wessex, one mile from his birthplace. The oak beams and inglenook fireplaces in our pretty, no-smoking restaurant complement head chef Russell Brown's excellent, award-winning food. This is prepared from top quality Dorset produce and is accompanied by a varied international wine list. AA Rosette / Egon Ronay Recommended.

Bed & Breakfast per night: single occupancy £49.00; double room £74.00
Dinner, Bed & Breakfast per person, per night: £48.00–£68.00 (min 2 nights)
Evening meal 1900 (last orders 2100)

Bedrooms: 6 double, 1 twin, 1 family room (6 are non-smoking)
Bathrooms: 8 en-suite
Parking for 19 Open: February–December
Cards accepted: Mastercard, Visa, Switch/Delta

Cerne Abbas Giant

EVEN WITHOUT ITS MOST FAMOUS landmark, Cerne Abbas in Dorset has many attractions. The town grew up around a Benedictine abbey founded in 987, and although only a few ancient remains of the abbey still stand, many of the prettiest houses date from the abbey's 500-year domination of the community. Later, the town flourished as a small market centre, but its decline in the 19th century meant that it never grew large or industrialised, and today it ranks as one of the prettiest villages in Dorset, complete with duckpond, village stocks, a holy well in the churchyard and a superb 14th-century tithe barn.

But what makes Cerne Abbas uniquely memorable is the enormous and extraordinary figure cut into the chalky hillside near by. Brandishing a knobbly club, the Cerne giant strides across the turf, arms outstretched, his naked form leaving little to the imagination. His origins and identity are obscure. Strangely, given that the abbey was a centre of literacy, there is no written record of the figure before 1754, but the current opinion is that the giant is most likely to be a representation of the Roman god Hercules, carved during the first few centuries AD.

Only two other similarly ancient hill-carvings exist in Britain – the White Horse of Uffington, Oxfordshire, and the Long Man of Wilmington, East Sussex. These were probably not the only ones; perhaps a whole panoply of colossal figures and beasts once marched across the English downland, only to be slowly smothered in vegetation and lost forever. The giant has survived through regular and rigorous 'scourings',

usually at seven-year intervals, a practice which was presumably, and rather surprisingly, condoned by the Benedictines despite the giant's obviously pagan nature and indecent nakedness. Today the National Trust is responsible for maintenance.

For obvious reasons the Cerne giant has always been regarded as something of a fertility symbol. It is thought that the village's annual spring revelries were held on a site near by, and to this day it is claimed that merely sitting on the giant's impressive 30ft (9 metre) member is a certain cure for infertility. This is not to be encouraged, however, because of the risk of eroding the carving's most prominent feature! Perhaps the best view of the Cerne giant is to be had from a viewpoint at the junction where Duck Street meets the A352 Sherborne–Dorchester road.

293 THE BELFRY COUNTRY HOTEL

 **HIGHLY COMMENDED**

Yarcombe, near Honiton, Devon EX14 9BD Tel (01404) 861234 Fax (01404) 861579

This small luxury hotel is tastefully converted from the Victorian village school. Each en-suite room is individually furnished, comprehensively equipped, and has lovely countryside views. The cosy candle-lit AA Rosette restaurant with log fire serves Jackie's scrumptious home cooking, using all fresh local produce. Ideally located for walking the countryside and coast, visiting the many National Trust properties, gardens and places of scenic beauty nearby, and a convenient stop-over en-route for Cornwall. Phone Jackie or Tony Rees for a hotel information package and brochure. www.westcountry_hotels.co.uk/belfry

Bed & Breakfast per night: single occupancy from £39.00–£44.00; double room from £59.00–£68.00
Dinner, Bed & Breakfast per person, per night: £39.00–£46.00 (min 2 nights)
Evening meal 1900 (last orders 2100)

Bedrooms: 3 double, 2 twin, 1 triple
Bathrooms: 6 en-suite
Parking for 10
Cards accepted: Mastercard, Visa, Amex, Switch/Delta

294 LEA HILL HOTEL

HIGHLY COMMENDED

Membury, Axminster, Devon EX13 7AQ Tel (01404) 881881 or (01404) 881388

14th-century hotel set in eight acres of grounds overlooking a secluded valley in peaceful Devon countryside, only ten miles from the coast. Mellow stone, oak beams and inglenook fireplaces enhance the relaxed, informal and friendly atmosphere. The beamed restaurant offers superb cuisine which is freshly prepared using local produce such as Lyme Bay seafood and Devonshire lamb and game. Lea Hill is ideally situated for touring the West Country, walking, bird-watching, golfing or simply relaxing away from it all.

Bed & Breakfast per night: single occupancy from £36.00; double room from £72.00
Dinner, Bed & Breakfast per person, per night: £55.00–£68.00
Lunch available: 1200–1400

Evening meal 1900 (last orders 2030)
Bedrooms: 7 double, 4 twin
Bathrooms: 11 en-suite
Parking for 50
Cards accepted: Mastercard, Visa, Amex, Switch/Delta

295 HORNSBURY MILL

HIGHLY COMMENDED

Eleighwater, Chard, Somerset TA20 3AQ Tel (01460) 63317 Fax (01460) 63317

A working watermill set in a five-acre beauty spot with character en-suite bedrooms and a locally renowned restaurant and bar open to non-residents. Attractions include the lake with many breeds of duck, the curious and bygones museum and speciality cream teas. Hornsbury Mill is open all year and is conveniently situated on the borders of Dorset, Devon and Somerset between Chard and Ilminster. Please contact the owners, Keith and Sarah Jane Lewin, for brochure and further details.

Bed & Breakfast per night: single occupancy max £59.50; double room max £75.00
Lunch available: 1200–1400
Evening meal 1900 (last orders 2100)

Bedrooms: 3 double, 1 twin, 1 triple
Bathrooms: 5 en-suite
Parking for 80
Cards accepted: Mastercard, Visa, Diners, Amex, Switch/Delta

296 THE PHEASANT

🌊🌊🌊🌊 **HIGHLY COMMENDED**

Seavington St Mary, Ilminster, Somerset TA19 0QH   Tel (01460) 240502 Fax (01460) 242388

The Pheasant Hotel is a beautifully converted 17th-century farmhouse with a wealth of olde-world charm nestling in the peaceful little village of Seavington St Mary, deep in the heart of Somerset. With its two sumptuous suites and six individually-designed and tastefully appointed en-suite bedrooms, the hotel provides the highest standards of luxury and comfort complemented by its cosy, welcoming bar with huge open inglenooks and beautiful oak-beamed restaurant.

Bed & Breakfast per night: single occupancy from £72.50–£105.00; double room from £95.00–£125.00
Evening meal 1930 (last orders 2130)

Bedrooms: 6 double, 2 twin
Bathrooms: 8 en-suite
Parking for 30
Cards accepted: Mastercard, Visa, Diners, Amex, Switch/Delta

297 GLENCOT HOUSE

🌊🌊🌊🌊 **HIGHLY COMMENDED**

Glencot Lane, Wookey Hole, Somerset BA5 1BH   Tel (01749) 677160 Fax (01749) 670210

Idyllically set in eighteen acres of gardens and parkland with river frontage, this elegantly furnished Victorian mansion offers high-class accommodation, excellent cuisine and friendly service. Facilities abound, with a small indoor pool, sauna, snooker, table-tennis, private fishing and more.

Bed & Breakfast per night: single room from £62.00–£75.00; double room from £86.00–£100.00
Dinner, Bed & Breakfast per person, per night: £64.00–£71.50 (min 2 nights)
Evening meal 1830 (last orders 2030)

Bedrooms: 3 single, 8 double, 2 twin
Bathrooms: 13 en-suite
Parking for 25
Cards accepted: Mastercard, Visa, Amex, Switch/Delta

298 BERYL

🌊🌊🌊 **HIGHLY COMMENDED**

Beryl, Wells, Somerset BA5 3JP   Tel (01749) 678738 Fax (01749) 670508

'Beryl' – a precious gem in a perfect setting. Small 19th-century Gothic mansion, set in peaceful gardens, one mile from the centre of Wells. Well placed for touring the area. Offers comfortable, well-equipped bedrooms and relaxed use of the beautifully furnished reception rooms. Dinner is served with elegant style using fresh produce from the vegetable garden and local supplies. Children and pets are welcome. Outdoor heated pool, June-September. Open all year, except Christmas.

Bed & Breakfast per night: single occupancy from £50.00–£65.00; double room from £65.00–£85.00
Dinner, Bed & Breakfast per person, per night: £52.50–£62.50
Evening meal 2000

Bedrooms: 3 double, 4 twin
Bathrooms: 7 en-suite
Parking for 14
Cards accepted: Mastercard, Visa

299 BOWLISH HOUSE

 HIGHLY COMMENDED

Coombe Lane, Shepton Mallet, Somerset BA4 5JD Tel (01749) 342022 Fax (01749) 342022

An elegant Georgian restaurant with rooms, wonderfully counterbalanced by the relaxed atmosphere. The award-winning restaurant and wine list are famous for their range and eclectic mix of modern classics and local produce. Shepton Mallet is a market town on the south-west slopes of the Mendip Hills, just ten minutes from the cathedral city of Wells. It is an ideal centre for exploring nearby Bath, Stourhead, Longleat, Glastonbury and Cheddar.

Bed & Breakfast per night: single occupancy from £48.00; double room from £58.00
Dinner, Bed & Breakfast per person, per night: from £55.00
Lunch available: first Sunday of each month, 1330–1400

Evening meal 1900 (last orders 2130)
Bedrooms: 2 double, 1 twin
Bathrooms: 3 en-suite
Parking for 10
Cards accepted: Mastercard, Visa, Amex, Switch/Delta

300 SWALLOW ROYAL HOTEL

 HIGHLY COMMENDED

College Green, Bristol BS1 5TA Tel (0117) 9255100 or (0117) 9255200 Fax (0117) 9251515

On College Green, next to the Cathedral, this elegant Victorian hotel has been fully restored and has reclaimed its rightful place as one of Bristol's finest hotels. 226 bedrooms and 16 suites equipped with private bathroom, individually-controlled air conditioning, satellite television, direct dial telephone with three extensions, tea and coffee-making facilities, mini-bar, hairdryer and trouser press. Full valet service is available. Cocktail bar and 'Queen Vic' pub. Roman-styled Swallow Leisure Club with heated indoor swimming pool, spa bath, sauna, steam room, fitness room, solarium.
CATEGORY 3

Bed & Breakfast per night: single room from £140.00–£150.00; double room from £160.00–£200.00
Dinner, Bed & Breakfast per person, per night: £75.00–£87.50 (min 2 nights, 2 sharing)
Evening meal 1900 (last orders 2215)

Bedrooms: 16 single, 104 double, 108 twin, 14 triple
Bathrooms: 242 en-suite
Parking for 200
Cards accepted: Diners, Amex

301 APSLEY HOUSE HOTEL

 HIGHLY COMMENDED

141 Newbridge Hill, Bath BA1 3PT Tel (01225) 336966 Fax (01225) 425462 E-mail apsleyhouse@easynet.co.uk

David and Annie Lanz warmly welcome guests into their elegant Georgian house. Beautifully proportioned reception rooms overlook the pretty garden. Fine antiques and oil paintings create a gracious but relaxed atmosphere. En-suite bedrooms are all individually decorated and furnished, offering TVs, direct dial telephones, and tea/coffee-making facilities. Breakfast is a delight, with full English breakfast and house specialities. Local information available. Just over one mile west of the city centre. Private car park. Licensed bar. www.gratton.co.uk/apsley

Bed & Breakfast per night: single occupancy from £50.00–£65.00; double room from £60.00–£100.00
Evening meal 1930 (last orders 2100)

Bedrooms: 6 double, 2 twin, 1 triple
Bathrooms: 9 en-suite
Parking for 10
Cards accepted: Mastercard, Visa, Amex, Switch/Delta

302 HOLLY LODGE

 DE LUXE

8 Upper Oldfield Park, Bath BA2 3JZ Tel (01225) 424042 or (01255) 339187 Fax (01225) 481138

This charming Victorian town house commands panoramic views of the city and is delightfully furnished with individually-designed bedrooms, some with four-posters, and superb bathrooms. Elegant and stylish, it is owned and operated with meticulous attention to detail by George Hall. Superb breakfasts are enjoyed in the appealing breakfast room with yellow and green decor. Furnished with antiques, this immaculate establishment makes a pleasant base for touring Bath and the Cotswolds.
www.scoot.co.uk/holly_lodge/

Bed & Breakfast per night: single room from £48.00–£55.00; double room from £75.00–£89.00

Bedrooms: 1 single, 4 double, 2 twin
Bathrooms: 7 en-suite
Parking for 8
Cards accepted: Mastercard, Visa, Diners, Amex, Switch/Delta

---

303 BLOOMFIELD HOUSE

 HIGHLY COMMENDED

146 Bloomfield Road, Bath BA2 2AS Tel (01225) 420105 Fax (01225) 481958

An elegant Georgian country house in a tranquil setting with glorious views over the city and with ample parking. French crystal chandeliers feature strongly and breakfast is served against a candlelit and open fire background. Half-tester and four-poster rooms, including the lavish principal bedroom of the Mayor and Mayoress of Bath (1902/03), are romatically presented. An easy ten minute walk to the city, and ideally situated for Somerset, Wessex and the south. www.bloomfield-house.co.uk

Bed & Breakfast per night: single room from £45.00–£55.00; double room from £70.00–£95.00

Bedrooms: 1 single, 6 double, 1 twin
Bathrooms: 5 en-suite, 3 private
Parking for 10
Cards accepted: Mastercard, Visa, Switch/Delta

---

304 SIENA HOTEL

 HIGHLY COMMENDED

24/25 Pulteney Road, Bath BA2 4EZ Tel (01225) 425495 Fax (01225) 469029 E-mail siena.hotel@dial.pipex.com

The Siena is one of the most attractive small hotels in Bath, situated within a few minutes' level walk from the centre. It is a fine example of early Victorian architecture, and is built within a walled garden, affording exceptional views of the city and the medieval Abbey. The interior combines elegant decoration with superb classical furnishings, creating an atmosphere of warmth and tranquillity. We pride ourselves on our quality accommodation, friendly approach and flexibility of service.

Bed & Breakfast per night: single room from £47.50–£65.00; double room from £65.00–£95.00

Bedrooms: 2 single, 8 double, 2 twin, 3 triple, 2 family rooms
Bathrooms: 17 en-suite
Parking for 16
Cards accepted: Mastercard, Visa, Diners, Amex, Switch/Delta

305 THE BATH TASBURGH HOTEL

🌊🌊🌊 HIGHLY COMMENDED

Warminster Road, Bath BA2 6SH Tel (01225) 425096 Fax (01225) 463842 E-mail reservations@bathtasburgh.co.uk

A beautiful Victorian mansion standing in lovely gardens with spectacular views, providing ideal country comfort in a city setting and convenient for the city centre. All bedrooms are en-suite, tastefully furnished and have many extras to ensure a comfortable, memorable stay. Four-poster and spacious family bedrooms, elegant drawing room and stunning conservatory & terrace. Licensed. Gourmet evening meals. Ample car parking. Friendly, professional service. Adjacent canal towpath provides a scenic walk into the city.

Bed & Breakfast per night: single room from
£48.00–£58.00; double room from £68.00–£90.00
Dinner, Bed & Breakfast per person, per night:
£54.00–£65.00
Evening meal 1930 (last orders 2000)

Bedrooms: 1 single, 7 double, 1 twin, 3 family rooms
Bathrooms: 12 en-suite
Parking for 15
Cards accepted: Mastercard, Visa, Amex, Switch/Delta

306 THE BATH SPA HOTEL

🌊🌊🌊🌊🌊 HIGHLY COMMENDED

Sydney Road, Bath BA2 6JF Tel (01225) 444424 Fax (01225) 444006 E-mail fivestar@bathspa.u-net.com

The award-winning Bath Spa Hotel, a former Georgian mansion, is set in seven acres of lovingly restored gardens just ten minutes' walk from the centre of Bath. The elegance of the city is recreated in a traditionally English style, combining exceptional comfort with attentive personal service and friendly informality. With a choice of restaurants – the cosmopolitan atmosphere of the Vellore, or the distinctive Alfresco in the Colonnade – and for relaxation, the Laurels Health and Leisure Spa. www.bathspahotel.com

Bed & Breakfast per night: single room from
£139.00–£159.00; double room from £169.00–£369.00
Dinner, Bed & Breakfast per person, per night:
£99.00–£239.00
Lunch available: 1200–1400

Evening meal 1800 (last orders 2200)
Bedrooms: 7 single, 45 double, 46 twin
Bathrooms: 98 en-suite   Parking for 156
Cards accepted: Mastercard, Visa, Diners, Amex,
Switch/Delta

307 CORSTON FIELDS FARM

Listed HIGHLY COMMENDED

Corston, Bath BA2 9EZ Tel (01225) 873305 or (0421) 379294 Fax (01225) 873305 E-mail corston.fields@3wa.co.uk

A 17th-century, Grade II listed farmhouse with stone mullion windows and big, wholesome bedrooms. Set in beautiful countryside, yet just a few miles from the romantic Roman city of Bath. Close to Wells and the city of Bristol. Come to shop, walk in the country, go to the theatre or watch Bath rugby – it's all possible from this ideal location. Corston Fields is a working farm: we love it and we hope you will enjoy it too!

Bed & Breakfast per night: single occupancy from
£30.00; double room from £44.00–£50.00

Bedrooms: 3 double, 1 twin
Bathrooms: 1 en-suite, 1 public
Parking for 10

At-a-glance symbols are explained on the flap inside the back cover

308 **COMBE GROVE MANOR HOTEL** AND COUNTRY CLUB  HIGHLY COMMENDED

Brassknocker Hill, Monkton Combe, Bath BA2 7HS Tel (01225) 834644 or (01225) 835533 Fax (01225) 834961

Set in 82 acres of gardens and woodlands with panoramic views, this 18th-century elegant manor house hotel, with its 21st-century sports and leisure amenities, hosts 40 individually-designed bedrooms, from modern de luxe to four-poster suites. There is a choice of two restaurants – the Georgian Restaurant (AA 2 Rosettes) offers superb cuisine and fine dining, while the Manor Vaults has a more relaxed atmosphere.

Bed & Breakfast per night: single occupancy from £100.00–£280.00; double room from £120.00–£300.00
Dinner, Bed & Breakfast per person, per night: £75.00–£160.00 (min 2 nights at weekends)
Lunch available: 1200–1430 (bar snacks all day)

Evening meal 1900 (last orders 2130)
Bedrooms: 27 double, 11 twin, 2 triple
Bathrooms: 40 en-suite   Parking for 200
Cards accepted: Mastercard, Visa, Diners, Amex, Switch/Delta

309 **CRICKLADE HOTEL AND COUNTRY CLUB**  HIGHLY COMMENDED

Common Hill, Swindon, Wiltshire SN6 6HA Tel (01793) 750751 Fax (01793) 751767

This beautiful and dignified house is set in extensive grounds, offering a range of sporting activities including a golf course with an on-site golf professional. The luxurious lounge, warmed by open fires in winter, extends through to a magnificent Victorian conservatory. All the bedrooms are smartly furnished and fully equipped. The first-class restaurant offers a varied and interesting menu with an emphasis on fresh local produce and careful presentation. Regular live entertainment, dinner dances and barbecues.

Bed & Breakfast per night: single room from £84.00–£100.00; double room from £105.00–£120.00
Dinner, Bed & Breakfast per person, per night: £63.00–£75.00 (min 2 nights, 2 sharing)
Lunch available: 1200–1400

Evening meal 1900 (last orders 2200)
Bedrooms: 8 single, 31 double, 6 twin, 1 triple
Bathrooms: 46 en-suite, 4 public
Parking for 100
Cards accepted: Mastercard, Visa, Amex, Switch/Delta

Key to Symbols

For ease of use, the key to symbols appears on the back of the cover flap and can be folded out while consulting individual entries. The symbols which appear at the end of each entry are designed to enable you to see at a glance what's on offer, and whether any particular requirements you have can be met. Most of the symbols are clear, simple icons and few require any further explanation, but the following points may be useful:

ALCOHOLIC DRINKS: Alcoholic drinks are available at all types of accommodation listed in the guide unless the symbol **UL** (unlicensed) appears. However, even in licensed premises there may be some restrictions on the serving of drinks, such as being available to diners only.

SMOKING: Some establishments prefer not to accommodate smokers, and if this is the case it will be indicated by the symbol ⚡. Other establishments may offer facilities for non-smokers such as no-smoking bedrooms and parts of communal rooms set aside for non-smokers. Please check at the time of booking if the non-smoking symbol does not appear.

PETS: The symbol 🐕 is used to show that dogs are not accepted in any circumstances. Some establishments will accept pets, but we advise you to check this at the time of booking and to enquire as to whether any additional charge will be made to accommodate them.

South & South East *England*

Portsmouth

▶ Folly Hill

When Gerald Tyrwhitt-Wilson, 14th Baron Berners, opened his 140ft (43m) folly to his friends in 1935 he displayed the following notice above the entrance: 'Members of the public committing suicide from this tower do so at their own risk'. Berners was an aristocratic eccentric, an accomplished painter, writer and composer, who entertained lavishly. Those who climb his folly (just outside Faringdon) are rewarded by a panoramic view of several counties stretching to the Berkshire Downs and the White Horse of Uffington (tel: 01367 242191).

▶ Castles of the Weald

The Weald is the wooded, fertile area of Kent and East Sussex lying between the North and South Downs. The region's historic prosperity and its proximity to London have ensured an array of impressive buildings, many of them castles. These include the fairy-tale Leeds Castle, near Maidstone, perched on two islands in the River Len, and, equally picturesque, ruined Scotney Castle (near Lamberhurst), the centrepiece of a stunning hillside garden. Hever, Knole, Penshurst (all Kent) and Bodiam (East Sussex) are other magnificent examples.

Ancient and modern

History pervades every pore of south-eastern England. Despite the prosperity and modernity of these bustling counties, there lies a Roman villa, Saxon church, Tudor cottage, Georgian townhouse or Victorian railway station around almost every corner. Sometimes, the juxtaposition of old and modern is striking; at Folkestone, for example, visitors can choose from an exhibition celebrating the engineering triumph of the Channel Tunnel or descend the steep cliffs to the Maritime Gardens in a lift built in 1885 and powered by water pressure. On other occasions, you will be hard-pushed to realise that you are still in the late 20th century. Stroll through Chiddingstone, near Tonbridge (and not that far from the M25) and you leave the modern world behind. The houses are half-timbered, many dating from the Elizabethan and Jacobean periods, but the feel is of an idyllic, timeless age. Or hire a rowing boat at Odiham and explore the Basingstoke Canal. Trees shade the calm, quiet backwaters, the only sounds the gentle splash of oar and rustle of leaves.

An Englishman's home...

The region specialises in gorgeous villages. Some, such as Chiddingstone, are celebrated, others less so. Into this latter category fall the following. Wherwell (near Andover) is a shrine to the thatcher's art that also enjoys a magnificent setting on the banks of the Test. Across the Solent on the Isle of Wight lies sleepy Shorwell, sheltering in a wooded valley beneath the closely grazed downs. In West Sussex, just three miles from Petworth – itself a delightful small town dominated by the majestic Petworth House – is Fittleworth, a straggling settlement that offers another group of picturesque stone or brick cottages at each twist of the woodland lanes. Flint is the prevailing material at Piddinghoe, just inland from Newhaven, where St John's Church has one of only three Norman round towers in Sussex. East Clandon, about four miles east of Guildford, is a compact

community of brick-and-tile houses surrounding two of the staples of village life – the church and the inn. Milton Abbas is all tranquillity now, but two centuries ago Lord Dorchester provoked outrage from its residents when he razed it to the ground – in order to improve his view – and rebuilt it in a wooded valley a mile away. The replacement, six miles (10km) from Blandford Forum, is made up of regularly spaced, thatched cob cottages, so later generations have benefited from the landlord's ruthlessness. Pusey, down a 'no through road' east of Faringdon, is another appealing estate village, this one guarded by venerable beech and horse-chestnut trees. Swanbourne, in the Vale of Aylesbury, has been attractively rebuilt since an 18th-century fire. Smithfield Close, however, survived the conflagration, and is a handsome group of whitewashed, 16th-century thatched cottages.

Choose a clear day...

The above villages make excellent centres to walk from, and most offer a pub for well-earned refreshment. If you believe all good walks should include some fine vistas, then try one of these four: Ditchling Beacon, a couple of miles north of Brighton, is arguably the best viewpoint in the South Downs. The stretch of the South Downs Way, leading west to the pair of windmills familiarly known as Jack and Jill, makes a rousing afternoon's hike. At the western end of the Way, and competing for the accolade of best viewpoint, is Butser Hill, highest point in the South Downs. The fort at Ditchling dates from the Iron Age; here Stone Age men and women flourished. The Queen Elizabeth Country Park – of which the hill is a part – provides leaflets for waymarked trails. Towards the northern end of the Chilterns – and at the end of the Ridgeway, a track used before the Romans arrived – is Ivinghoe Beacon; views extend to London, out over the Bedfordshire plain and south-west to the Chilterns, home to glorious, underrated countryside. The final vantage point is beside the Cerne Abbas giant, that uncompromising symbol of male fertility etched on the Dorset downs. And Dorset comprises the entire view: untaxing, unspoilt and ineffably beautiful.

Walk this way

Many of the long-distance paths in south-eastern England follow the ridges of chalk downland, leading you past countless such viewpoints. With other rights-of-way criss-crossing these paths at regular intervals, it is a simple matter to devise shorter, circular walks. The 100-mile (161km) South Downs Way follows ancient tracks and old droveways in East and West Sussex and Hampshire. The North Downs Way, running 153 miles (246km) from Farnham to Canterbury, explores scenery of such splendour – sometimes wooded, sometimes grassland – it is hard to believe that for much of its length London is less than 30 miles (48km) away. The Ridgeway keeps to the tops of the Chilterns for its eastern stretch, descending to cross the Thames at Goring Gap, where it meets the Thames Path. A recent creation, this trail follows England's most famous river from source in Gloucestershire to the Thames Barrier at Woolwich, availing itself of 126 footbridges en route. The region has other longer paths that seek out the remoter corners of the countryside. Hampshire has the Hangers Way (17 miles (27km) through beechwoods between Alton and Petersfield) and The Solent Way (60 miles (96.5km) from Milford-on-Sea to Emsworth), and others besides. The Isle of Wight Coast Path circles the island in 69 glorious miles (111km).

How the other half lived

Those who enjoy that most intriguing of pastimes – having a good look round somebody else's house – can indulge themselves to their heart's content and without conscience. The choice is so wide that it can be a matter of choosing your scale, which starts at the very, very grand, such as Windsor Castle, Blenheim Palace, Osborne House, Waddesdon Manor and Goodwood House, and includes some comparatively modest houses. Closer to this end of the spectrum is the 14th-century Alfriston Clergy House, the first property purchased by the National Trust

▶ Pallant House

Built in 1712, Chichester's Pallant House (tel: 01243 774557) is an interesting setting for a modern-art collection. Each room, lovingly restored, reflects a period in the house's history and contains furniture, porcelain, textiles, even pictures from the period. But amongst all this grace and refinement, the raw colour and abstract form of the modern paintings on its walls strike an exciting note of contrast. Picasso, Sutherland, Nash, Piper, Moore and others are represented, most donated by Walter Hussey, Dean of Chichester Cathedral from 1955 to 1977.

▶ Brownsea Island

A trip from busy Poole Quay across Poole Harbour to Brownsea Island is a voyage to a different world. Though once the site of a (failed) china clay industry, for most of its history Brownsea has remained isolated, even neglected. For some crucial years, between 1925 and 1961, the island was cut off from all outside influences by a reclusive owner. Now owned by the National Trust, it has remained unspoilt and undeveloped, a haven for red squirrels and the secretive sika deer. (Tel: 01202 707744.)

► **The Bloomsbury Group in Sussex**

Inside the 12th-century church at Berwick, near Eastbourne, a surprise awaits. Its walls are covered with astonishing modern murals, created in the 1940s by Duncan Grant, Vanessa Bell and her son, Quentin Bell. The three, who lived at nearby Charleston Farmhouse, were members of an eccentric affiliation of writers and artists, the Bloomsbury Group. Charleston became a gathering place for the group and was vividly decorated in accordance with their artistic ideals. Virginia Woolf lived not far away, at Monk's House (NT), Rodmell. (Tel: 01323 411400.)

► **Mad Jack Fuller**

Nineteenth-century patron of the arts, bon viveur and local squire, 'Mad' Jack Fuller lives on thanks to his abiding passion for follies. His grave in the churchyard at Brightling, East Sussex, is a 25ft (7.5m)-high stone pyramid. Despite his wish to be interred at table, dressed for dinner and resplendent in top hat, he rests – in conventional repose – in the ground below. Nearby edifices include the 'Tower', a gothic-looking building with a battlemented top, and the Sugar Loaf, reputedly built in a night to enable Fuller to 'win' a bet that the spire of Dallington church was visible from his windows.

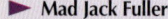

for just £10 in 1896. Lamb House, in the near-perfect town of Rye, was the home of the novelist Henry James; the 18th-century building is surrounded by an attractive garden. Other, less celebrated historic homes include: Rousham House, a 17th-century Oxfordshire mansion now full of portraits but once used as a Royalist garrison in the Civil War; Haseley Manor, a rambling house of several periods happily rescued from dereliction in the 1970s; Dorney Court, Eton, a 15th-century brick-and-timber house in the same ownership for almost 500 years; Chettle House, near Blandford Forum, an appealingly idiosyncratic, small Baroque country-house that feels – and is – very much a family home.

The coast is clear

England's southern coast has long been a playground for London, ensuring that most resorts offer a bewildering array of amenities. Margate, Eastbourne, Brighton, Bournemouth and Shanklin, amongst others, have long welcomed huge numbers of visitors. Escaping the hurly-burly can be more of a challenge on this stretch of coastline, but try Minnis Bay, on Kent's north-facing shore, west of Margate; Pevensey Bay, between Bexhill and Eastbourne; the sand dunes west of Littlehampton; Bracklesham Bay, near Selsey Bill; Lepe, a small stretch of sand and shingle facing the Isle of Wight; Luccombe Bay, ten minutes' walk from Shanklin; and Shipstal Point, giving on to a quiet stretch of Poole Harbour.

The artistic year

The cultural capital for livelier, broad-minded souls is Brighton, with its avant-garde galleries, arthouse cinemas and never-ending supply of clubs. The Brighton Festival – held each May, and one of England's largest celebrations of the arts – includes events such as conducted walks through Victorian cemeteries, dance, theatre, jazz and classical music. Not far away, Arundel puts out the bunting in August and invites you to open-air theatre in the castle grounds, jazz, fireworks and classical concerts. The centrepiece of the Canterbury Festival is the cathedral – used for operatic performances – while other venues host drama, dance and much more, each October. Similarly, Chichester Festival's focal point is its Norman cathedral, though the refurbished ballroom of Goodwood House has also been called into service in the past; the July festivities add exhibitions of contemporary sculpture and lectures to the round of concerts and plays. Guildford holds two festivals each year: music in March and books in October. Henley makes the most of its superb Thames-side setting when theatre takes to the streets and bridges of the town each July. At the end of September and in early October, it is the turn of Windsor to stage musical and literary events, some held in the Castle itself. And for four weeks in February and March, the dance world turns its attention to north-western Surrey, the home of the Woking Dance Umbrella.

A break with history

Most of the festival towns and cities are ideal for short breaks. There are a hundred other attractive bases suitable for a weekend away, of which these form an eclectic sample. Winchester, the nation's capital until the reign of Canute, claims the longest cathedral in Europe and an impressive collection of Georgian townhouses, too. Midhurst, a busy market town beneath the South Downs, seems only to have glorious 16th-, 17th- and 18th-century buildings, some of the best in the appealingly named Knockhundred Row. Tunbridge Wells's prosperity arrived with the discovery of its chalybeate springs in 1606, and it has barely looked back since. Modern-day visitors can approach the springs along The Pantiles, a shopping area of sublime beauty. Arrive in early June and a cricket festival at one of the country's most picturesque grounds is in full swing. Hungerford, on the banks of the Kennet and close to more superb walking country, is a paradise for antique hunters. Thame, on the river of the same name, is equally popular with those not averse to spending an evening in a fine old coaching inn; the town boasts four that date from the 15th century.

Contact numbers

Eurotunnel Exhibition Centre, Folkestone (tel: 01303 270111)
Basingstoke Canal (tel: 01252 370073)
The South Downs Way (tel: 01903 741234)
The North Downs Way (tel: 01622 696185)
The Ridgeway (tel: 01865 810224)
The Thames Path (tel: 01865 810224)
Hangers Way (tel: 01705 59504)
Solent Way (tel: 0345 626424)
Isle of Wight Coast Path, Shanklin Tourist Information Centre (tel: 01983 862942)
Windsor Castle (tel: 01753 831118)
Blenheim Palace, Woodstock (tel: 01993 811091)
Osborne House, Isle of Wight (tel: 01983 200022)
Waddesdon Manor, Aylesbury (tel: 01296 651211)
Goodwood House, Chichester (tel: 01243 774107)
Alfriston Clergy House (tel: 01323 870001)
Lamb House, Rye (tel: 01892 890651)
Rousham House, Bicester (tel: 01869 347110)
Haseley Manor, Arreton, Isle of Wight (tel: 01983 865420)
Dorney Court, Eton (tel: 01628 604638)
Brighton Festival (tel: 01273 292950)
Arundel Festival (tel: 01903 883690)
Canterbury Festival (tel: 01227 452853)
Chichester Festival (tel: 01243 785718)
Guildford International Music Festival (tel: 01483 259167)
Guildford Book Festival (tel: 01483444334)
Henley Festival (tel: 01491 410482)
Windsor Festival (tel: 01753 623400)
Woking Dance Umbrella (tel: 0181 741 8354)

► Sandham Memorial Chapel

This chapel, at Burghclere in Berkshire, was built to house an extraordinary series of wall-paintings by the artist Stanley Spencer. He served in the army medical corps during World War I, and the murals record the everyday humdrum soldiers' duties: floor-cleaning, bed-making, laundry-sorting and a whole variety of other chores, but painted with exaggerated proportions and stylised perspective so that the scenes take on an aura of significance and horror. The chapel is dominated by a great Resurrection on the wall behind the altar (tel: 01635 278394).

Sir Stanley Spencer CBE RA

► The Gardens of Stowe

Perhaps the finest statement of the art of the 18th-century garden lives on at Stowe, near Buckingham. John Vanbrugh, William Kent, James Gibbs and 'Capability' Brown – the most talented gardeners and architects of their day – went to great lengths to create a landscape remodelled and replanted to look as natural as possible, in order to match the aesthetic blueprint of ancient Rome. To this end, grottoes were built, lakes dug, columns erected and monuments – thirty, all told – sited with consummate care. The National Trust is now restoring these majestic gardens.

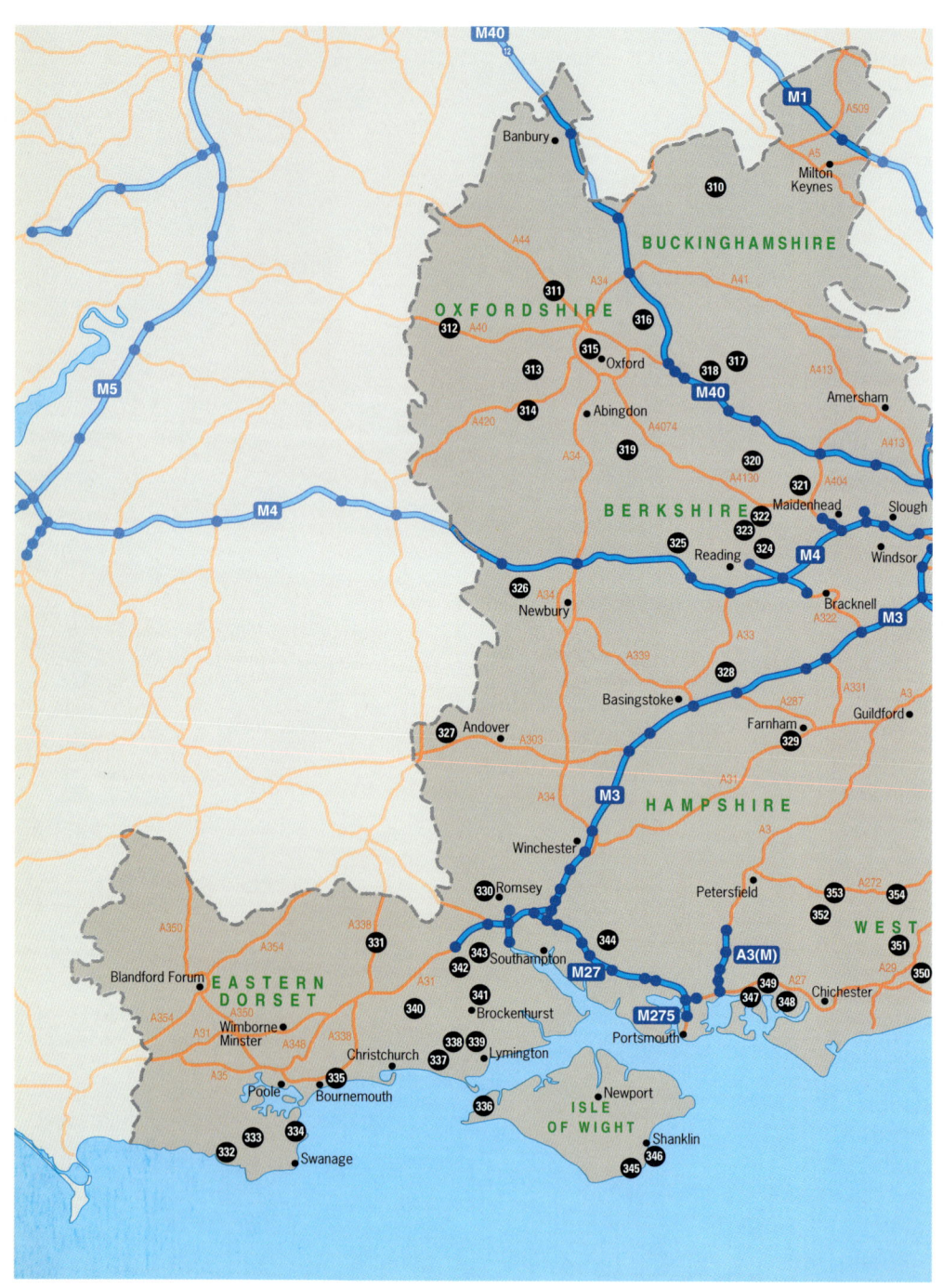

Colin Earl Cartography

310 VILLIERS HOTEL

 HIGHLY COMMENDED

3 Castle Street, Buckingham, Buckinghamshire MK18 1BS Tel (01280) 822444 Fax (01280) 822113

When we created Villiers Hotel from the old Swan and Castle Inn, we set out to build a very special and individual hotel. Drawing upon the character of the four-hundred-year-old hostelry we included the highest quality facilities and services, with comfort a priority for you, our guest – a home away from home. Henry's, our elegant air-conditioned restaurant, has just been awarded its second AA Rosette for exceptional cuisine.

Bed & Breakfast per night: single room from £69.00–£85.00; double room from £89.00–£135.00
Lunch available: 1230–1400
Evening meal 1900 (last orders 2230)

Bedrooms: 3 single, 18 double, 17 twin
Bathrooms: 38 en-suite
Parking for 36
Cards accepted: Mastercard, Visa, Diners, Amex, Switch/Delta

311 SHIPTON GLEBE

DE LUXE

Woodstock, Oxford, Oxfordshire OX20 1QQ Tel (01993) 812688 Fax (01993) 813142 E-mail phase@patrol.i-way.co.uk

This lovely country house, set in nine acres of garden/parkland, is situated on the edge of historic Woodstock, close to Blenheim Palace. All the rooms are en-suite, luxuriously furnished, and incorporate sitting room facilities. Breakfasts are served in the conservatory overlooking the gardens, and evening meals – available by prior arrangement – can be served in the elegant dining room. You will find that Shipton Glebe is the perfect setting for that special and relaxing few days away.

Bed & Breakfast per night: single occupancy from £50.00–£70.00; double room from £70.00–£85.00
Dinner, Bed & Breakfast per person, per night: £75.00–£80.00
Evening meal 1930 (last orders 2030)

Bedrooms: 1 double, 1 twin, 1 family room
Bathrooms: 3 en-suite, 1 public
Cards accepted: Mastercard, Visa, Switch/Delta

312 BURFORD HOUSE HOTEL

HIGHLY COMMENDED

99 High Street, Burford, Oxford, Oxfordshire OX18 4QA Tel (01993) 823151 Fax (01993) 823240

Situated in one of the Cotswold's most historic towns, Burford House is perfectly placed for exploring this lovely area. Run with care by owners Jane and Simon Henty, importance is placed on comfort, a relaxed atmosphere and attention to detail, and the house is cosy and intimate with a wealth of personal touches. Wonderful breakfasts are served and guests can return to traditional afternoon tea in the sitting rooms or delightful courtyard garden. A warm welcome awaits.

Bed & Breakfast per night: single occupancy from £75.00–£110.00; double room from £80.00–£120.00
Lunch available: 1200–1415

Bedrooms: 6 double, 1 twin
Bathrooms: 7 en-suite
Cards accepted: Mastercard, Visa, Amex, Switch/Delta

313 PINKHILL COTTAGE

≋≋ HIGHLY COMMENDED

45 Rack End, Standlake, Witney, Oxfordshire OX8 7SA Tel (01865) 300544

A charming 17th-century thatched cottage in half-acre gardens fronting the River Windrush in a quiet Oxfordshire village, offering exclusive, private bed & breakfast accommodation for two. The old stable has been transformed into a sitting room from which leads a staircase to the hayloft – now an airy double bedroom with en-suite shower room. Many of the original beams are a feature of our cottage. Standlake is ideal for touring Oxford and the Cotswolds.

Bed & Breakfast per night: single occupancy from £30.00–£32.00; double room from £40.00–£44.00

Bedrooms: 1 double
Bathrooms: 1 en-suite
Parking for 1

314 FALLOWFIELDS COUNTRY HOUSE HOTEL

≋≋≋≋ HIGHLY COMMENDED

Kingston Bagpuize with Southmoor, Oxford, Oxfordshire OX13 5BH Tel (01865) 820416 Fax (01865) 821275 E-mail stay@fallowfields.com

The Fallowfields' recipe – take near-organic garden produce, add meticulously chosen meat and fish, mix in a three-hundred-year-old (in parts) manor farmhouse, add interesting company, personal care of the owners, and serve in a candle-lit dining room, preferably by a log fire – leave with your bank manager still talking to you and you have the perfect recipe for a stay on business or pleasure. 'The next step is heaven' said one guest. AA Rosette.

Bed & Breakfast per night: single occupancy from £87.50–£105.00; double room from £110.00–£155.00
Dinner, Bed & Breakfast per person, per night: £82.00–£108.00
Evening meal 2000 (last orders 2100)

Bedrooms: 6 double, 2 twin, 2 triple
Bathrooms: 10 en-suite, 1 public
Parking for 23
Cards accepted: Mastercard, Visa, Amex, Switch/Delta

315 MARLBOROUGH HOUSE HOTEL

Listed HIGHLY COMMENDED

321 Woodstock Road, Oxford, Oxfordshire OX2 7NY Tel (01865) 311321 Fax (01865) 515329 E-mail enquiries@marlbhouse.win-uk.net

Our immaculate, spacious, privately-owned hotel is located in an attractive leafy area of Victorian houses, one and a half miles from the city centre, but with easy access to the town. Bedrooms are equipped with a kitchenette containing fridge, microwave and area for light food preparation, direct dial telephone, television with four Sky channels, together with comfortable chairs, dining table and desk. Restaurants and shops are located within a ten-minute walk from the hotel.
www.oxlink.co.uk/oxford/hotels/marlborough.html

Bed & Breakfast per night: single room £62.50; double room £73.00

Bedrooms: 2 single, 8 double, 4 twin, 2 triple
Bathrooms: 16 en-suite, 1 public
Parking for 6
Cards accepted: Mastercard, Diners, Amex, Switch/Delta

316 STUDLEY PRIORY HOTEL

≈≈≈≈ HIGHLY COMMENDED

Horton cum Studley, Oxford, Oxfordshire OX33 1AZ Tel (01865) 351203 or (01865) 351254 Fax (01865) 351613 E-mail res@studley-priory.co.uk

Timeless seclusion characterises the wooded setting of Studley Priory, whose exterior has scarcely altered since Elizabethan times. Enjoy fine views of the Chilterns and surrounding countryside. Our AA 2 Rosette restaurant offers modern English cooking complemented by our outstanding wine list. A short drive away are the dreaming spires of Oxford and magnificent Blenheim Palace at Woodstock. Public rooms and master bedrooms contain antique furniture. Log fires in public rooms in the winter months.
www.lattargotmls.co.uk

Bed & Breakfast per night: single room from £105.00–£135.00; double room from £140.00–£210.00
Dinner, Bed & Breakfast per person, per night: £90.00–£120.00 (min 2 nights)
Lunch available: 1200–1345

Evening meal 1930 (last orders 2130)
Bedrooms: 3 single, 9 double, 5 twin, 1 suite
Bathrooms: 18 en-suite Parking for 101
Cards accepted: Mastercard, Visa, Diners, Amex, Switch/Delta

317 THE OXFORD BELFRY

≈≈≈≈ HIGHLY COMMENDED

Milton Common, Thame, Oxfordshire OX9 2JW Tel (01844) 279381 Fax (01844) 279624

A privately-owned and extended hotel, situated on the A40 near junctions 7 and 8 of the M40, ten minutes from historic Oxford. The hotel is an ideal location for touring the Thames, the Chilterns, Oxford and the Cotswolds. One hour from London and Birmingham, with Heathrow a 45-minute drive away. Reflections Leisure Club includes a heated indoor pool, sauna, sunbed, mini-gym and relaxation area. Charming oak-panelled restaurant with an AA Rosette for fine food.

Bed & Breakfast per night: single occupancy from £95.00–£105.00; double room from £130.00–£170.00
Dinner, Bed & Breakfast per person, per night: £75.00–£95.00 (min 2 nights, 2 sharing)
Lunch available: 1230–1400

Evening meal 1930 (last orders 2130)
Bedrooms: 70 double, 39 twin, 20 double executive, 2 suites
Bathrooms: 131 en-suite Parking for 200
Cards accepted: Mastercard, Visa, Diners, Amex, Switch/Delta

318 THE DAIRY

≈ HIGHLY COMMENDED

Moreton, Thame, Oxfordshire OX9 2HX Tel (01844) 214075 Fax (01844) 214075

This former milking parlour, set in over four acres, provides a beautiful, peaceful and comfortable stay. All bedrooms are bright and airy and include hairdryers, writing tables, fresh flowers, biscuits and comfortable sofas and chairs. There is a large open plan lounge with views of the Chilterns. The property is very convenient for London, either by train (50 minutes from local station), coach or car. Oxford is 20 minutes by car.

Bed & Breakfast per night: single occupancy from £52.00; double room from £75.00

Bedrooms: 2 double
Bathrooms: 2 en-suite
Parking for 6
Cards accepted: Amex

Entries are cross referenced by number to the maps on pages 158–159

319 ROOKS ORCHARD

HIGHLY COMMENDED

Little Wittenham, Abingdon, Oxfordshire OX14 4QY Tel (01865) 407765 Fax (01865) 407765 E-mail jonathan.welfare@which.net

A pretty black and white 17th-century listed house which is full of character, with beams, inglenooks and period furniture. The house, surrounded by large attractive gardens, is next to a nature reserve with public access, and the River Thames runs through the village. Rooks Orchard is within easy reach of Abingdon (5 miles), Wallingford (4 miles), Didcot (4 miles) and Oxford (10 miles). There is always an extremely good breakfast which includes local farm produce and home-made and home-grown fresh food.

Bed & Breakfast per night: single occupancy from £26.00–£30.00; double room from £46.00–£50.00

Bedrooms: 2 double
Bathrooms: 1 en-suite, 1 private
Parking for 6

The landmarks of White Horse Hill

THE LAMBOURN DOWNS of south Oxfordshire, rising up bare and smooth from the Vale of the White Horse, are steeped in ancient history. Around 5000 years ago our ancestors settled here, built their forts, buried their dead and walked their pathways; today the downs are liberally sprinkled with the relics of their existence. Some sites have been excavated, but alongside the scant archaeological evidence, a vein of myth and legend has come down over the centuries to provide explanations for the mysterious landmarks.

Dominating the valley which is named after it, the strange elongated shape of a galloping horse is cut into the chalk near Uffington. The Iron Age tribes who lived in the nearby hillfort are believed to have carved it in about 50BC as a representation of the horse goddess, Epona. Possibly the oldest chalk carving in the country, it is, intriguingly, the only one which faces right. In more recent centuries the white horse became the focus of a seven-yearly tradition: people would climb the hill to 'scour' the accumulated weeds and debris from the horse to the accompaniment of fairground revels.

Just below the horse is a mound known as Dragon's Hill. Whether natural or man-made is unknown, but local legend asserts that this is where St George killed the dragon. The patches of bare chalk on its top and sides, the story goes, were formed by hot streams of dragon's blood, over which the grass can never grow.

Running along the ridge of the downs, just south of the White Horse, is the Ridgeway. This track – used by people of the New Stone Age, the builders of Stonehenge – is one of the oldest roads in Britain. It leads south-west past Wayland's Smithy, a neolithic burial chamber dating from around 2800BC. This remote spot is one of many places throughout Europe (usually either caves or burial mounds) imagined as the home of Wayland, the fearsome Saxon blacksmith-god.

The figure of the smith is also associated, somewhat menacingly, with another curiosity: a strangely-shaped stone beside the road leading south from Kingston Lisle, just east of the White Horse. The 'Blowing Stone', as it is called, was supposedly brought here by a blacksmith living in the nearby cottage who could blow into its many holes to create a gruesome, moaning roar. Another legend grew up that King Alfred summoned his troops to battle by blowing through the stone.

320 THE STONOR ARMS HOTEL

HIGHLY COMMENDED

Stonor, Henley-on-Thames, Oxfordshire RG9 6HE Tel (01491) 638866 Fax (01491) 638863

A privately-owned country hotel and restaurant, the 18th-century Stonor Arms is the perfect retreat, with its award-winning restaurant, elegant accommodation and intimate walled garden. We offer all the charms of a country home away from home in a peaceful, yet accessible, setting. Scenic Henley-on-Thames, the Royal Regatta and the university town of Oxford are a comfortable drive away. The village of Stonor itself offers stunning countryside and excellent walks.

Bed & Breakfast per night: single occupancy £95.00;
double room from £115.00–£140.00
Dinner, Bed & Breakfast per person, per night:
£62.50–£87.50 (min 2 nights)
Lunch available: 1200–1400

Evening meal 1900 (last orders 2130)
Bedrooms: 4 double, 6 twin
Bathrooms: 10 en-suite
Parking for 26
Cards accepted: Mastercard, Visa, Amex, Switch/Delta

321 DANESFIELD HOUSE

HIGHLY COMMENDED

Medmenham, Marlow-on-Thames, Buckinghamshire SL7 2EY Tel (01628) 891010 Fax (01628) 890408

Danesfield House offers one of England's finest award-winning country house hotels, ideally set within the Chiltern Hills in an area of outstanding natural beauty, and yet within only one hour of London. Panoramic views of the River Thames from luxurious bedrooms, a beautiful terrace brasserie and the AA 2 Rosette Oak Room restaurant have helped establish Danesfield as a very popular destination.

Bed & Breakfast per night: single room from
£145.00–£155.00; double room from £175.00–£300.00
Lunch available: 1200–1400
Evening meal 1800 (last orders 2200)

Bedrooms: 9 single, 57 double, 18 twin, 3 family rooms
Bathrooms: 87 en-suite
Parking for 130
Cards accepted: Mastercard, Visa, Diners, Amex,
Switch/Delta

322 THE KNOLL

HIGHLY COMMENDED

Crowsley Road, Shiplake, Henley-on-Thames, Oxfordshire RG9 3JT Tel (01189) 402705 Fax (01189) 403789 E-mail milpops2@aol.com

The Knoll provides the perfect accommodation for an idyllic holiday or short stay. Beautifully restored by local craftsmen and fitted out with every modern convenience, you will be able to relax after a day's sightseeing or riverside walk in this private home with extensive landscaped gardens. The Knoll is situated in the quiet village of Shiplake, just two miles from Henley-on-Thames. Only 28 miles from London, you are also within easy driving distance of Windsor and Oxford.

Bed & Breakfast per night: double room from
£50.00–£55.00

Bedrooms: 1 double, 1 twin
Bathrooms: 2 en-suite
Parking for 4

323 HOLMWOOD

HIGHLY COMMENDED

Shiplake Row, Binfield Heath, Henley-on-Thames, Oxfordshire RG9 4DP Tel (0118) 947 8747 Fax (0118) 947 8637

Holmwood is an elegant Georgian country house with a galleried hall, mahogany doors and marble fireplaces. The house is set in three acres of beautiful gardens with extensive views over the Thames valley. The large bedrooms are furnished with antique and period furniture – all have bathrooms en-suite, colour TV and tea/coffee-making facilities. Holmwood is convenient for Windsor, Oxford, London and Heathrow. Nearby are several pubs offering excellent evening meals. CATEGORY 3

Bed & Breakfast per night: single room £35.00; double room £55.00

Bedrooms: 1 single, 2 double, 2 twin
Bathrooms: 5 en-suite
Parking for 8
Cards accepted: Mastercard, Visa, Switch/Delta

324 THE GREAT HOUSE AT SONNING

HIGHLY COMMENDED

Thames Street, Sonning-on-Thames, Reading, Berkshire RG4 6UT Tel (0118) 969 2277 Fax (0118) 944 1296

Situated in the beautiful conservation village of Sonning, parts of The Great House date back to pre-Elizabethan times. With a four-acre estate and positioned on one of the loveliest stretches of the Thames, the hotel offers accommodation in five different areas. The elegant Moorings Restaurant overlooks the gardens and offers a choice of menu at luncheon and dinner. The cosy Ferryman's Bar serves a selection of real ales and is open all day.

Bed & Breakfast per night: single room from £118.00–£138.00; double room from £155.00–£192.50
Dinner, Bed & Breakfast per person, per night: from £64.50 (min 2 nights, Friday–Sunday only)
Lunch available: 1230–1430 (1500 on Sunday)

Evening meal 1900 (last orders 2215)
Bedrooms: 6 single, 25 double, 8 twin, 2 triple
Bathrooms: 41 en-suite   Parking for 100
Cards accepted: Mastercard, Visa, Diners, Amex, Switch/Delta

325 THE COPPER INN HOTEL & RESTAURANT

HIGHLY COMMENDED

Church Road, Pangbourne, Reading, Berkshire RG8 7AR Tel (0118) 984 2244 Fax (0118) 984 5542

Georgian coaching inn, carefully restored in 1995, next to the old parish church and with secluded gardens. This is a good centre for touring the valley of the River Thames and visiting Oxford, Henley and Windsor. The hotel takes pride in its friendly service, comfortable lounges and bedrooms, and its cuisine. Michel Rosso, the new proprietor, comes from the Alpes Maritimes and the cooking, whilst based on the best local produce, owes much to the recipes and flavours of his native Provence.

Bed & Breakfast per night: single room from £60.00–£100.00; double room from £90.00–£115.00
Dinner, Bed & Breakfast per person, per night: from £65.00 (min 2 nights, Friday–Sunday only)
Lunch available: 1200–1430 (last orders)

Evening meal 1900 (last orders 2200)
Bedrooms: 2 single, 14 double, 5 twin, 1 triple
Bathrooms: 22 en-suite   Parking for 20
Cards accepted: Mastercard, Visa, Diners, Amex, Switch/Delta

At-a-glance symbols are explained on the flap inside the back cover

326 HOLT LODGE

Listed HIGHLY COMMENDED

Kintbury, Hungerford, Berkshire RG17 9SX Tel (01488) 668244 Fax (01488) 668244

Holt Lodge is situated near the village of Kintbury in the Kennet valley, between the river and the Hampshire downs. The house is a quiet and secluded Queen Anne farmhouse surrounded by its large mature garden and farm pastures and woodland. The rooms are well furnished in the old fashioned manner and have all the facilities expected of a Highly Commended place to stay.

Bed & Breakfast per night: single room £22.00; double room £44.00
Evening meal 1930 (last orders 2130)

Bedrooms: 1 single, 1 twin, 1 double/triple
Bathrooms: 1 private, 1 public
Parking for 8

Romsey Abbey

Elizabeth Bowtell

IF EVER A BUILDING deserved to be better known, it is Romsey's parish church. It was built as part of a Benedictine nunnery, survived Henry VIII's dissolution of the monasteries because the people of Romsey bought it for £100, and is today one of the most flawless pieces of Norman architecture in Europe. It sits close to the River Test, its squat grey tower visible behind Romsey's market square. Inside is an untampered, uncluttered beauty that stops you in your tracks as you enter: tall round columns, perfectly proportioned rounded arches, superb arcading, zig-zagging, exuberantly carved capitals.

Stand at the west end and notice how, as your eye moves up the Nave toward the main altar, each bay is earlier in style than the last, for building work began at the east end, on the site of an earlier church, in about 1120 and progressed westwards, being completed about 1250. It makes a perfect textbook on Norman architecture. Then walk up the South Aisle to the South Transept to find the simple memorial to Earl Mountbatten, assassinated in 1979. The Mountbatten estate, Broadlands (tel: 01794 505010), is in Romsey. Further up the South Aisle, and in the Retrochoir, are some particularly delightful carved capitals: several scalloped with birds and beasts. The one on the last pillar on the left of the South Aisle, together with its corresponding one in the North Aisle, tells a busy story. At the end of the South Aisle is one of the

abbey's most precious treasures: a little low-relief Saxon white stone crucifix set in the rounded wall behind the altar. There is another, larger, similarly dated to about 1000, outside, on the west wall of the South Transept. Pass the 12th-century wall painting in the Retrochoir, and from the North Aisle look across the Chancel to the three storeys of Norman arches. The arcading above the main arches is unique to Romsey: within each bay (the zig-zagging on the arches is wonderful here) is a pair of smaller arches with a small column in the space above. From the Chancel there is a clear view down the Nave. In the North Transept look for the 16th-century, Italian-style wooden painted reredos. Finally, turn left out of the South Door to see the carving above the Abbess's Doorway and the second Saxon crucifix. And all around the building look up at the corbels, a delightfully lively gallery of faces and creatures.

327 MAY COTTAGE

HIGHLY COMMENDED

Thruxton, Andover, Hampshire SP11 8LZ Tel (01264) 771241 or (0468) 242166 Fax (01264) 771770

May Cottage dates back to 1740 and is situated in the heart of this picturesque tranquil village with a Post Office and old inn. A most comfortable home with en-suite rooms, all having colour television, radio and tea tray. Guests' own sitting/dining room. Just off the A303, an ideal base for visiting ancient cities, stately homes and gardens, yet within easy reach of ports and airports. All home cooking.

Bed & Breakfast per night: single room from
£25.00–£30.00; double room from £45.00–£50.00

Bedrooms: 1 single, 3 twin
Bathrooms: 2 en-suite, 1 private
Parking for 4

328 TYLNEY HALL HOTEL

DE LUXE

Rotherwick, Basingstoke, Hampshire RG27 9AZ Tel (01256) 764881 Fax (01256) 768141 E-mail reservations@tylneyhall.com

Amidst sixty six acres of Hampshire countryside lies Tylney Hall, a privately-owned, Grade II listed country house hotel. The one hundred and ten bedrooms are beautifully decorated and fitted with all modern amenities. The award-winning Oak Room restaurant offers innovative menus for those dining for business or pleasure, complemented by an extensive wine cellar and attentive, yet discreet, service. Twelve individually designed function suites cater for up to one hundred people, whilst extensive and exclusive leisure facilities allow guests to relax in the luxurious surroundings.

Bed & Breakfast per night: single occupancy from
£115.00–£285.00; double room from £145.00–£310.00
Dinner, Bed & Breakfast per person, per night:
£148.00–£338.00 (with table d'hôte dinner)
Lunch available: 1230–1400 (last orders 1330)

Evening meal 1930 (last orders 2130)
Bedrooms: 95 double, 15 twin
Bathrooms: 110 en-suite
Parking for 120
Cards accepted: Mastercard, Diners, Amex, Switch/Delta

329 THE BISHOP'S TABLE HOTEL & RESTAURANT

HIGHLY COMMENDED

27 West Street, Farnham, Surrey GU9 7DR Tel (01252) 710222 Fax (01252) 733494 E-mail bishops.table@btinternet.com

An elegant, award-winning hotel where hospitality is at its best. All bedrooms are individually decorated. The walled garden is a walk into another world. The restaurant is well known and offers an excellent cuisine, including a full vegetarian menu.

Bed & Breakfast per night: single room from £85.00;
double room from £100.00
Dinner, Bed & Breakfast per person, per night: from
£105.00
Lunch available: 1230–1345

Evening meal 1900 (last orders 2145)
Bedrooms: 6 single, 9 double, 2 twin
Bathrooms: 17 en-suite
Cards accepted: Mastercard, Diners, Amex

At-a-glance symbols are explained on the flap inside the back cover

330 HIGHFIELD HOUSE

≋ ≋ ≋ HIGHLY COMMENDED

Newtown Road, Awbridge, Romsey, Hampshire SO51 0GG Tel (01794) 340727 Fax (01794) 341450

Set in an unspoilt rural village in a delightful position with charming gardens. Home cooking a speciality. Close to Mottisfont Abbey (National Trust) and Hillier Arboretum. Twelve miles from Winchester and Salisbury. Fishing, golf and horse-riding can be arranged. On-site parking.

Bed & Breakfast per night: double room from
£50.00–£55.00
Evening meal 1900

Bedrooms: 1 double, 2 twin
Bathrooms: 3 en-suite, 1 public
Parking for 10

331 THE THREE LIONS

≋ ≋ HIGHLY COMMENDED

Stuckton, Fordingbridge, Hampshire SP6 2HF Tel (01425) 652489 Fax (01425) 656144

Built in 1863, The Three Lions nestles on the edge of the New Forest and is personally owned and run by Mike and Jayne Womersley. The rooms are all en-suite, airy and very peaceful, overlooking well-manicured gardens and the forest behind. There is also an open-air whirlpool therapy spa for residents' use. The restaurant is highly rated in all major UK food guides with three AA Rosettes and a 150-bin wine list.

Bed & Breakfast per night: double room from
£65.00–£75.00
Dinner, Bed & Breakfast per person, per night:
£55.00–£60.00 (min 2 nights, continental breakfast)
Lunch available: 1200–1400

Evening meal 1900 (last orders 2100)
Bedrooms: 2 double, 1 twin
Bathrooms: 3 en-suite
Parking for 40
Cards accepted: Mastercard, Visa, Switch/Delta

332 KIMMERIDGE FARMHOUSE

≋ ≋ HIGHLY COMMENDED

Kimmeridge, Wareham, Dorset BH20 5PE Tel (01929) 480990

Enjoy a relaxing holiday in our picturesque farmhouse, with views of Kimmeridge Bay across 700 acres of farmland. Spectacular walks along the coastal paths, or inland across the Purbeck Hills surrounding the ruins of Corfe Castle. Nearby are Lulworth Cove and Castle, Studland Bay, Poole, Bournemouth and a wide choice of excellent places to eat. Spacious and attractively furnished rooms overlooking a peaceful garden. Home-cooked breakfast of your choice. A warm welcome assured.

Bed & Breakfast per night: double room from
£40.00–£42.00

Bedrooms: 2 double, 1 twin
Bathrooms: 3 en-suite
Parking for 3

333 MORTONS HOUSE HOTEL

HIGHLY COMMENDED

East Street, Corfe Castle, Wareham, Dorset BH20 5EE Tel (01929) 480988 Fax (01929) 480820

Mortons House is a 400-year-old Elizabethan manor in this fairytale village, built in the shape of an E to honour Queen Elizabeth I. The hotel offers both the history and charm of a private country house beautifully situated in the heart of the Purbeck Hills with the heritage coast close by. Seventeen character en-suite bedrooms, acclaimed cuisine (AA Rosette), log fire, pretty walled gardens and car parking. Open throughout the year. Special Christmas three-day holiday.

Bed & Breakfast per night: double room from £90.00–£100.00
Dinner, Bed & Breakfast per person, per night: £50.00–£68.00 (min 2 nights, 2 sharing)
Lunch available: 1200–1400

Evening meal 1900 (last orders 2030)
Bedrooms: 13 double, 3 twin, 1 family room
Bathrooms: 17 en-suite
Parking for 35
Cards accepted: Mastercard, Visa, Diners, Amex

334 FAIRFIELDS HOTEL

HIGHLY COMMENDED

Studland Bay, Dorset BH19 3AE Tel (01929) 450224 Fax (01929) 450224

A small family-run hotel situated in a National Trust village, with magnificent views over Studland Bay to the Isle of Wight. A perfect place to relax in all seasons for those who appreciate good food, friendly service and an award-winning wine list. We use the very best of local produce, and herbs and vegetables from our garden. We welcome and cater for the needs of children, as well as discerning adults.

Bed & Breakfast per night: single room from £32.00–£45.00; double room from £64.00–£90.00
Dinner, Bed & Breakfast per person, per night: £45.00–£57.00 (min 2 nights)
Lunch available: 1200–1400

Evening meal 1900 (last orders 1945)
Bedrooms: 2 single, 5 double, 1 triple, 4 family rooms
Bathrooms: 12 en-suite, 1 public
Parking for 16   Open: March–December
Cards accepted: Mastercard, Visa, Switch/Delta

335 NORFOLK ROYALE HOTEL

HIGHLY COMMENDED

Richmond Hill, Bournemouth, Dorset BH2 6EN Tel (01202) 551521 Fax (01202) 299729

This luxuriously restored Edwardian hotel, situated within a minute's walk from theatres, shops, gardens and golden beaches, provides the perfect blend of friendly and efficient service to ensure a relaxing short break. The Orangery Restaurant offers international cuisine and a fine wine list. The individually-designed bedrooms, studios and suites and the dome-covered pool set in the lovely garden make this the perfect location for that special occasion. CATEGORY 3

Bed & Breakfast per night: single room from £95.00–£115.00; double room from £135.00–£175.00
Dinner, Bed & Breakfast per person, per night: £59.50–£75.00 (min 2 nights)
Lunch available: 1200–1400

Evening meal 1900 (last orders 2200)
Bedrooms: 9 single, 46 double, 32 twin, 8 triple
Bathrooms: 95 en-suite   Parking for 88
Cards accepted: Mastercard, Visa, Diners, Amex, Switch/Delta

336 SENTRY MEAD HOTEL

HIGHLY COMMENDED

Madeira Road, Totland Bay, Isle of Wight PO39 0BJ Tel (01983) 753212 Fax (01983) 753212

A tranquil location by the sea, most comfortable and relaxing surroundings, superb food, personal care and attention to guests' needs all add together to make Sentry Mead that 'somewhere special' place. Our imaginative menus, including vegetarian dishes, incorporate the best of English cuisine with European flavours and our very own flair. Sentry Mead's position in the west of the Island makes it an ideal retreat and a perfect base for walking. Well-behaved dogs welcome.

Bed & Breakfast per night: single room from £30.00–£40.00; double room from £60.00–£80.00
Dinner, Bed & Breakfast per person, per night: £45.00–£55.00
Lunch available: 1200–1400

Evening meal 1900 (last orders 2000)
Bedrooms: 2 single, 5 double, 3 twin, 3 triple, 1 family room
Bathrooms: 14 en-suite
Parking for 10
Cards accepted: Mastercard, Visa, Amex, Switch/Delta

337 CHEWTON GLEN HOTEL, HEALTH & COUNTRY CLUB

DE LUXE

Christchurch Road, New Milton, Hampshire BH25 6QS Tel (01425) 275341 Fax (01425) 272310 E-mail reservations@chewtonglen.com

A very warm welcome awaits you here. Great emphasis is placed on service, with the restaurant being renowned for the quality of its food and wines. All bedrooms are individually decorated, and most have a balcony or terrace with a beautiful view. The health club offers a full range of health and fitness facilities, including an indoor pool and gymnasium. Beauty therapy appointments also available. Nine-hole golf course within grounds. www.chewtonglen.com

Dinner, Bed & Breakfast per person, per night: £170.00–£310.00 (min 2 nights at weekends)
Lunch available: 1230–1345
Evening meal 1930 (last orders 2130)

Bedrooms: 53 double
Bathrooms: 53 en-suite
Parking for 125
Cards accepted: Mastercard, Visa, Diners, Amex, Switch/Delta

338 THE NURSE'S COTTAGE

HIGHLY COMMENDED

Station Road, Sway, Lymington, Hampshire SO41 6BA Tel (01590) 683402 Fax (01590) 683402 E-mail nurses.cottage@lineone.net

Nothing equals a visit to this cosy New Forest cottage, for over 50 years home to Sway's successive District Nurses. Lovingly refurbished in recent years, the award-winning guest accommodation offers every possible creature comfort, while chef/proprietor Tony Barnfield's enterprising dinner menu and extensive wine list make this the perfect escape for that very special occasion. Invariably fully booked months ahead, advance reservations are essential. The Garden Room Restaurant is open to non-residents for dinner.

Bed & Breakfast per night: single room from £50.00–£60.00; double room £85.00
Dinner, Bed & Breakfast per person, per night: £45.00–£70.00 (min 2 nights)
Lunch available: by arrangement

Bedrooms: 1 single, 1 double, 1 twin
Bathrooms: 3 en-suite
Parking for 4
Cards accepted: Mastercard, Visa, Amex, Switch/Delta

339 STRING OF HORSES

Mead End Road, Sway, Lymington, Hampshire SO41 6EH Tel (01590) 682631

HIGHLY COMMENDED

A secluded hotel set in two acres of grounds. Experience the luxury of individually-designed bedrooms – several with four-poster beds – each with its own fantasy bathroom and offering every facility. Sample the delights of our intimate, award-winning candlelit restaurant. The perfect setting for newly-weds, second honeymooners and couples. Heated outdoor swimming pool. Excellent location for horse-riding, yachting, golfing and exploring the New Forest. Regrettably, we are unable to accommodate children.

Bed & Breakfast per night: double room from £90.00–£110.00
Dinner, Bed & Breakfast per person, per night: £66.00–£76.00
Lunch available: 1230–1345 (Sunday only)

Evening meal 1900 (last orders 2130)
Bedrooms: 7 double, 1 twin
Bathrooms: 8 en-suite
Parking for 26
Cards accepted: Mastercard, Visa, Amex, Switch/Delta

340 BURBUSH FARM

Pound Lane, Burley, Ringwood, Hampshire BH24 4EF Tel (01425) 403238 Mobile (0411) 381924 Fax (01425) 403238

HIGHLY COMMENDED

A warm and friendly welcome awaits you at Burbush Farm, situated in the heart of the New Forest and nestling in twelve acres of peace and tranquillity. Cosy lounge with log fire in winter months and Aga-cooked breakfasts presented on fine Spode china. Every care and attention is given during your stay in this beautifully presented character farmhouse. Ideal centre for golf, riding (stables and paddocks available), cycling (hire available), sailing and walking. All the bedrooms are extremely comfortable and have en-suite facilities. A short walk to the village, which has restaurants and public houses.

Bed & Breakfast per night: single occupancy £30.00; double room from £44.00–£50.00

Bedrooms: 3 double
Bathrooms: 3 en-suite
Parking for 150

341 WHITLEY RIDGE COUNTRY HOUSE HOTEL

Beaulieu Road, Brockenhurst, Hampshire SO42 7QL Tel (01590) 622354 Fax (01590) 622856

HIGHLY COMMENDED

A charming Georgian country house hotel, formerly a royal hunting lodge, in five acres of New Forest parkland, Whitley Ridge has a very good reputation for its cuisine and friendly service. All en-suite bedrooms have recently been refurbished to a high standard and overlook extensive grounds which include a tennis court. In winter, log fires burn on cooler evenings, and the candlelit dining room (AA 2 Rosettes) creates a special atmosphere. Special midweek inclusive rates available.

Bed & Breakfast per night: single room from £66.00–£70.00; double room from £92.00–£110.00
Dinner, Bed & Breakfast per person, per night: £51.00–£75.00
Lunch available: 1200–1400 (Sunday only)

Evening meal 1900 (last orders 2030)
Bedrooms: 2 single, 9 double, 3 twin
Bathrooms: 14 en-suite   Parking for 28
Cards accepted: Mastercard, Visa, Diners, Amex, Switch/Delta

342 PARKHILL COUNTRY HOUSE HOTEL

HIGHLY COMMENDED

Beaulieu Road, Lyndhurst, Hampshire SO43 7FZ Tel (01703) 282944 Fax (01703) 283268

Graciously Georgian, Parkhill has a romantic setting in a superb elevated position amid beautiful grounds complete with great trees, stone statues, picturesque lake, secluded swimming pool, putting green and croquet lawn. All around is the peace, profusion and sylvan beauty of the New Forest. Delightful bedrooms conform to the highest standard and beautiful public rooms, with roaring log fires throughout the cooler months, open out onto terraces and lawns. The spacious dining room offers a cuisine to delight. www.scoot.co.uk/parkhill_country

Bed & Breakfast per night: single occupancy from £80.00–£160.00; double room from £100.00–£160.00
Dinner, Bed & Breakfast per person, per night: £67.00–£101.00 (min 2 nights)
Lunch available: 1200–1400

Evening meal 1900 (last orders 2130)
Bedrooms: 11 double, 5 twin, 3 triple
Bathrooms: 19 en-suite   Parking for 81
Cards accepted: Mastercard, Visa, Diners, Amex, Switch/Delta

343 WOODLANDS LODGE HOTEL

HIGHLY COMMENDED

Bartley Road, Woodlands, New Forest, Hampshire SO40 7GN Tel (01703) 292257 Fax (01703) 293090 E-mail woodlands_lodge@nortels.ltd.uk

Luxuriously restored Georgian country house hotel. Our gardens have direct access to the New Forest. The peaceful and relaxing setting enables you to enjoy luxury without ostentation and unwind from the stress that is all too common today. The beautiful well-equipped bedrooms are all en-suite with showers and baths, all with whirlpool. Other features include a four-poster, balcony and real flame fires. See the inside front cover for more information. www.nortels.ltd.uk/hotel

Bed & Breakfast per night: single occupancy from £45.00–£79.00; double room from £118.00–£170.00
Dinner, Bed & Breakfast per person, per night: £69.00–£92.25 (2 sharing)
Evening meal 1900 (last orders 2100)

Bedrooms: 16 double, 1 twin
Bathrooms: 17 en-suite
Parking for 40
Cards accepted: Mastercard, Visa, Switch/Delta

344 BOTLEY PARK HOTEL, GOLF & COUNTRY CLUB

HIGHLY COMMENDED

Winchester Road, Boorley Green, Botley, Southampton, Hampshire SO3 2UA Tel (01489) 780888 Fax (01489) 789242

Set in 176 acres of parkland golf course, within easy reach of M3/M27 motorways and 60 minutes from London, Botley Park offers 100 well appointed bedrooms with en-suite facilities. Enjoy our 18-hole golf course, driving range and putting green, squash and tennis courts, large gymnasium, aerobics dance studio, sauna and steam rooms, indoor heated swimming pool and spa pool. We also have a croquet lawn and petanque terrain, snooker room, and beauty salon. A choice of two bars, or dine in our award-winning restaurant. CATEGORY 1

Bed & Breakfast per night: single occupancy from £60.00–£200.00; double room from £60.00–£220.00
Dinner, Bed & Breakfast per person, per night: £50.00–£100.00
Evening meal 1900 (last orders 2145)

Bedrooms: 36 double, 64 twin
Bathrooms: 100 en-suite
Parking for 250
Cards accepted: Mastercard, Visa, Diners, Amex, Switch/Delta

(345) THE ROYAL HOTEL

〰〰〰〰〰 HIGHLY COMMENDED

Belgrave Road, Ventnor, Isle of Wight PO38 1JJ Tel (01983) 852186 Fax (01983) 855395 E-mail royalhotel@zetnet.co.uk

Walk into The Royal and step back to an era of elegance, class and 'Empire': Queen Victoria herself enjoyed the charm of this delightful hotel. Lovingly restored to true Victorian splendour, The Royal has fifty five recently refurbished en-suite bedrooms, immaculate gardens with heated swimming pool and an AA 2 Rosette award-winning restaurant. Imaginative menus are expertly prepared, beautifully presented and changed daily to make evenings at The Royal a very special occasion.

Bed & Breakfast per night: single room from £45.00–£64.00; double room from £90.00–£150.00
Dinner, Bed & Breakfast per person, per night: £65.00–£95.00
Lunch available: 1200–1400

Evening meal 1900 (last orders 2115)
Bedrooms: 5 single, 19 double, 5 twin, 19 double/twin, 7 family rooms   Bathrooms: 55 en-suite   Parking for 55
Cards accepted: Mastercard, Visa, Diners, Amex, Switch/Delta

Isle of Wight Geology

NO PART OF THE Isle of Wight's complex geology is unaffected by the action of the waves. The sea has periodically inundated the land and then retreated, laying down sediments and battering away at them, carving out dramatic cliffs and steep-sided valleys and creating some of the most spectacular coastal scenery in southern England.

The island is bisected by a high chalk ridge running east–west and rising to a height of some 650ft (198m). At its western end this chalk band forms a narrow headland pointing out to sea, shaped by the waves into the spectacular snow-white cliffs of Freshwater Bay and, at its furthest extremity, eroded into a series of jagged, white teeth poking from the sea: the famous Needles (shown below).

The character of the landscape north and south of the band of chalk differs markedly. The soils of the northern half of the island were laid down about 60 million years ago, in sedimentary layers of sand (crushed quartz) and clay. At Alum Bay, just north of the Needles, some of these layers have been exposed by the sea to create an extraordinary phenomenon. Mineral impurities have changed the colour of the usually white quartz, creating an amazing variety of coloured sands: white, black, green, red and yellow.

On the southern side of the island, ancient earth movements have exposed sedimentary layers laid down between 120 and 65 million years ago. Of these, the Wealden group, Wight's oldest rocks, meet the sea in just two places,

one north of Sandown, the other along the south-west coast. They were deposited when dinosaurs roamed the area and now yield some of the richest sources of dinosaur bones in Europe. On the beach at Hanover Point is Pine Raft, the fossilised remains of tree-trunks, some beautifully preserved, with annular growth rings still visible.

The southernmost region of the island is a complex arrangement of soft gault clay sandwiched between harder layers of sandstone. The gault, known as 'blue slipper', creates a highly unstable lubricant layer, causing the hard strata above to collapse periodically in giant landslips. Between Shanklin and Chale, each of the distinctive terraces falling down to the sea represents a different landslip. Known as the Undercliff, this picturesque terrain is the largest area of coastal landslip in north-western Europe.

The Museum of Isle of Wight Geology at Sandown (tel: 01983 404344) records the island's geological history and displays some spectacular fossil remains.

346 CHINE COURT HOTEL

Popham Road, Shanklin, Isle of Wight PO37 6RG   Tel (01983) 862732 Fax (01983) 862732

Welcome to Chine Court. A truly elegant Victorian residence, lavishly furnished and decorated throughout. Standing in large grounds, it commands magnificent sea views from its elevated cliff-top position. Beautifully appointed public rooms include a large luxurious bar lounge, dry lounges and an elegant Victorian dining room offering a sumptuous five course dinner with a full choice of traditional and continental dishes. The hotel offers peace and tranquillity and a high degree of comfort and Victorian grace and charm.

Bed & Breakfast per night: single room from £25.00–£32.00; double room from £50.00–£64.00
Dinner, Bed & Breakfast per person, per night: £35.00–£42.00 (min 2 nights)
Evening meal 1830 (last orders 1915)

Bedrooms: 3 single, 8 double, 6 twin, 5 triple, 4 family rooms
Bathrooms: 25 en-suite, 1 public
Parking for 24
Open: April–October

Fishbourne and Bignor

IN 1960, A WORKMAN digging a trench across empty pasture at Fishbourne, near Chichester, uncovered some ancient building material; the site later revealed the remains of one of the most magnificent Roman palaces anywhere in Britain. It was not the first fortuitous discovery of substantial Roman remains in the Chichester area. In 1811, a farmer ploughing fields near Bignor, just a few miles to the north-east, struck a large stone, actually a water basin from another impressive Roman villa.

Whoever once lived at Fishbourne (tel: 01243 785859) were citizens of ever-increasing wealth and importance. Excavations show the progression of the building from a modest timber construction to a vast, elaborately-decorated palace, fitted with every luxury and convenience of the time. The chief glory of Fishbourne is its mosaics. Room after room is floored with tiny tesserae, or tiles, laid during the 1st and 2nd centuries to create a variety of patterns, some geometric in design and austere in colour, others vivid and elaborate. The finest and most intact of the mosaics represents Cupid riding on a dolphin surrounded by exotic sea-monsters and exuberant designs of urns and tendrils.

Amazingly, only a quarter of the original layout of the palace can be seen; the rest lies beneath a main road and nearby houses.

The villa at Bignor (tel: 01798 869259) was a less ostentatious residence, but between the 3rd and 4th centuries AD it also increased dramatically in size, perhaps to accommodate a growing extended family. Upon completion it was one of the largest villas in the country and stood upon an important site close to the military road, Stane Street. The mosaics, though less numerous than those at Fishbourne, are some of the best in the country. Laid in later centuries than those at Fishbourne, they display an interesting contrast: at Bignor the decoration is elaborate and sophisticated, showing an assured mastery of the mosaic technique. Most memorable perhaps is the lugubrious allegorical figure of winter, well muffled against the cold.

Archaeological evidence has thrown light on the fate of both buildings. Lumps of molten lead and charred timbers indicate that Fishbourne was destroyed by a terrible fire in the late 3rd century and was never rebuilt. By contrast Bignor, it seems, was simply abandoned sometime in the 5th century and left to moulder gently into the ground. Both are now open to the public.

347 MILLSTREAM HOTEL AND RESTAURANT

HIGHLY COMMENDED

Bosham Lane, Bosham, Chichester, West Sussex PO18 8HL Tel (01243) 573234 Fax (01243) 573459

A beautifully appointed country manor house dating from 1701, set in a picturesque quayside village, only four miles west of Chichester. The friendly staff will make you feel very welcome. Bedrooms are all individually furnished, with every modern facility. The Millstream Restaurant is renowned for its superb food and extensive wine list and has been awarded an AA Rosette for food excellence. Enjoy walking on the beautiful shoreline or the rolling South Downs. Fishbourne Roman Villa, Goodwood and Chichester Festival Theatre are all within easy reach.

Bed & Breakfast per night: single room from £69.00–£72.00; double room from £109.00–£115.00 Dinner, Bed & Breakfast per person, per night: £55.00–£75.00 (min 2 nights) Lunch available: 1230–1400

Evening meal 1900 (last orders 2130) Bedrooms: 5 single, 18 double, 9 twin, 1 suite Bathrooms: 33 en-suite Parking for 44 Cards accepted: Mastercard, Visa, Diners, Amex, Switch/Delta

348 HATPINS

HIGHLY COMMENDED

Bosham Lane, Old Bosham, Chichester, West Sussex PO18 8HG Tel (01243) 572644 Fax (01243) 572644

From the moment you walk through the door you know that you are entering a very special home, with the atmosphere normally reserved for an English country house hotel. The owner, Mary Waller, a former designer of hats and wedding dresses, has used her creative talents to build up her emporium into a bed & breakfast delight. Every bedroom has beautiful drapes, pillows and bed coverings, and every cushion has care and attention lavished upon it. However long you stay, Hatpins offers you an experience to savour.

Bed & Breakfast per night: single occupancy from £25.00–£50.00; double room from £50.00–£80.00

Bedrooms: 4 double, 1 twin Bathrooms: 3 en-suite, 1 private Parking for 3

349 THE BROOKFIELD HOTEL

HIGHLY COMMENDED

Havant Road, Emsworth, Hampshire PO10 7LF Tel (01243) 373363 Fax (01243) 376342 E-mail hermit@mcmhil.com

Situated in the fishing village of Emsworth, between historic maritime Portsmouth and the cathedral city of Chichester. Landscaped gardens give a peaceful setting in which to relax and unwind. Friendly, personal service and attention to detail are reflected in the Hermitage Restaurant, with its nationally award-winning wine list and use of fresh produce prepared to order.

Bed & Breakfast per night: single room from £58.00–£65.00; double room from £85.00–£120.00 Dinner, Bed & Breakfast per person, per night: £69.50–£74.95 Lunch available: 1200–1400

Evening meal 1900 (last orders 2130) Bedrooms: 5 single, 25 double, 10 twin Bathrooms: 40 en-suite Parking for 80 Cards accepted: Mastercard, Visa, Diners, Amex, Switch/Delta

At-a-glance symbols are explained on the flap inside the back cover

350 BURPHAM COUNTRY HOUSE HOTEL

HIGHLY COMMENDED

Burpham, Arundel, West Sussex BN18 9RJ Tel (01903) 882160 Fax (01903) 884627

Nestling in a fold of the famous Sussex South Downs, the hotel offers the most perfect location for a 'Stress Remedy Break'! The hamlet of Burpham is totally peaceful and unspoilt and the walks are truly spectacular. The dining room offers a regularly changing menu using only the best ingredients. Swiss-born Marianne Walker and husband George – the resident owners – are justly proud of their AA Rosette award-winning cuisine. The comfort offered here is truly memorable. Please mention this guide when booking. Special breaks available.

Bed & Breakfast per night: single room from £40.00;
double room from £82.00–£100.00
Dinner, Bed & Breakfast per person, per night:
£63.50–£73.50
Evening meal 1915 (last orders 2045)

Bedrooms: 1 single, 6 double, 3 twin
Bathrooms: 10 en-suite
Parking for 12
Cards accepted: Mastercard, Visa, Amex

Arundel

VIEWED FROM THE SOUTH-WEST the attractive West Sussex town of Arundel has something of a French air. The warm red of clay rooftiles spills down a steep slope crowned by the Gothic-style Catholic cathedral and the huge fortifications of Arundel Castle. Both these buildings – and most of the town, for that matter – have strong connections with the Dukes of Norfolk, the family that has, in one sense or another, looked down upon the townsfolk for seven centuries. The castle, commanding a strategically important gap on the edge of the South Downs, was built in the 11th century. During the Civil War it suffered such damage at the hands of the Parliamentarians that little of the Norman original survives. Dating in large part from the 19th century, the battlements were designed as romantic rather than practical features. In the film version of *The Madness of King George* Arundel took on the starring role of Windsor Castle. It is open to the public (tel: 01903 883136).

The cathedral is dedicated to St Philip Howard, 13th Earl of Arundel, who was martyred in 1595 for his Catholic faith. Not to everyone's taste, it was designed in 1870 by one JA Hansom, inventor of the eponymous cab. Of greater architectural significance is the late 14th-century church of St Nicholas. One half, full of monuments to past Dukes of Norfolk, forms the Fitzalan Chapel where Catholic services are held; Anglican services are held in the other.

Over the past 20 years Arundel has also become a picturesque venue for international cricket with the touring team traditionally playing their opening game here against Lavinia, Duchess of Norfolk's XI. The town can also boast an intriguing museum dedicated to toys and militaria (tel: 01903 882908), though one of the most pleasant ways to pass time is to wander along streets full of Georgian and Victorian frontages (often concealing Tudor interiors). High Street, Maltravers Street and Tarrant Street are three of the best.

One theory about how Arundel came by its name claims it is a corruption of *hirondelle*, French for swallow. Whatever the truth, the town enjoys at least two avian connections; swallows appear on Arundel's coat of arms while near by is one of the South's best reserves for swans, geese, ducks and waders. Keen-eyed visitors to the Wildfowl and Wetlands Trust (tel: 01903 883355) may even be lucky enough to glimpse (or more probably hear the grunting of) the elusive water rail.

351 WHITE HORSE INN

⚜⚜⚜ HIGHLY COMMENDED

The Street, Sutton, Pulborough, West Sussex RH20 1PS Tel (01798) 869221 Fax (01798) 869291

Sutton is a picture-postcard village tucked away at the foot of the South Downs. Great sensitivity has been used to bring our charming Georgian inn up to the standards expected by the discerning traveller, whilst retaining its essential character. The bedrooms are elegantly furnished, each with its own spacious bathroom. The food has a strong emphasis on traditional country cooking, enhanced by a selection of other well-chosen dishes. Log fires in the winter and the garden in the summer! A no-smoking policy applies to bedrooms.

Bed & Breakfast per night: single occupancy £48.00; double room from £58.00–£68.00
Lunch available: 1200–1400
Evening meal 1900 (last orders 2145)

Bedrooms: 4 double, 2 twin
Bathrooms: 5 en-suite, 1 private shower
Parking for 10
Cards accepted: Mastercard, Visa, Amex

352 PARK HOUSE HOTEL

⚜⚜⚜⚜ HIGHLY COMMENDED

Bepton, Midhurst, West Sussex GU29 0JB Tel (01730) 812880 Fax (01730) 815643

Beautifully situated country house hotel nestling in the South Downs, within easy reach of Goodwood racecourse and Chichester Festival Theatre. A quiet village location and beautifully furnished accommodation, with fourteen en-suite bedrooms, make this hotel the perfect retreat. Home-cooked food is served in the elegant dining room. Set in nine acres of grounds with two grass tennis courts, putting and croquet lawns, 9-hole pitch and putt course and heated swimming pool. Conference facilities available. Fully licensed. www.Freepages.co.uk/parkhouse_hotel/

Bed & Breakfast per night: single room from £45.00–£80.00; double room from £90.00–£140.00
Dinner, Bed & Breakfast per person, per night: £65.00–£90.00
Evening meal 2000

Bedrooms: 1 single, 6 double, 6 twin, 1 family room
Bathrooms: 14 en-suite, 1 public
Parking for 40
Cards accepted: Mastercard, Visa, Diners, Amex, Switch/Delta

353 THE ANGEL HOTEL

⚜⚜⚜ HIGHLY COMMENDED

North Street, Midhurst, West Sussex GU29 9DN Tel (01730) 812421 Fax (01730) 815928

The Angel Hotel is a large 16th-century coaching inn located in the historic market town of Midhurst. Sympathetically restored by owners Peter Crawford-Rolt and Nicholas Davies, the hotel retains many features from its Tudor origins. Each of the bedrooms and suites have been individually designed and four-poster beds grace the larger suites. Many of the bedrooms have wonderful views over the Elizabethan rose gardens and Cowdray Castle beyond. Good food, impeccably presented and served, is central to the hotel's approach and has won many awards.

Bed & Breakfast per night: single room from £85.00–£120.00; double room from £95.00–£165.00
Dinner, Bed & Breakfast per person, per night: £67.50–£95.00 (min 2 nights)
Lunch available: 1200–1430

Evening meal 1800 (last orders 2200)
Bedrooms: 4 single, 12 double, 12 twin
Bathrooms: 28 en-suite   Parking for 40
Cards accepted: Mastercard, Visa, Diners, Amex, Switch/Delta

354 EEDES COTTAGE

Listed HIGHLY COMMENDED

Bignor Park Road, Bury Gate, Pulborough, West Sussex RH20 1EZ Tel (01798) 831438

Eedes Cottage is a quiet country house, totally surrounded by farmland, and is under the personal charge of the proprietors, Jane and David Hare. The house stands in its own grounds of two acres which are maintained in immaculate condition. Children and dogs are welcome and your horse can be accommodated in our own stables. Ideal for easy access to Arundel, Chichester and the Sussex coast.

Bed & Breakfast per night: single occupancy from £22.50–£25.00; double room from £40.00–£45.00

Bedrooms: 1 double, 2 twin
Bathrooms: 1 en-suite, 2 public
Parking for 15

355 THE OLD TOLLGATE RESTAURANT & HOTEL

HIGHLY COMMENDED

The Street, Bramber, Steyning, West Sussex BN44 3WE Tel (01903) 879494 Fax (01903) 813399

In a lovely old Sussex village nestling at the foot of the South Downs, standing on the original Tollhouse site, a perfect blending of the old with the new. Award-winning, carvery-style restaurant – a well-known and popular eating spot – offers a magnificent hors d'oeuvres display followed by a vast selection of roasts, pies and casseroles, with delicious sweets and cheeses to add the final touch. Luxuriously-appointed bedrooms, including two four-posters with jacuzzi baths, and two suites.

Bed & Breakfast per night: single occupancy from £68.95–£91.95; double room from £75.90–£98.90
Dinner, Bed & Breakfast per person, per night: £56.90–£68.40 (2 sharing)
Lunch available: 1200–1345

Evening meal 1900 (last orders 2130)
Bedrooms: 21 double, 10 twin
Bathrooms: 31 en-suite Parking for 60
Cards accepted: Mastercard, Visa, Diners, Amex, Switch/Delta

356 ADELAIDE HOTEL

 HIGHLY COMMENDED

51 Regency Square, Brighton, East Sussex BN1 2FF Tel (01273) 205286 Fax (01273) 220904 E-mail adelaide@pavilion.co.uk

This elegant Regency townhouse hotel centrally situated in Brighton's premier seafront square offers, among its hallmarks, a warm welcome, friendly service and delicious food. All the bedrooms include the extras that guarantee a relaxing and comfortable stay. Brighton's extensive and diverse shopping, many restaurants, theatre, etc., are all within easy walking distance, and parking is available in the square. An ideal centre from which to explore the Sussex hinterland. Discounted leisure breaks available.

Bed & Breakfast per night: single room from £41.00–£60.00; double room from £65.00–£82.00

Bedrooms: 3 single, 7 double, 1 twin, 1 triple
Bathrooms: 12 en-suite, 1 public
Cards accepted: Mastercard, Visa, Diners, Amex, Switch/Delta

357 ARLANDA HOTEL

 HIGHLY COMMENDED

20 New Steine, Brighton, East Sussex BN2 1PD   Tel (01273) 699300 Fax (01273) 600930 E-mail arlanda@brighton.co.uk

The Arlanda Hotel is owned by Ken and Karenza Mathews. Karenza played table tennis for England and was twice England Champion. Sport has taken Ken and Karenza to many parts of the world and they have stayed in all kinds of hotels! They use their experience to ensure that their guests are well looked after, with warmth, comfort and good food being priorities. The hotel is licensed and offers excellent accommodation close to the heart of Brighton.

Bed & Breakfast per night: single room from £25.00–£36.00; double room from £46.00–£80.00
Lunch available: 1200–1400
Evening meal 1800 (last bookings 1600)

Bedrooms: 4 single, 3 double, 4 twin, 1 triple
Bathrooms: 12 en-suite
Cards accepted: Mastercard, Visa, Diners, Amex

358 SHELLEYS HOTEL

 HIGHLY COMMENDED

High Street, Lewes, East Sussex BN7 1XS   Tel (01273) 472361 Fax (01273) 483152

The town of Lewes, which is well known to opera lovers who attend the celebrated annual Glyndebourne Opera Festival, is nestled among the picturesque South Downs. Shelleys offers the highest standard of comfort. A short break can offer you the chance to explore some beautiful scenery, shop for antiques and visit the attractions of Brighton – about twenty minutes away – before returning to a peaceful country house hotel, renowned for its service and cuisine.

Bed & Breakfast per night: single room £127.50; double room from £174.00–£245.00
Dinner, Bed & Breakfast per person, per night: £76.00–£96.00 (min 2 nights, 2 sharing)
Lunch available: 1215–1415

Evening meal 1900 (last orders 2115)
Bedrooms: 1 single, 9 double, 9 twin
Bathrooms: 19 en-suite   Parking for 25
Cards accepted: Mastercard, Visa, Diners, Amex, Switch/Delta

359 SOUTH PADDOCK

 HIGHLY COMMENDED

Maresfield Park, Uckfield, East Sussex TN22 2HA   Tel (01825) 762335

A comfortable country house, beautifully furnished with an atmosphere of warmth and elegance. All rooms face south, overlooking three and a half acres of mature gardens, landscaped for attractive colouring throughout the year. A peaceful setting for relaxing on the terrace, beside the fishpond and fountain or in spacious drawing rooms with log fires. Centrally located, 41 miles from London and within easy reach of Gatwick, the channel ports, Glyndebourne, Nymans, Sissinghurst and Chartwell. Good restaurants locally.

Bed & Breakfast per night: single occupancy from £35.00–£39.00; double room from £53.00–£57.00

Bedrooms: 1 double, 2 twin
Bathrooms: 2 private, 1 public
Parking for 6

360 ASHDOWN PARK HOTEL

DE LUXE

Wych Cross, Forest Row, East Sussex RH18 5JR Tel (01342) 824988 Fax (01342) 826206 E-mail sales@ashdownpark.co.uk

Ashdown Park Hotel is an impressive Victorian mansion set in the heart of Ashdown Forest, yet within easy reach of London, Gatwick Airport and the South Coast. Each of the bedrooms and suites are beautifully decorated, many with breathtaking views of the gardens and parkland that encompass the hotel. The award-winning Anderida Restaurant offers an unforgettable dining experience which can be enjoyed following an energetic or relaxing visit to our extensive Country Club. www.ashdownpark.co.uk

Bed & Breakfast per night: single room from £115.00–£285.00; double room from £145.00–£305.00
Dinner, Bed & Breakfast per person, per night: £92.50–£175.00 (min 2 nights, 2 sharing)
Lunch available: 1230–1400

Evening meal 1930 (last orders 2130)
Bedrooms: 6 single, 42 double, 47 twin
Bathrooms: 95 en-suite   Parking for 120
Cards accepted: Mastercard, Visa, Diners, Amex, Switch/Delta

Rudyard Kipling and Bateman's

AS SOON AS RUDYARD KIPLING set eyes upon Bateman's he knew he wanted it as his home: 'That's her! The only she!' he exclaimed, 'Make an honest woman of her – quick!' He then explored every room, finding 'no shadow of ancient regrets, stifled miseries, nor any menace'.

The beautiful manor house near Burwash in Sussex (tel: 01435 882302) indeed has an atmosphere of venerable serenity. Built from warm local sandstone, its rooms all dark panelling and polished old wood, it is a perfect example of the English Jacobean manor house, almost unaltered since its completion in 1634. Of its early history little is known save that it may have been built by a prosperous Wealden ironmaster (17th-century Burwash was at the heart of a thriving iron industry). A large, rambling place with an oddly asymmetrical frontage, it is surrounded by large trees and the beautiful gardens the Kiplings created there.

Kipling was a successful author when he came to Bateman's. Literary acclaim had come early to him and by his late twenties he was already well-known in London intellectual circles. In 1892 he married Caroline Balestier and spent the next four years at her family's estates in America, where he wrote his famous Jungle Book. Kipling then returned to England and settled at Rottingdean, a village not far from Burwash, where a beautiful public garden has been created in his memory, adjacent to his former home The Elms. The years there, however, were clouded by the death of his six-year-old daughter from pneumonia, and after only a year or so the hunt began for a new house. After years of searching, Bateman's became his next, and final, home.

The Bateman's years were productive: here he wrote, amongst other works, Traffics and Discoveries, Puck of Pooks Hill, Rewards and Fairies, and the poems If and The Glory of the Garden. After his death in 1936, Caroline Kipling lived on at Bateman's for a further three years, finally bequeathing the house to the National Trust as a memorial to her husband. Many of the furnishings now on display belonged to the Kiplings, and particularly evocative is the author's study, barely touched since the day of his death. The table where he wrote, in front of the window, still bears his writing implements and paraphernalia and the view is of a little grassy knoll, immortalised in his writings as Pooks Hill.

Bateman's in Sussex

Entries are cross referenced by number to the maps on pages 158–159

361 WHITE LODGE COUNTRY HOUSE HOTEL

HIGHLY COMMENDED

Sloe Lane, Alfriston, Polegate, East Sussex BN26 5UR Tel (01323) 870265 Fax (01323) 870284

An Edwardian building set in five acres overlooking Alfriston village. All bedrooms are individually decorated with every facility, the majority having either extensive downland or village views. We have three lounges (one non-smoking) and our Orchid Restaurant, with views over the Cuckmere valley, offers freshly-prepared daily and à la carte menus accompanied by an extensive wine list. Alfriston village is a particularly attractive oasis of calm in the glorious South Downs and our welcome really makes the White Lodge 'Somewhere Special'.

Bed & Breakfast per night: single room from £50.00–£80.00; double room from £100.00–£150.00
Dinner, Bed & Breakfast per person, per night: £70.00–£95.00
Lunch available: 1215–1330

Evening meal 1915 (last orders 2130)
Bedrooms: 3 single, 7 double, 6 twin, 1 triple
Bathrooms: 17 en-suite   Parking for 25
Cards accepted: Mastercard, Visa, Diners, Amex, Switch/Delta

362 BRAYSCROFT HOTEL

HIGHLY COMMENDED

13 South Cliff Avenue, Eastbourne, East Sussex BN20 7AH Tel (01323) 647005 Fax (01323) 720705 E-mail Brayscroft@compuserve.com

Brayscroft is an elegant, small hotel in an attractive, tree-lined avenue of red brick Edwardian houses. Just moments from the seafront and a few minutes' walk from the bandstand, western lawns, theatres and Devonshire Park. Thoughtfully equipped guest rooms have stylish en-suite facilities, colour televisions and well-stocked hospitality trays. The hotel enjoys an excellent reputation for the quality of its food. For the comfort of guests, smoking is not allowed in guest or public rooms.

Bed & Breakfast per night: single room max £24.00; double room max £48.00
Dinner, Bed & Breakfast per person, per night: max £34.00
Evening meal 1800 (last orders 1900)

Bedrooms: 1 single, 2 double, 2 twin
Bathrooms: 5 en-suite

363 CONQUERORS

HIGHLY COMMENDED

Stunts Green, Herstmonceux, Hailsham, East Sussex BN27 4PR Tel (01323) 832446

With its commanding views over 1066 country, Conquerors was built, to the highest standards, in the 1930s. Peaceful and secluded in its parkland setting of outstanding natural beauty, Conquerors is only one mile from several old village inns and restaurants. Famous houses, castles and gardens are within easy touring distance, as are the historic towns of Hastings, Battle, Royal Tunbridge Wells, Brighton and Eastbourne. Conquerors aims to offer complete comfort in total tranquillity. CATEGORY 3

Bed & Breakfast per night: single occupancy from £22.00–£28.00; double room from £40.00–£50.00

Bedrooms: 1 double, 2 twin
Bathrooms: 2 en-suite, 1 private
Parking for 25

364 MANOR FARM OAST

☷☷ HIGHLY COMMENDED

Windmill Orchard, Workhouse Lane, Icklesham, Winchelsea, East Sussex TN36 4AJ Tel (01424) 813787 Fax (01424) 813787

A three roundel oasthouse built in the 19th century and nestling in acres of apple and cherry orchards. A truly peaceful haven of luxury, ideally situated for country walks or coastal visits. Set in 1066 Country, within easy reach of Rye, Winchelsea, Battle and Hastings. Christmas house parties catered for – solve the murder mystery in front of open log fires whilst enjoying traditional fare. Credit cards accepted. Licensed.

Bed & Breakfast per night: single occupancy from £35.00–£38.00; double room from £50.00–£60.00 Dinner, Bed & Breakfast per person, per night: £68.00–£78.00 Evening meal 1900 (last orders 2000)

Bedrooms: 2 double, 1 twin Bathrooms: 2 en-suite, 2 private Parking for 10 Cards accepted: Mastercard, Switch/Delta

---

365 FLACKLEY ASH HOTEL & RESTAURANT

☷☷☷☷ HIGHLY COMMENDED

London Road, Peasmarsh, Rye, East Sussex TN31 6YH Tel (01797) 230651 Fax (01797) 230510

A Georgian country house hotel, set in beautiful gardens with croquet and putting lawns. Indoor swimming pool and leisure centre with gym, saunas, whirlpool spa, steam room and flotation tank. Beauty salon offering aromatherapy massage. Warm, friendly atmosphere, fine wines and good food (AA Rosette). Well situated for visiting the castles and gardens of East Sussex and Kent and the ancient Cinque port of Rye. Golf, bird-watching, country or seaside walks, potteries and steam trains are some of the attractions in the area.

Bed & Breakfast per night: single occupancy from £75.00–£90.00; double room from £115.00–£145.00 Dinner, Bed & Breakfast per person, per night: £69.00–£85.00 (min 2 nights) Lunch available: 1230–1345

Evening meal 1900 (last orders 2130) Bedrooms: 27 double, 13 twin, 1 triple, 1 family room Bathrooms: 42 en-suite   Parking for 60 Cards accepted: Mastercard, Visa, Diners, Amex, Switch/Delta

---

366 OXNEY FARM

☷☷ HIGHLY COMMENDED

Moons Green, Wittersham, near Tenterden, Kent TN30 7PS Tel (01797) 270558 or 0850 219830 Fax (01797) 270958 E-mail oxneyf@globalnet.co.uk

A warm 'home from home' welcome from Eve and Brian Burnett, together with excellent food, await you at Oxney Farm. Convenient for the Channel Tunnel and ports, the spacious well-furnished comfortable farmhouse, with luxurious indoor pool, lies midway between Tenterden and Rye in peaceful rural surroundings. The area is steeped in history, scenery and culture. Our miniature horses and ponies add their charm to the friendly country house atmosphere. A no smoking house. Eurocards accepted. Directions: from Tenterden or Rye, B2082 to Wittersham, at Swan Inn turn into Swan Street, Oxney Farm is 1.3 miles (2.1km) along on left. www.users.globalnet.co.uk/~oxneyf

Bed & Breakfast per night: single occupancy from £25.00–£30.00; double room from £50.00–£60.00 (reductions for stays of more than 3 nights)

Bedrooms: 2 double, 1 twin Bathrooms: 2 en-suite, 1 private Parking for 6 Cards accepted: Mastercard, Visa, Switch/Delta

367 LITTLE SILVER COUNTRY HOTEL

≋≋≋≋ HIGHLY COMMENDED

Ashford Road, St Michaels, Tenterden, Kent TN30 6SP   Tel (01233) 850321 Fax (01233) 850647

Little Silver Country Hotel is set in its own landscaped gardens. The restaurant provides an intimate, tranquil atmosphere where local produce is enjoyed, pre-dinner drinks and after dinner coffee are offered in the beamed sitting room with its log fire. Breakfast is served in a Victorian conservatory overlooking the waterfall rockery. Luxury bedrooms, tastefully and individually designed, some with four-posters and jacuzzi baths, others with brass beds. Facilities for disabled. Personal attention, care for detail, warmth and friendliness create a truly memorable experience. RAC Restaurant Award.

🛉 CATEGORY 3

Bed & Breakfast per night: single occupancy from £60.00–£80.00; double room from £85.00–£110.00
Dinner, Bed & Breakfast per person, per night: £60.00–£85.00 (min 3 nights)
Lunch available: 1200–1400 (pre-booked only)

Evening meal 1830 (last orders 2200)
Bedrooms: 5 double, 3 twin, 1 triple, 1 family room
Bathrooms: 10 en-suite
Parking for 50
Cards accepted: Mastercard, Visa, Switch/Delta

The Royal Military Canal

WALK ALONG THE BANKS of the Royal Military Canal today in the company of none other than swans and the occasional angler, and it is hard to believe that such a peaceful haven of wildlife was created with the purpose of keeping Napoleon's marauding armies at bay. It was thought the French would try to land on the beaches between Hastings and Folkestone, and the suggestion was that a canal be built along the top of the Romney Marshes as a defensive barrier. There would be a road running parallel behind it to enable troops to move in safety and the canal would have regular dog-legs so that cannons, placed at each kink, could fire along the entire length. With the enthusiastic backing of Pitt the Younger, who was just beginning his second term as Prime Minister in 1804, this amazing feat of engineering was soon under way. There were problems and delays in its construction, however, and by the time it was completed the French had been defeated at Trafalgar and the threat of invasion was over. The whole thing was just one costly military folly. The canal saw some commercial use until the railway opened in 1851 but it was never busy. From the start it was used to control the drainage of the Romney Marshes and this is still a vital role.

The Royal Military Canal Path is waymarked along its 27-mile (43.5km) length. At its eastern end it starts in Hythe, where rowing boats may be hired in summer, then it runs out into agricultural land, yellow waterlilies spreading across its surface. The whole canal is exceptionally rich in wildlife. The section between Hamstreet and Appledore is in the hands of the National Trust. You may see swans anywhere along the canal, but always at Appledore. The section between Appledore and Rye is perhaps the most interesting as the military road is still in use, and the path on top of the bank, where sheep rest beneath the trees, gives a good view of the whole thing. On the one side is the canal, the towpath and the front drain and, on the other, the military road and the back drain. At Iden Lock the canal runs into the River Rother as far as Rye, and from there the path runs across marshland past Henry VIII's Camber Castle to Winchelsea, and on across Pett Level to end in Cliff End. Rye Tourist Information Centre (tel: 01797 2266960) has more details.

Tim Ratledge/Sealand Aerial Photography

368 PLAYDEN COTTAGE GUESTHOUSE

 HIGHLY COMMENDED

Military Road, Rye, East Sussex TN31 7NY Tel (01797) 222234

On the old Saxon shore, less than a mile from Rye town and on what was once a busy fishing harbour, there is now only a pretty cottage with lovely gardens, a pond and an ancient right of way. The sea has long receded and, sheltered by its own informal gardens, Playden Cottage looks over the River Rother and across the sheep-studded Romney Marsh. It offers comfort, peace, a care for detail – and a very warm welcome. www.theaa.co.uk/hotels

Bed & Breakfast per night: single occupancy from
£42.00–£62.00; double room from £56.00–£62.00
Dinner, Bed & Breakfast per person, per night:
£40.00–£74.00
Evening meal by arrangement

Bedrooms: 1 double, 2 twin
Bathrooms: 3 en-suite, 1 public
Parking for 7
Cards accepted: Mastercard, Visa

369 JEAKE'S HOUSE

 HIGHLY COMMENDED

Mermaid Street, Rye, East Sussex TN31 7ET Tel (01797) 222828 Fax (01797) 222623 E-mail jeakeshouse@btinternet.com

Jeake's House stands on the most famous cobbled street in medieval Rye. Bedrooms have been individually restored to create a very special atmosphere, combining traditional elegance and luxury with modern amenities. Oak-beamed and panelled bedrooms with brass, mahogany or four-poster beds overlook the marsh and rooftops to the sea. Vegetarian or traditional breakfast is served in the galleried former chapel where soft chamber music and a roaring fire will make your stay a truly memorable experience. Private car park nearby.
www.s-h-systems.co.uk/hotels/jeakes.html

Bed & Breakfast per night: single room from
£25.50–£59.00; double room from £49.00–£89.00

Bedrooms: 1 single, 7 double, 1 twin, 2 triple, 1 family room
Bathrooms: 9 en-suite, 2 private, 2 public
Cards accepted: Mastercard, Visa, Amex

370 RYE LODGE HOTEL

 HIGHLY COMMENDED

Hilders Cliff, Rye, East Sussex TN31 7LD Tel (01797) 223838 Fax (01797) 223585 E-mail info@ryelodge.demon.co.uk

Premier position on East Cliff, close to the historic 14th-century Landgate, High Street shops and restaurants. De luxe rooms, all en-suite with luxurious bathrooms, remote control colour TVs, direct-dial telephones and hospitality trays. Room service with breakfast in bed as late as you like. Candle-lit dinners in the elegant Terrace Room, with delicious food and an extensive, well-chosen wine list. Tastefully furnished, where elegance is the keynote in a relaxed atmosphere with really caring service. Own car park.
www.ryelodge.demon.co.uk

Bed & Breakfast per night: single room from
£49.50–£75.00; double room from £65.00–£110.00
Dinner, Bed & Breakfast per person, per night:
£49.50–£69.50 (min 2 nights)
Evening meal 1900 (last orders 2100)

Bedrooms: 2 single, 11 double, 7 twin
Bathrooms: 20 en-suite
Parking for 20
Cards accepted: Mastercard, Visa, Diners, Amex,
Switch/Delta

371 EASTWELL MANOR HOTEL

DE LUXE

Eastwell Park, Boughton Lees, Ashford, Kent TN25 4HR Tel (01233) 213000 Fax (01233) 635530

Eastwell Manor dates back to 1069 and lies within 62 acres of tranquil gardens and grounds amidst a 3,000-acre estate. Today, lovingly restored, it is one of England's finest country house hotels with an AA 3 Rosette award-winning restaurant. An oak-panelled dining room, lounges, open log fires and individually furnished bedrooms complete the atmosphere of a splendid country house where fine cuisine and attentive service make for a memorable stay. In early summer 1999 nineteen courtyard apartments will become operational, providing an additional 38 en-suite bedrooms.

Bed & Breakfast per night: single occupancy from
£150.00–£330.00; double room from £187.00–£360.00.
Lunch available: 1200–1430 (1200–1530 on Sunday)
Evening meal 1930 (last orders 2130)

Bedrooms: 10 double, 13 twin
Bathrooms: 23 en-suite
Parking for 112
Cards accepted: Mastercard, Visa, Diners, Amex

372 THE HYTHE IMPERIAL

HIGHLY COMMENDED

Princes Parade, Hythe, Kent CT21 6AE Tel (01303) 267441 Fax (01303) 264610

An impressive sea-front resort hotel set within fifty acres in the historic Cinque port of Hythe. All the rooms enjoy sea or garden views with executive, four-poster, half-tester or jacuzzi rooms and suites available. Conference facilities available for up to two hundred and fifty, as well as superb leisure facilities, including 9-hole golf course, indoor swimming pool, luxurious spa bath, steam room, sauna, gym, sunbed, tennis, croquet, beauty salon and hairdressing.

Bed & Breakfast per night: single room from
£94.50–£114.50; double room from £124.00–£164.00.
Dinner, Bed & Breakfast per person, per night:
£72.00–£92.00 (min 2 nights)
Lunch available: 1230–1400

Evening meal 1900 (last orders 2100)
Bedrooms: 17 single, 43 double, 40 twin
Bathrooms: 100 en-suite Parking for 202
Cards accepted: Mastercard, Visa, Diners, Amex,
Switch/Delta

373 THE OLD VICARAGE

DE LUXE

Chilverton Elms, Hougham, Dover, Kent CT15 7AS Tel (01304) 210668 Fax (01304) 225118

South East England Tourist Board 'Bed & Breakfast of the Year' 1997. Guests are welcomed in a warm and relaxed style at this Victorian country house, elegantly furnished with lovely antiques and pictures. Situated in the peaceful Elms Vale with outstanding views, yet only minutes from Dover, The Old Vicarage provides everything for your stay to the highest standards and in spacious comfort. Large informal gardens. Log fires in winter. Secure parking. An ideal base for touring East Kent.

Bed & Breakfast per night: double room from
£55.00–£65.00
Evening meal by arrangement

Bedrooms: 3 double, 1 double/family
Bathrooms: 2 en-suite, 2 private
Parking for 10
Cards accepted: Mastercard, Visa

At-a-glance symbols are explained on the flap inside the back cover

374 LODDINGTON HOUSE HOTEL

 HIGHLY COMMENDED

14 East Cliff, (Seafront - Marine Parade), Dover, Kent CT16 1LX Tel (01304) 201947 Fax (01304) 201947

Loddington House is a Regency Grade II listed building on the seafront, with panoramic views over the harbour and English Channel. The famous Dover Castle and White Cliffs form a spectacular backdrop to the property. Canterbury, Sandwich and Deal are all a short distance away, making it an excellent holiday choice for exploring Kent, or for a trip to France. Freshly prepared quality food, table d'hôte or à la carte, with a good selection of wines.

Bed & Breakfast per night: single room from £35.00–£45.00; double room from £52.00–£56.00; Dinner, Bed & Breakfast per person, per night: £41.50–£45.50
Evening meal 1830 (last orders 2000)

Bedrooms: 1 single, 3 double, 2 twin
Bathrooms: 4 en-suite, 2 private
Parking for 3
Cards accepted: Mastercard, Visa, Amex

Dickens' Kent

FOR EIGHT DAYS IN LATE JUNE Broadstairs, on Kent's eastern coast, is thronged with characters in Victorian dress, parading the streets and participating in period cricket matches, bathing parties and other amusements. They are here for the Dickens festival, a literary event first staged in 1937 to mark the centenary of Dickens' first visit, and held annually ever since.

When Dickens came to Broadstairs he was 25 years old and on the point of achieving nationwide fame with the publication of *The Pickwick Papers*. He had spent part of his childhood in the Kent town of Chatham and had become well-acquainted with the county from accompanying his father on long country walks. For 14 years he frequently spent summer and autumn months in Broadstairs, eventually leasing Fort House, a fine residence overlooking Viking Bay. Now called Bleak House and open to the public as a museum (tel: 01843 862224), it is thought to have inspired its namesake in Dickens' famous novel, for it stands, tall and solitary, on the cliffs far above Broadstairs. Visitors may see rooms inhabited by the author, including the study where he completed *David Copperfield* and planned *Bleak House*. Also in Broadstairs is the Dickens House Museum (tel: 01843 862853) once the home of Miss Mary Strong, an eccentric woman who was probably the inspiration for one of Dickens' most colourful creations, Miss Betsey Trotwood, David Copperfield's aunt.

In 1856, Dickens purchased Gad's Hill Place, near Rochester, which he had admired as a boy, and always dreamed of owning. This substantial house, now a private school, is occasionally open to the public (details from Rochester's Tourist Information Centre, tel: 01634 843666). The town also provided inspiration for many places in Dickens's works. Eastgate House was both Nun's House School in *The Mystery of Edwin Drood* and Westgate House in *The Pickwick Papers*. Now the Rochester Dickens Centre (tel: 01634 844176), it recreates scenes and characters from the author's best-known works. In its gardens an elaborately carved Swiss chalet was a gift to Dickens from an actor friend who sent it to Higham station in 58 packing cases. It once stood in the shrubbery at Gad's Hill and in it Dickens wrote his last words before his death in 1870. Further Dickensian associations may be followed up using *The Dickens Trail*, available from local tourist information centres.

375 THE CHURCHILL

HIGHLY COMMENDED

Dover Waterfront, Dover, Kent CT17 9BP Tel (01304) 203633 Fax (01304) 216320

The Churchill, Dover's only waterfront hotel, is situated in a beautiful Regency crescent, nestling under the famous White Cliffs, with views over the English Channel. A total of sixty eight bedrooms, all with en-suite facilities, satellite television, direct dial telephone, trouser press, and tea and coffee-making facilities. Our spacious executive rooms also feature mini bars and bathrobes. Within the hotel is Winston's Restaurant, which offers a wide variety of classic English cuisine, with panoramic views over the English Channel. An alternative is a bar snack or light meal in the bar. Special offers and weekend breaks available on request.

Bed & Breakfast per night: single room from £64.00; double room from £93.00
Dinner, Bed & Breakfast per person, per night: from £57.50

Bedrooms: 6 single, 37 double, 20 twin, 5 family rooms
Bathrooms: 68 en-suite
Cards accepted: Mastercard, Visa, Diners, Amex, Switch/Delta

376 WALLETT'S COURT COUNTRY HOUSE HOTEL, RESTAURANT & SPA

HIGHLY COMMENDED

Westcliffe, St-Margarets-at-Cliffe, Dover, Kent CT15 6EW Tel (01304) 852424 Fax (01304) 853430 E-mail wallettscourt@compuserve.com

Wallett's Court is an 'historic building of Kent' – a restored 17th-century manor house with a truly authentic sense of history. In a lovely rural setting with far-reaching views towards St. Margaret's Bay, Dover and the famous White Cliffs. The AA 3 Rosette restaurant, highly acclaimed in major guides, is under the personal supervision of Chris Oakley and his family. New for 1999 is a barn conversion within the grounds housing a Romanesque excercise pool, hydrotherapy spa, steam room and sauna.
www.wallettscourt.com

Bed & Breakfast per night: single occupancy from £60.00–£100.00; double room from £75.00–£120.00
Dinner, Bed & Breakfast per person, per night: £62.50–£85.00
Evening meal 1900 (last orders 2100)

Bedrooms: 11 double, 2 twin, 3 triple
Bathrooms: 16 en-suite
Parking for 20
Cards accepted: Mastercard, Visa, Diners, Amex, Switch/Delta

377 DUNKERLEY'S RESTAURANT & HOTEL

HIGHLY COMMENDED

19 Beach Street, Deal, Kent CT14 7AH Tel (01304) 375016 Fax (01304) 380187

Dunkerley's is an AA 2 Rosette family-run restaurant and hotel which enjoys commanding views over the English Channel. We are renowned for our fresh local seafood and offer a warm and friendly welcome to hungry and weary travellers. We have sixteen comfortable and spacious Victorian bedrooms and have recently introduced an informal bar-bistro. Deal, which is rich in maritime history, generously accommodates the inquisitive. And for sport, the town and nearby Sandwich offer fishing and four excellent golf courses.

Bed & Breakfast per night: single occupancy from £35.00–£45.00; double room from £50.00–£70.00
Dinner, Bed & Breakfast per person, per night: £43.00–£63.00
Lunch available: 1200–1500

Evening meal 1800 (last orders 2200)
Bedrooms: 5 double, 7 twin, 4 family rooms
Bathrooms: 16 en-suite
Cards accepted: Mastercard, Visa, Diners, Amex, Switch/Delta

At-a-glance symbols are explained on the flap inside the back cover

378 YORKE LODGE

HIGHLY COMMENDED

50 London Road, Canterbury, Kent CT2 8LF Tel (01227) 451243 Fax (01227) 462006 E-mail yorke-lg@dircom.co.uk

A spacious and elegant Victorian townhouse, close to the city and recently restored to its period splendour, Yorke Lodge offers hotel-standard rooms at bed & breakfast prices. The beautiful bedrooms are all en-suite, with colour television and all modern amenities. There is a fully stocked library and a private car park. Enjoy a traditional English breakfast in the themed dining room (early breakfasts catered for). Close to channel ports and local attractions. Whether for business or pleasure, let us make your stay in Canterbury a memorable one. www.users.dircom.co.uk/~yorke-lg

Bed & Breakfast per night: single room from
£25.00–£30.00; double room from £45.00–£50.00

Bedrooms: 1 single, 2 double, 1 triple, 2 family rooms
Bathrooms: 6 en-suite
Parking for 4
Cards accepted: Mastercard, Visa, Diners

379 THE RINGLESTONE INN & FARMHOUSE HOTEL

HIGHLY COMMENDED

Ringlestone Hamlet, Harrietsham, Maidstone, Kent ME17 1NX Tel (01622) 859900 Fax (01622) 859966 E-mail michelle@ringlestone.com

Situated on the North Downs in the heart of Kent, just ten minutes from Leeds Castle, this character Kentish farmhouse is surrounded by eight acres of tranquil gardens and farmland. Luxuriously furnished in rustic oak throughout, with a canopied four-poster bed in the Elderflower Room. Opposite, the famous 16th-century Ringlestone Inn is recommended in major guides for help-yourself buffet lunch and interesting evening Kentish fare incorporating English fruit wines in the traditional recipes. www.ringlestone.com/ringlestone

Bed & Breakfast per night: single occupancy from
£79.00–£89.00; double room from £89.00–£99.00
Dinner, Bed & Breakfast per person, per night:
£70.50–£75.50 (2 sharing)
Lunch available: 1200–1400

Evening meal 1900 (last orders 2130)
Bedrooms: 1 double, 2 twin
Bathrooms: 3 en-suite Parking for 74
Cards accepted: Mastercard, Visa, Diners, Amex,
Switch/Delta

380 TANYARD

HIGHLY COMMENDED

Wierton Hill, Boughton Monchelsea, Maidstone, Kent ME17 4JT Tel (01622) 744705 Fax (01622) 741998

Tanyard is a medieval country house hotel perched on a ridge with far-reaching views across the weald of Kent. All six bedrooms have en-suite facilities and are furnished with antiques combined with modern comforts. The top-floor suite, which is heavily beamed, has a spa bath and is particularly popular. The no smoking restaurant seats twenty eight and is in the oldest part of the building, dating from 1350. The modern English cuisine uses only fresh local produce. AA 2 Rosettes.

Bed & Breakfast per night: single room from
£65.00–£85.00; double room from £105.00–£150.00
Dinner, Bed & Breakfast per person, per night:
£81.50–£114.00
Evening meal 1900 (last orders 2100)

Bedrooms: 1 single, 3 double, 2 twin
Bathrooms: 6 en-suite
Parking for 20   Open: February–mid October
Cards accepted: Mastercard, Visa, Diners, Amex,
Switch/Delta

381 WILLINGTON COURT

 HIGHLY COMMENDED

Willington Street, Maidstone, Kent ME15 8JW Tel (01622) 738885 Fax (01622) 631790

Charming Grade II listed building, tastefully furnished and including antiques and a four-poster bed. All bedrooms have private facilities, television, hospitality tray, hairdryer, trouser press, plus extras for that touch of luxury. Guests can relax in the lounges. Smoking is restricted to the 'smokers' lounge, adjacent to the conservatory. Enjoy the restful and friendly atmosphere. An ideal location for visiting National Trust and other local historic properties, including nearby Leeds Castle. Gourmet dinners and fine wines available.

Bed & Breakfast per night: single occupancy from £28.00–£40.00; double room from £44.00–£54.00
Dinner, Bed & Breakfast per person, per night: £45.00–£60.00
Lunch available: 1230–1430

Evening meal 1900 (last orders 2000)
Bedrooms: 2 double, 1 twin
Bathrooms: 2 en-suite, 2 private
Parking for 6
Cards accepted: Mastercard, Diners, Amex

382 COULSDON MANOR HOTEL

HIGHLY COMMENDED

Coulsdon Court Road, Coulsdon, Croydon, Surrey CR5 2LL Tel (0181) 668 0414 Fax (0181) 668 3118

Set in 140 acres of parkland, a large part of which is laid down as a challenging 18-hole golf course. Fifteen miles from central London and Gatwick, and easily accessible from all parts of the South East via the M25, M23, A23 or A22. A restored manor house with thirty five delightful bedrooms – many with enchanting views over the golf course – an award-winning restaurant and Reflections Leisure Club offering squash, sunbed, gymnasium, racketball, aerobics, sauna and steam.

Bed & Breakfast per night: single occupancy from £104.00–£114.00; double room from £130.00–£150.00
Dinner, Bed & Breakfast per person, per night: £75.00–£85.00 (min 2 nights, 2 sharing)
Evening meal 1900 (last orders 2130)

Bedrooms: 16 double, 19 twin
Bathrooms: 35 en-suite
Parking for 200
Cards accepted: Mastercard, Diners, Amex, Switch/Delta

383 TRIPLE DUTCH

HIGHLY COMMENDED

64 Seymour Avenue, Ewell, Epsom, Surrey KT17 2RR Tel (0181) 873 0170 Fax (0181) 873 0170 E-mail tripledutch@mcmail.com

Triple Dutch offers a unique opportunity to experience true Dutch hospitality in a luxury family home. The house enjoys panoramic views of peaceful open countryside and woodlands. Set on the border between Surrey and London, it is an ideal location for no-hassle visits to London, 25 minutes by train, and/or touring beautiful Surrey and Sussex. A wide range of skilfully-cooked evening meals is available by prior arrangement. Non-smoking. There are two friendly resident cats. www.tripledutch.mcmail.com

Bed & Breakfast per night: single room £25.00; double room £35.00
Evening meal 1800 (last orders 2000)

Bedrooms: 1 double, 1 twin
Bathrooms: 1 en-suite, 1 private
Parking for 2

384 RICHMOND GATE HOTEL AND GATES ON THE PARK RESTAURANT  HIGHLY COMMENDED

Richmond Hill, Richmond, Surrey TW10 6RP Tel (0181) 940 0061 Fax (0181) 332 0354

One of Richmond's leading hotels is to be found at the top of Richmond Hill, adjacent to the Royal Park and Richmond Terrace, where Turner painted his famous view of the Thames between Hampton Court and Kew Gardens. Exceptional cuisine is prepared to order in 'Gates on the Park Restaurant' which has been awarded two AA Rosettes, whilst afternoon tea in the club lounge or walled garden is a memorable experience. 'Cedars', our health and leisure club, includes a 20m pool, spa, sauna, steam room, gym, aerobics studio and health and beauty suite.

Bed & Breakfast per night: single room from £110.00–£131.00; double room from £130.00–£175.00
Lunch available: 1230–1430
Evening meal 1800 (last orders 2200)

Bedrooms: 18 single, 32 double, 15 twin, 1 triple
Bathrooms: 66 en-suite
Parking for 50
Cards accepted: Mastercard, Visa, Diners, Amex, Switch/Delta

Epsom Derby

THE DERBY, THE MOST FAMOUS horserace in the world, was first run in 1780, and has attracted huge audiences of ordinary people ever since. 'On Derby Day,' wrote Charles Dickens, 'a population rills and surges and scrambles through the place, that may be counted in millions.' Dickens was surely exaggerating, but so great was the race's popularity in the second half of the 19th century that parliament was suspended for the day. Currently crowds of some 100,000 or so attend the race, held on the first Saturday in June.

The Derby is named after the 12th Earl of Derby, Edward Smith Stanley, who, together with his colourful uncle, General John Burgoyne, organised the first contest for three-year old fillies in 1779. The race over Epsom Downs was named 'The Oaks' after Burgoyne's rambling house,

once a pub, near Epsom, and was won by Derby's filly, Bridget. At the celebration dinnner which followed, Derby planned a second race for three-year-old colts and fillies, to be named after himself. On 4 May 1780 the first Derby took place – and a great English tradition was born. Both races continue to run, with The Oaks taking place the day before the Derby.

During its 200-year history the race has had more than its fair share of dramatic occurrences.

In 1913 the suffragette, Emily Davison, was killed when she threw herself in front of the King's horse, a deliberate act of martyrdom designed to generate maximum publicity. More recently, in 1981, the crowds thrilled to the most dramatic Derby win ever, when the legendary colt Shergar, ridden by Walter Swinburn, won effortlessly by a clear 10 lengths. Two years later Shergar was kidnapped from the Aga Khan's stud in Ireland, and to this day his fate remains a mystery.

From a racing point of view, the course over the Epsom Downs is supremely challenging. Run early in the season when the going can be heavy, the undulating and twisting one-and-a-half-mile (2.4km) course requires great stamina. Rising 150ft (46m) in the first four furlongs, it then falls 100ft (30.5m) in varying gradients to the famous Tattenham Corner, before rising again towards the finishing post. The difficulties of winning such an event make the Derby a true test of equine greatness.

Tickets for the Derby and Oaks may be obtained by ringing 01372 470047. 'Derby Experience' tours of the racecourse (tel: 01372 726311) are available throughout the year.

385 THE EXCELSIOR

HIGHLY COMMENDED

Bath Road, West Drayton, Middlesex UB7 0DU Tel (0181) 759 6611 Fax (0181) 759 3421

A modern, international hotel overlooking Heathrow airport. Heathrow's largest hotel, with 828 bedrooms and eight suites, offering an informal and relaxed atmosphere. Relaunched at the end of 1998 is The Crown Club – a separate, luxurious wing featuring 258 bedrooms with a contemporary feel. There is an excellent choice of restaurants and bars. Guests are able to relax and unwind in our well-equipped health and leisure club, or perhaps visit some of the superb local tourist attractions, including Windsor Castle, Hampton Court and Legoland.

Bed & Breakfast per night: from £87.95 (weekends only)
Lunch available: 1130–1430
Evening meal 1815 (last orders 2300)

Bedrooms: 5 single, 526 double, 278 twin, 19 triple
Bathrooms: 828 en-suite
Parking for 540
Cards accepted: Mastercard, Visa, Diners, Amex, Switch/Delta

386 FIVE SUMNER PLACE HOTEL

Listed HIGHLY COMMENDED

South Kensington, London SW7 3EE Tel (0171) 584 7586 Fax (0171) 823 9962 E-mail no.5@dial.pipex.com

This delightful award-winning hotel is situated in South Kensington, one of the most fashionable areas of London. The hotel itself has been sympathetically restored to recreate the ambience and style of a bygone era. Family-owned and run, it offers excellent service and personal attention. All rooms are luxuriously appointed and come with private en-suite facilities, telephone, colour television, trouser press and full buffet breakfast. www.dspace.dial.pipex.com/no.5

Bed & Breakfast per night: single room from £75.00–£95.00; double room from £120.00–£141.00
Dinner, Bed & Breakfast per person, per night: £60.00–£95.00

Bedrooms: 3 single, 5 double, 5 twin
Bathrooms: 13 en-suite, 1 public
Cards accepted: Mastercard, Visa, Amex

387 HOTEL NUMBER SIXTEEN

HIGHLY COMMENDED

16 Sumner Place, London SW7 3EG Tel (0171) 589 5232 Fax (0171) 584 8615 E-mail reservations@numbersixteenhotel.co.uk

Situated in South Kensington, Number Sixteen has been created from four Victorian town houses. Offering style, elegance and seclusion, guests are encouraged to make themselves at home. There is a relaxed informality about the drawing room and the library, where everyone is invited to pour themselves a drink from the honour bar. The conservatory opens onto an award-winning garden. The comfortable well-appointed bedrooms are individually decorated with a combination of antique and traditional furnishings. www.numbersixteenhotel.co.uk

Bed & Breakfast per night: single room from £90.00–£125.00; double room from £160.00–£190.00

Bedrooms: 9 single, 23 double, 4 triple
Bathrooms: 33 en-suite, 2 private, 1 private shower
Cards accepted: Mastercard, Visa, Diners, Amex, Switch/Delta

388 BLOOMS HOTEL

〰〰〰 HIGHLY COMMENDED

7 Montague Street, London WC1B 5BP Tel (0171) 323 1717 Fax (0171) 636 6498

Blooms Hotel is an elegant 18th-century town house with a walled garden, offering relaxation and tranquillity. With twenty seven bedrooms, it is conveniently located next to the British Museum and a ten-minute walk from the theatre district and Oxford Street for shopping. Theatre tickets, restaurant reservations and transport from and to the airport can be arranged. A light menu is available in our bar/lounge area; there is also 24-hour room service.

Bed & Breakfast per night: single room from
£125.00–£165.00; double room from £185.00–£200.00

Bedrooms: 5 single, 13 double, 9 twin
Bathrooms: 27 en-suite
Cards accepted: Mastercard, Visa, Diners, Amex, Switch/Delta

---

389 THE PARK LANE HOTEL

〰〰〰〰 HIGHLY COMMENDED

Piccadilly, London W1Y 8BX Tel (0171) 499 6321 Fax (0171) 499 1965

Located in the heart of Mayfair on London's Piccadilly; overlooking Green Park and Buckingham Palace; within walking distance of the high fashion shops of Bond Street and Knightsbridge; nearby theatres of the West End; Royal Academy; and Westminster Abbey. 305 rooms, 39 suites, garage parking (capacity 180 cars), 24 hour room service. Palm Court with Champagne Bar. Ballroom and meeting facilities, business centre. French restaurant 'The Brasserie on the Park'. Smart rooms for the business traveller.

Bed & Breakfast per night: single room from £260.00;
double room from £280.00
Evening meal 1900 (last orders 2300)

Bedrooms: 42 single, 100 double, 100 twin, 20 triple,
38 family rooms
Bathrooms: 300 en-suite   Parking for 150
Cards accepted: Mastercard, Visa, Diners, Amex,
Switch/Delta

---

390 AUCKLANDS

Listed HIGHLY COMMENDED

25 Eglington Road, North Chingford, London E4 7AN Tel (0181) 529 1140 Fax (0181) 508 3837

Comfortable Edwardian family home on the edge of London, where an open fire and caring owners welcome guests as friends. We are within easy reach of Stansted and London City airports, just five minutes' walk to the station (lifts offered), 25 minutes to Liverpool Street station, and 35 minutes to Oxford Circus. We are right on the edge of Epping Forest, where you can enjoy relaxing walks or play a game of golf at the local course. We have one king-size double room, one twin, and a super bathroom. Enjoy our secluded garden with its small swimming pool (May to September). We serve good food and offer lunches by arrangement. The resident cat will tolerate guide-dogs only.

Bed & Breakfast per night: single occupancy from
£32.50–£35.00; double room from £60.00–£70.00
Dinner, Bed & Breakfast per person, per night:
£47.50–£55.00
Lunch available: 1130–1430 (or packed lunch)

Evening meal 1700 (last orders 2300)
Bedrooms: 1 double, 1 twin
Bathrooms: 1 public

SYMBOLS

For ease of use, the key to symbols appears on the back of the cover flap and can be folded out while consulting individual entries. The symbols which appear at the end of each entry are designed to enable you to see at a glance what's on offer, and whether any particular requirements you have can be met. Most of the symbols are clear, simple icons and few require any further explanation, but the following points may be useful:

ALCOHOLIC DRINKS

Alcoholic drinks are available at all types of accommodation listed in the guide unless the symbol UL (unlicensed) appears. However, even in licensed premises there may be some restrictions on the serving of drinks, such as being available to diners only. You may wish to check this in advance.

SMOKING

Some establishments prefer not to accommodate smokers, and if this is the case it will be indicated by the symbol ⚞. Other establishments may offer facilities for non-smokers such as no-smoking bedrooms and parts of communal rooms set aside for non-smokers. Please check at the time of booking if the non-smoking symbol does not appear.

PETS

The symbol 🐕 is used to show that dogs are not accepted in any circumstances. Some establishments will accept pets, but we advise you to check this at the time of booking and to enquire as to whether any additional charge will be made to accommodate them.

BOOKING CHECKLIST

When enquiring about accommodation remember to state your requirements clearly and precisely. It may be necessary or helpful to discuss some or all of the following points:

- Your intended arrival and departure dates.
- The type of accommodation you require. For example, a twin-bedded room, a private bath and WC, whether the room has a view or not.
- The terms you require, such as room only; bed & breakfast; bed, breakfast and evening meal (half board); bed, breakfast, lunch and evening meal (full board).
- If you have any children travelling with you, say how old they are and state their accommodation requirements, such as a cot, and whether they will share your room.
- Any particular requirements, such as a special diet or a ground-floor room.
- If you think you are likely to arrive late in the evening, mention this when you book. Similarly, if you are delayed on your journey

a telephone call to inform the management may well help avoid any problems on your arrival.

- If you are asked for a deposit or the number of your credit card, find out what the proprietor's policy is if, for whatever reason, you can't turn up as planned – see 'cancellations' opposite.
- Exactly how the establishment's charges are levied – see below.

Misunderstandings can easily occur over the telephone, so it is advisable to confirm in writing all bookings, together with special requirements. Please mention that you learnt of the establishment through *Somewhere Special*. Remember to include your name and address, and please enclose a stamped, addressed envelope – or an international reply coupon if writing from outside Britain. Please note that the English Tourist Board does not make reservations; you should address your enquiry directly to the establishment.

PRICES

The prices given throughout this publication will serve as a general guide, but you should always check them at the time of booking. The following information may prove useful when determining how much a trip may cost:

- Prices were supplied during the autumn of 1998 and changes may have occurred since publication.
- Prices include VAT where applicable.
- You should check whether or not a service charge is included in the published price.
- Prices for double rooms assume occupancy by two people; you will need to check whether there is a single person supplement.
- Half board means the price for the room, breakfast and evening meal per person per day.
- A full English breakfast is not always included in the quoted price; you may be given a continental breakfast unless you are prepared to pay more.
- Establishments with at least four bedrooms or eight beds are obliged to display in the reception area or at the entrance overnight accommodation charges.
- Reduced prices may apply for children; check exactly how these reductions are calculated, including the maximum age for the child.
- Prices are often much cheaper for off-peak holidays; check to see whether special off-season packages are available.

DEPOSITS AND ADVANCE PAYMENTS

For reservations made weeks or months ahead a deposit is usually payable which will be deducted from the total bill at the end of your stay.

Some establishments, particularly the larger hotels in big towns, now require payment for the room upon arrival if a prior reservation has not

been made. Regrettably this practice has become necessary because of the number of guests who have left without settling their bills. If you are asked to pay in advance, it is sensible to see your room before payment is made to ensure that it meets your requirements.

If you book by telephone and are asked for your credit card number, you should note that the proprietor may charge your credit card account even if you subsequently cancel the booking. Ask the owner what his or her usual practice is.

CREDIT/CHARGE CARDS

Any credit/charge cards that are accepted by the establishment are indicated at the end of the written description. The abbreviations used in this guide are:

Mastercard – Mastercard/Eurocard

Visa – Visa/Barclaycard

Diners – Diners

Amex – American Express

Switch/Delta – Direct debit card

If you intend to pay by either credit or charge card you are advised to confirm this at the time of booking. Please note that when paying by credit card, you may sometimes be charged a higher rate for your accommodation in order to cover the percentage paid by the proprietor to the credit card company. Again find this out in advance.

When making a booking, you may be asked for your credit card number as 'confirmation'. The proprietor may then charge your credit card account if you have to cancel the booking, but if this is the policy, it must be made clear to you at the time of booking – see below.

CANCELLATIONS

When you accept offered accommodation, including over the telephone, you are entering into a legally binding contract with the proprietor. This means that if you cancel a reservation or fail to take up all or part of the accommodation booked, the proprietor may be entitled to compensation if the accommodation cannot be re-let for all or a good part of the booked period. If you have paid a deposit, you will probably forfeit this, and further payment may well be asked for.

However, no such claim can be made by the proprietor until after the booked period, during which time every effort should be made to re-let the accommodation. It is therefore in your interests to advise the management immediately in writing if you have to cancel or curtail a booking. Travel or holiday insurance, available quite cheaply from travel agents and some hotels, will safeguard you if you have to cancel or curtail your stay.

And remember, if you book by telephone and are asked for your credit card number, you should check whether the proprietor intends charging your account should you later cancel your reservation. A

proprietor should not be able to charge for a cancellation unless he or she has made this clear at the time of your booking and you have agreed. However, to avoid later disputes, we suggest you check whether he or she intends to make such a charge.

SERVICE CHARGES AND TIPPING

Some establishments levy a service charge automatically, and, if so, must state this clearly in the offer of accommodation at the time of booking. If the offer is accepted by you, the service charge becomes part of the contract. If service is included in your bill, there is no need for you to give tips to the staff unless some particular or exceptional service has been rendered. In the case of meals, the usual tip is 10% of the total bill.

TELEPHONE CALL CHARGES

There is no restriction on the charges that can be made by hotels for telephone calls made from their premises. Unit charges are frequently considerably higher than telephone companies' standard charges in order to defray the costs of providing the service. It is a condition of being awarded a national Crown classification that the telephone unit charges are displayed alongside the telephone. However, it may not always be clear how these compare with the standard unit charge. Before using a hotel telephone, particularly for long-distance calls, you should enquire how much extra you will be paying per unit.

SECURITY OF VALUABLES

It is advisable to deposit any valuables for safe-keeping with the management of the establishment in which you are staying. If the management accept custody of your property they become wholly liable for its loss or damage. They can however restrict their liability for items brought on to the premises and not placed in their special custody to the minimum amounts imposed by the Hotel Proprietors Act, 1956. These are the sum of £50 in respect of one article and a total of £100 in the case of one guest. In order to restrict their liability the management must display a notice in the form required by the Act in a prominent position in the reception area or main entrance of the premises. Without this notice, the proprietor is liable for the full value of the loss or damage to any property (other than a motor car or its contents) of a guest who has booked overnight accommodation.

FEEDBACK

Let us know about your holiday. We welcome suggestions about how the guide itself may be improved.

Most establishments welcome feedback. Please let the proprietor know if you particularly enjoyed your stay. We sincerely hope that you have no cause for complaint, but should you be dissatisfied or have any problems, make your complaint to the management at the time of the incident so that immediate action may be taken.

The English Tourist Board, Jarrold Publishing and Celsius cannot guarantee the accuracy of the information in this guide and accept no responsibility for any error or misrepresentation. All liability for any loss, disappointment or damage caused by reliance upon the information contained in this guide, or in the event of bankruptcy or liquidation or cessation of trade of any company, individual or firm mentioned, is hereby excluded. All establishments listed are bound by the Trades Description Acts of 1968 and 1972 when describing and offering accommodation and facilities, but we strongly recommend that prices and other details should be confirmed at the time of booking.

Details listed were believed correct at time of going to press. It is advisable to telephone in advance to check the details have not altered and to discuss any specific requirements.

CODE OF CONDUCT

All establishments appearing in this guide have agreed to observe the following Code of Conduct:

1 To ensure high standards of courtesy and cleanliness; catering and service appropriate to the type of establishment.

2 To describe fairly to all visitors and prospective visitors the amenities, facilities and services provided by the establishment, whether by advertisement, brochure, word of mouth or any other means. To allow visitors to see accommodation, if requested, before booking.

3 To make clear to visitors exactly what is included in all prices quoted for accommodation, meals and refreshments, including service charges, taxes and other surcharges. Details of charges, if any, for heating or for additional services or facilities available should also be made clear.

4 To adhere to, and not to exceed, prices current at time of occupation for accommodation or other services.

5 To advise visitors at the time of booking, and subsequently, of any change, if the accommodation offered is in an unconnected annexe, or similar, or by boarding out, and to indicate the location of such accommodation and any difference in comfort and amenities from accommodation in the main establishment.

6 To give each visitor, on request, details of payments due and a receipt if required.

7 To deal promptly and courteously with all enquiries, requests, reservations, correspondence and complaints from visitors.

8 To allow an English Tourist Board representative reasonable access to the establishment, on request, to confirm that the Code of Conduct is being observed.

INDEX

INDEX